WHAT IS LIFE?

The Originality, Irreducibility

VALUE INQUIRY BOOK SERIES

VIBS

Volume 51

a volume in
Central-European Value Studies
CEVS
H. G. Callaway, Editor

WHAT IS LIFE?
The Originality, Irreducibility, and Value of Life

Josef Seifert

Rodopi

Amsterdam - Atlanta, GA 1997

Cover design by Chris Kok based on a photograph, ©1984 by Robert Ginsberg, of statuary by Gustav Vigeland in the Frogner Park, Oslo, Norway.

∞ The paper on which this book is printed meets the requirements of "ISO 9706:1994, Information and documentation - Paper for documents - Requirements for permanence".

ISBN: 90-420-0381-2

Printed in The Netherlands

... in everything the essence is identical with the ground of its being, and here, in the case of living things, their being is to live, and of their being and their living the soul in them is the cause or source.

Aristotle, *De Anima*, Book 1, 412 a 1-5

Let the foregoing suffice as our account of the views concerning the soul which have been handed down by our predecessors; let us now dismiss them and make, as it were, a completely fresh start, endeavouring to give a precise answer to the question, What is soul?

Aristotle, *De Anima*, Book 2, 415 b 12-14

The idea of life in its immediacy is in the last analysis only the creative ... soul ... the principle that makes a beginning and moves itself.

Georg Wilhelm Friedrich Hegel, *Wissenschaft der Logik*, vol. 2, 249 f.

This [supreme] life ... is light, because it is love.

Gabriel Marcel, *Sein und Haben,* p. 249

Dedicated in profound friendship
to Roy Heyne, Jr., M. D.,
and
to his dear wife Elizabeth Heyne

CONTENTS

EDITORIAL FOREWORD

Josef Seifert's *What Is Life?* is the first contribution to the *Central-European Value Studies* from the International Academy for Philosophy in the Principality of Liechtenstein, one of the co-sponsoring organizations of the CEVS special series. Professor Seifert is also on the Board of Editors of the special series. Thus, I would like to take this opportunity to welcome Professor Seifert and his book to CEVS.

Seifert argues with scholarly depth against scientific reductionism in our understanding of life, and he challenges the reader in an examination of the grounds for recognizing the dignity of life. These are important and worthy topics which repay reflection. I am certain that Seifert's contributions in this work hold out considerable potentiality for learned dialogue on the topics he addresses. We look forward to seeing further books from Seifert and from his colleagues in Liechtenstein.

H. G. Callaway
Editor, CEVS

PREFACE

Josef Seifert takes up the classic question, "What is Life?," in critical reflection upon the lectures that were published in English under this title in 1944 by the Austrian Nobel Laureate in physics, Erwin Schrödinger. Schrödinger's groundbreaking efforts to connect the leading edges of the physical and biological sciences in his little book were the culminating work that I had to study in my final college course on the Natural Sciences at the University of Chicago in 1955. But Schrödinger's approach to the question of life remained that of the scientist. Fifty years later, Seifert shows with subtle care that the very question is a philosophical one, and therefore it must be treated by the methods and distinctions of philosophical study.

Life, philosophically questioned, calls for understanding of its irreducible essence. A biological or physical approach that seeks to explain living organisms in terms of mechanism and matter misses the very life of life. Seifert turns upon the question his lifetime of familiarity with the grand traditions of philosophy. Centuries of thought are brought to life in this study of the central question of life. In the spirit of philosophical dialogue, Seifert's closing chapter takes the agreeable format of question and answer. This groundbreaking contribution is a scholarly yet spirited defense of the dignity of life.

Robert Ginsberg
Executive Editor

ACKNOWLEDGEMENTS

I wish to acknowledge the support I have received, in completing the final version of this book, through a grant of the Swiss National Foundation for the Sciences (*Schweizerischer Nationalfonds*) which supported a research project under my direction on the philosophical aspects of the concept of health.[1] This research into the philosophic dimensions of the concept of physical and mental health led to many improvements of this book on life. The philosophy of life here presented, which I had completed in earlier drafts before undertaking the health project, proved useful for the completion of the tasks of the research project on health.

My gratitude extends to the Pontifical Academy of the Sciences, in particular to Mons. Ing. Renato Dardozzi, whose invitation to participate as an expert in the Plenary Session of the Academy on "The Emergence of Complexity in Mathematics, Physics, Chemistry, and Biology," and to speak on the irreducibility of life to chaotic and non-chaotic physical systems became the origin of this book. I would probably never have written it without his invitation. I wish to express my cordial thanks to those scientists and illustrious members of the Academy who participated in the discussion following the presentation of my paper, for having posed the questions contained in Chapter Five of this book and for having given me valuable critical suggestions.[2]

My thankfulness addresses itself as well to those who have read carefully different versions of the manuscript of this book and have made helpful comments on them. I think here in particular of two distinguished philosophers and friends, Roderick Chisholm and Rocco Buttiglione, and of Alejandro Serani, professor of medicine. The philosopher Dr. John White, my dear friend, collaborator, and former student, made significant stylistic and philosophic comments on the present book for which I thank him cordially. I am grateful to Dmitry Atlas, who has examined the text from the perspective of a philosopher and of a physicist. In addition to his careful critical reading of the text, I owe to him more precise elaborations on the laws of physics which I touch in this book. Benefits of like nature I have also received from his brother Valery Atlas to whom I am especially indebted for his having directed my attention, through his paper, "On the Principle of Complementarity," to the contributions of Niels Bohr on the nature and irreducibility of life.[3] My gratitude extends likewise to Dr. med. Paulina Taboada who has examined scrupulously many biological aspects of the present work, to Dr. Kateryna Fedoryka and to Patricia Donohue-White who have made many helpful philosophical suggestions regarding the problem "What is life?" during our joint research work on the philosophical concept of health.

I thank also the Executive Editor of this series, Robert Ginsberg, for accepting this work, for his many helpful suggestions, and for the discrete and generous way with which he applied to my text his strict editorial prescriptions regarding style, especially the elimination of so-called "sexist" language (for example, the elimination of the English "man" in the sense of human being (*Mensch*) or the introduction of "he or she" as personal pronoun for "person"). I had informed him rather rudely of the fact that I regard a so-called "non-sexist style" as a misunderstanding of the trans-gender-meaning of these terms and as a linguistic barbarism that affects the substance of language and philosophical thought by eliminating central notions as, for example, man/*Mensch* or the non-gender-related use of masculine and feminine pronouns, as well as simple (uncomplicated) pronouns for persons and human beings, and introduces instead the "he or she" or the horrible *s/he*. He not only received my objections calmly and patiently but applied his principles in such a subtle and generously easy-going way that I have to admit that they became almost natural to me. This does not prevent me from preferring the classical use of language and from thinking that it has nothing to do with "sexism." Just as no German will take the pronoun "*sie*" ("she") for *Person* as a sign that persons are considered feminine and men are excluded in German, no normal user of the English pronoun "he" for persons will have a "sexist" meaning in mind. Instead, Thomas of Erfurt (or Duns Scotus) seem to be right here in distinguishing in the *Grammatica speculativa* four kinds of gender, insisting on the "inclusive" or "common" one where masculine or feminine forms and pronouns include both male and female members. Besides the *masculinum*, *femininum*, and *neutrum*, according to them, a fourth "common" gender (*sexus commune*) occurs, namely, as the author of the *Grammatica speculativa* points out quite well (and to recognize this would in my opinion avoid the sexist interpretation of male or female inclusive pronouns), there is a special *discretio sexus*, the *genus commune*. In its linguistic form the *genus commune* is either masculine or feminine (*quod nec differt a masculino nec a feminino*) but in its meaning comprises both sexes within itself, as, for example, in *homo* (man) when this term signifies human persons as such.[4]

I am grateful to Hofrat Dr. Eberhard Tiefenthaler, a pioneer librarian who died too young from cancer, for having created a wonderful place and atmosphere in form of the *Landesbibliothek Vorarlberg* in Bregenz, in whose *Kuppelsaal* I completed large portions and the final redaction of my book, drawing from the extraordinary beauty and rich historical and spiritual atmosphere of this place in which more than 2,000 years of European culture come to life. Mindful of these benefits and of bonds of friendship between his family and mine, I feel that this book, the first one I completed in this library, belongs especially to his memory and to his family.

I wish to thank especially Mrs. Veronika Albicker for the care which she invested in typesetting and preparing this manuscript for publication.

Finally, I thank heartily my wife, who has given me much human and moral support in my work, and my entire family for their patience with my using too much precious time which should have belonged to them, for the completion of this book.

The book is dedicated to my dear brother-in-law and sister-in-law and friends Dr. Roy Heyne, Jr., and Liz (Elizabeth) Heyne who are deeply committed to their medical work and at the same time intensely interested in questions of philosophy, particularly in those which regard the nature and value of human life.

25 January 1997

Introduction

EMPIRICAL KNOWLEDGE AND PHILOSOPHY FACE TO FACE WITH LIFE: A FRESH START, 50 YEARS AFTER SCHRÖDINGER

Some fifty years ago, the Austrian physicist and Nobel Laureate Erwin Schrödinger wrote a groundbreaking book, entitled *What Is Life?*,[1] which influenced significantly theoretical discoveries in biology and might even have given rise to the ensuing developments in the life-sciences that culminated in the discovery by James Dewey Watson and Francis Harry Compton Crick, in 1953, of the double helix of the chromosomes as bearers of genetic information.[2]

Schrödinger's book is outstanding from a scientific point of view and because of its position in the history of science, but also in view of its philosophical contributions, introducing striking concepts and terms as, for example, "negative entropy" to get at the irreducible newness of life, and suggesting innovative ideas – which were verified empirically only later – such as that precise "genetic information" lies hidden at the origins of the development of organisms.

The search for something like genetic codes had its roots not only in some suggestions of twentieth-century scientists but also in twentieth-century philosophy of life. For instance, Conrad-Martius has presented an outstanding defense of a new version of "preformism" that is much akin to the idea of genetic codes.[3] The basic ideas which inspired the search for a genetic code are much older, however, and go back to the Presocratics, to Aristotle, to Clemens of Alexandria's "*spermata tou logou*" and to Augustine's "seminal reasons," as well as to "preformists" and some "epigeneticists" who participated in the philosophical debates regarding biology from the eighteenth to the twentieth century.

In putting Schrödinger's work into perspective and taking from it an absolutely singular historical role as the origin of crucial insights about life, I do not deny its extraordinary significance in the field of philosophy and theory of life. Schrödinger's work contains many strikingly original ideas which became seminal for diverse future developments. For instance, Ludwig von Bertalanffy speaks of the "irreversible entropy" in the physical universe in contrast to the "negentropy" or "reversible thermodynamics" characteristic of life.[4] Using the term "negentropy," he is implying that the second law of thermodynamics, which asserts the tendency, within a closed system, to reach a state of highest probability which is also a state of greatest disorder, is here replaced by its opposite: negentropy. In other words, the tendency toward supreme disorganization, and thus a fundamental law of the life-less physical universe, is reversed in living organisms where we find a tendency to higher order, greater complexity, and higher forms of energy and organization. Bertalanffy likewise applied these concepts in his original theory of life, which remains significant to this day, under the name of "The General Systems Theory."[5]

Similar ideas, however, are found also in Schrödinger who came across many of his theses and insights by philosophical reflections which he pursued as a physicist who was struck by the apparent physical inexplicability of life and who explored the possibilities of physicalistic explanations of the phenomenon of life and their limits. He approached the question of life from his viewpoint as the leading quantum physicist of the time. Yet he did not reflect mainly on the possibilities and limits of specific quantum mechanical explanations of biological data and on hidden physical properties of the phenomena observed in organisms, but he reflected instead on the basic facts of life known to everyone.

Remarkably enough, few, if any, comparably significant recent books on the question "What is life?" written by a biologist or a philosopher appear to exist – with exceptions such as Plessner's *Stufen des Organischen und der Mensch* and some of Conrad-Martius's works.[6] These are undoubtedly in many respects more important books on life than Schrödinger's work. To them I shall frequently refer. They also have the advantage of making reference to more recent developments in biology. Some of them, moreover, explore the question "What is Life?" quite extensively and philosophically.[7]

Classical sources also exist, as, for example, Aristotle's writings on the essence of life, *De Anima,* Immanuel Kant's *Critique of Judgment,* and others, which contain perennial contributions to a philosophy of nature and of life and which I regard as much more important works than Schrödinger's book. Yet these classical writings presuppose an entirely outdated biology and, for this reason, cannot be – in their entirety – the basis of a sufficient contemporary philosophy of life. For while philosophical methods of essential analysis do not depend in their content or method on the results of the empirical sciences, they are related to them and inspired by them, especially when they treat such a "substantially interdisciplinary" or "multidisciplinary" issue as life.

Some might think that Hans Jonas's *The Phenomenon of Life* is another exception to my judgment of the singular importance of Schrödinger's book. But one can argue against this thesis. For Jonas's work is a collection of essays that do not exclusively relate to the theme of life and do not pursue this topic at great systematic length or depth. Besides, the most remarkable insights of his book refer to points other than the essence of life, for example, to the historical reversal, which, in recent centuries, regards not living things but dead matter as primary phenomenon and as preceding life. Jonas shows brilliantly that much of modern thought on life stands under the verdict and "climate of a universal ontology of death."[8] Yet all of these insights refer to other problems than that of the nature of life. Many other notable insights of Jonas refer to the lived body and sense perception rather than to the central question of Schrödinger's book, namely, "What is life?".[9] Furthermore, while Jonas's book contains more specifically philosophical thoughts than Schrödinger's, and while it conveys striking philosophical insights, it appears a less important work on life than Schrödinger's book, for it is less rigorously argued yet more rhetorical, and for this reason leaves the reader dissatisfied, especially when seeking an answer to the question of what life is.

I am not concerned here, however, with judgments about historical figures and the rank of their work but with the question "What is life?" itself. Thus, it is proper for me as philosopher to follow the great physicist's lead and ask myself fifty years later with equal seriousness: "What is life?"[10] Although it may have been the physicist Schrödinger who has asked "What is life?" with greater intensity than any other thinker in our century, this is a question whose answer concerns the biologist more than the physicist, and the philosopher even more than the biologist, for it is a philosophical question.

This philosophical question deserves a better answer than the one Schrödinger's book provides, even if a philosophically speaking better book than his will probably have less influence on the development of science than Schrödinger's work exerted – paradoxically – partly through its worst philosophical element: its reductionism. Saying this, I do not wish to deny that the remarks made by him, rather casually, on the idea of genetic information were quite influential too, and have nothing to do with reductionism.

Both philosophical discoveries and philosophical errors can inspire empirical scientific findings, for manifold and complicated mutual relationships exist between philosophical and empirical knowledge. The complex and dialectical relationships between philosophy and science forbid us also to assume that the scientific success of some theories, such as that of evolution or that of the relativity of time, automatically guarantees the truth of the philosophic assumptions underlying a given scientific theory. For example, the success of non-Euclidean geometry in modern physics or the success of a theory of physics based on the concept of the relativity of time do not prove the truth of the philosophical transition from Hendrik Antoon Lorentz to Albert Einstein or of Einstein's purely philosophical thesis that time itself is relative. Lorentz could explain the same phenomena with his non-relative theory of time as Einstein did with relativity. He distinguished, on the basis of similar empirical observations as those Einstein made, "apparent" from "real" time. Einstein later identified what Lorentz (for good philosophical reasons) had called *apparent* time with real time and proclaimed the relativity of real time. But these are pure philosophical theses and philosophical *interpretations* of empirical data. Consequently, the truth of Einstein's philosophical conceptions in the light of which he interpreted his influential scientific discoveries and theories is in no way guaranteed by the practical success and universal acceptance of his relativity theory in the scientific world. The same is true of Charles Darwin's theory of evolution. Ditto applies also to Werner Heisenberg's philosophical theses connected with the uncertainty relation that led him mistakenly to deny much supremely evident metaphysical as well as epistemological evidence: for example, the absolute validity of the principles of excluded middle and of causality and the determinate essence of each real thing. Neither success nor consensus is identical with truth or guarantees it.

Even ideological or clearly false philosophical ideas, if we try to prove them by means of science, often lead to positive scientific discoveries. For example, a radical materialist reductionism that believes in the possibility of producing life from non-living chemical substances, or even of human beings from animals, a reductionism that I will refute by philosophical arguments, led to many experiments and important discoveries, in Russia and elsewhere.

In view of this possibility that false philosophical ideas play a positive role in the acquisition of empirical discoveries, the purely philosophical aspects of a reductionist and materialist theory of life, and specifically of the theory of evolution (inasmuch as this theory assumes an immanent development leading from pure matter to humanity), cannot be justified simply by reference to their fruitfulness for empirical research. While Darwin's theory of evolution as well as modern versions of it led to many scientific discoveries of similarities among species, of hereditary laws, etc., this fact alone does not justify the belief that the philosophical ideas of Darwin are true, even though he derived them in some fashion from observational evidence or more precisely, in spite of the fact that he used them successfully in the interpretation of empirical facts.[11]

Incidentally, the history of the theory of evolution and of its various stages and degrees of radicality is far from simple. Darwin himself did not use the term "evolution" except in the later versions of his *The Origin of Species.* It was mainly Herbert Spencer and later Ernst Haeckel who introduced the kind of evolutionary religion that dominated the philosophy of life of the nineteenth and twentieth centuries. Moreover, the hereditary laws were discovered chiefly, as is generally known, by a great scientist who was in no way a reductionist or materialist, the priest Gregor Johann Mendel.

Even the most radical metaphysical versions of the theory of evolution may lead, however, in spite of their falsity, to significant scientific discoveries. Teilhard de Chardin defended the evolutionary thesis in the radical sense of a continuous development from life-less matter through all forms of life up to the "cosmic Christ" (*le Christique*), which involves a kind of evolution of the world into God. In a less radical form, Grichka and Igor Bogdanov defend an evolutionary concept of life within which any essential difference between living and life-less beings is overlooked. Their view also involves a reductionism according to which life is only characterized by a higher degree of order and complexity, as well as of information, when compared with life-less substances. Undoubtedly, their philosophical ideas may have led them to scientific discoveries, but this does not prove in any way the truth of their philosophical opinions.

As clearest proof of the possibility that false philosophical assumptions occasionally lead to the success of experimental science note that even Adolf Hitler's grotesque and vicious racism and the criminal medical experiments performed on Jewish women in Ravensbrück based on this racism may have led to discoveries in medicine regarding biological racial differences or surgical techniques and infectious diseases.

At the same time, we must remain conscious of the fact that false philosophical ideas frequently and logically lead to serious impediments of empirical discoveries. As was demonstrated by one of the greatest human embryologists of our century, Erich Blechschmidt of the University of Göttingen, the evolutionism of Darwin, Spencer, and Haeckel and their ideas about individual morphogenesis and ontogenesis repeating within the human embryonic development phylogenesis led to serious prejudices and false assumptions regarding human embryology and other empirical matters. Blechschmidt created an important center for the study of human embryos and the largest library of photos and other representations of human embryos in the world, at the University of Göttingen. He proved that the phenomena which were taken to be human gills by many scholars, from Ernst Haeckel until today, are in reality *Beugefalten* (folds) and were mistakenly thought to be gills for ideological reasons.[12] The ideology of evolution led to other errors as well, such as the failure to take note of "missing links" between species.

A similarly ambiguous relationship between experimental science and philosophy could be shown regarding philosophical materialism, which led to many empirical discoveries but also to serious prejudices that barred the progress of experimental science. Especially in the area of empirical brain-mind research, countless empirical findings were ignored or brushed aside by materialists and determinists. In contrast, scientists who overcame the error of the negation of freedom, such as Sir John Eccles, rediscovered ignored evidence for the power of subjectivity and voluntary action on the brain, or even conducted for the first time the experiments necessary to obtain the evidence.

In contrast to philosophical errors, which can have both good and bad results for empirical science, philosophical truths *per se* can never lead to scientific regress. Only their one-sided and therefore false interpretation can lead to regress, as, for example, the exaggerated role assigned to the knowledge of necessary and evident essences by Aristotle and even more by some of his followers, or any other wrong absolutistic role assigned to *a priori* knowledge which ignores the wide fields of study that require empirical methods. In this sense, Stanley L. Jaki showed that a false apriorism led to impediments for empirical science for centuries.[13]

Philosophical insights and discoveries as such can never prevent experimental findings. On the contrary, they can lead to experimental findings and scientific progress. As, for example, Sir John Eccles showed, the philosophical recognition of freedom, and thus of an extrinsic causal influence on the brain, led to important experiments and evidence in brain research, the discovery and the correct interpretation of which would have been hardly thinkable without the proper philosophical conception of freedom.[14]

Thus, both false philosophical ideas or fanatic ideologies, by accident, as well as true philosophical insights, quite naturally, can play an inspiring role for empirical scientific discoveries. The influence of empirical findings on philosophical research and discovery is a similarly complex issue but not our theme here. Though they are mutually related in many ways philosophical analysis and empirical investigation of life have entirely different and irreducible tasks and methods. Therefore, empirical life-sciences can never dispense us from the task of philosophical analysis.

Schrödinger's *What Is Life?* became influential both through its positive contributions and through its false reductionist ideas. In contrast to his great discoveries about the irreducible newness of life, we also find in Schrödinger's book an ultimate reductionism which seeks to reduce life in the last analysis to new and deeper laws of physics and of the inanimate nature. In this respect, he is quite similar to Michael Polanyi, who wrote superb essays on the irreducibility of life to the laws of physics and chemistry but then writes that this irreducibility of life is only relative to the present state of natural science:

> When I say that life transcends physics and chemistry, I mean that biology cannot explain life in our age by the current workings of physical and chemical laws.[15]

In contrast, the present book will defend the *absolute irreducibility of life*. Now, in view of what I have said, Schrödinger's *What Is Life?*– and I say this with all due admiration – cannot replace a properly philosophical study of life. The book is no properly philosophical work, however many merits it possesses and however many empirical discoveries it inspired, and whether it did so by the true philosophical insights it contains or by its mistaken materialist reductionism. Schrödinger's book implies a philosophy of life that is not only lacking in professional rigor but also involves many traces of an unphilosophical or even anti-philosophical reductionism that can only be overcome by a phenomenological and properly philosophical return to the intelligible "thing itself" which life is.[16]

Other books on the nature of life, many of which contain substantial contributions toward an adequate bio-philosophy, nevertheless appear too limited to take up the whole challenge of Schrödinger's book to philosophers: to answer the question about the essence of life. In the following, therefore, I shall take a fresh look at the question "What is life?," and answer it from a philosophical point of view – not hiding from myself the extreme difficulties associated with such an enterprise.

The reader will encounter in the text of this work some technical philosophical terms the use of which I deem unavoidable to convey the properly philosophical insights intended by me – although I try to explain these terms right away and in a common language the meaning of which should be universally accessible.

The reader might also find it helpful to use Chapter Five as a sort of guide and commentary for all other chapters and sections of the present work. For that chapter expresses succinctly many central ideas of this book and is relatively free of technical jargon. (I mean here by jargon both "technical terms" that are unintelligible to the interested non-philosopher but also those known only to one group of philosophers but not to another.) In Chapter Five – which originated in real dialogues concerning this book with representatives of biosciences, physics, cosmology, astronomy, and others – questions are addressed which many readers might pose to themselves and might wish to address to the author when reading his book.

In the real dialogues from which Chapter Five originated, many of the disasters became apparent that take place when philosophers intrude into the field of science, and some of those which frequently occur when scientists try to do philosophy.

Yet the farthest thing from my mind is to discourage either the philosophical adventures of scientists or the reflections of philosophers on the subject-matter and results of scientific investigations. Quite the contrary, philosophers today should turn close attention to those questions which scientists debate at the present moment of world history: new medical techniques, new definitions of life and death, genetic codes, evolution, the Big Bang, and the like. For the trans-disciplinary unity of being itself demands that we view the world from all those diverse sides which open themselves only to the different disciplines and to their different methods; at the same time, we should not forget the need to complement the limited knowledge obtained by means of our own disciplines through the cognitions acquired in others.

As a matter of fact, in the course of the dialogues with natural scientists which gave rise to this book, the need clearly emerged for scientists today to philosophize, or, more precisely, to develop a science open to philosophy; and *vice versa,* the need arises today more forcefully than before for philosophers not to ignore the great discoveries of science. Each scientific question has philosophical sides. Any isolation that imprisons members of single disciplines in their own compartmentalized fields of study will easily lead to reductionistic explanations and to errors. Such isolation and the errors ensuing therefrom have become more fateful today than they have ever been in the past. For incredibly fast and radical developments have taken place in the interdisciplinary fields of theory and investigation. Many new questions, definitions of life and death, and many other theoretical elements and new modes of praxis emerged in medicine and other fields of research and practical life, and they touch the whole of humanity – both the private and the political life of every human person.

Many significant scientific discoveries, as, for example, Darwin's theory of evolution and Einstein's theory of relativity, as well as the errors that are frequently linked to them, affect our *Weltanschauung* and our very lives. Simultaneously, they involve inevitably ethical and other philosophical questions and positions. This is particularly obvious in medicine and issues of medical ethics. What is true of medicine is true also of the basic concepts of the life-sciences, and even more so of sociology or of psychology, and of the humanities. Therefore, I hope to make not only a contribution to philosophy but also one which will turn out significant for the representatives in the empirical life-sciences and for all of us, members of a humanity which profits from a better understanding of life, and in particular of human life. Human life is gravely threatened not only by the horrors of abuses of the empirical knowledge and techniques of the life-sciences but also by the philosophical errors and misconceptions which lie at the bottom of these abuses.

In this context, special significance must be assigned not only to a general philosophical analysis of life *per se*, and of biological life, but also to the entirely new and deeper phenomenon of specifically *human* life and to an investigation of its higher value and dignity. Ultimately, only in the light of these forms and sources of the dignity of life can an ethics of experimentation and of the application of empirical research in society be judged. Precisely in this area the philosopher can make the most decisive contribution to the understanding of life and to the banishing of those evil spirits which a misguided and unphilosophical empirical science almost necessarily, though unwittingly, unleashes. The investigations into the new essence and dignity of human life are presented in Chapters Three and Four. Chapter Five then has a synoptic character and confronts a number of objections raised by scientists to the defense of the irreducibility of life to chaotic and non-chaotic physical systems.

One

ON THE METAPHYSICAL ESSENCE AND ABSOLUTE IRREDUCIBILITY OF LIFE: THE MANY MEANINGS OF LIFE – AND A BRIEF DISCOURSE ON METHOD

1. Introductory Remarks on the Essence of Life as *Bios* and *Zoee*

In his *Metaphysics*, Aristotle observes that we speak of being in many senses,[1] and he is certainly right in this. It is no less correct to say, "Of life we speak in many senses."

Some of the many meanings of life which will not be treated here include the purely "sensitive" life of animals (in contradistinction to that of plants), but also the difference between the actualized mental life – as opposed to its dormant state – as well as many further actualization within the actualized mental life, as, for example, a given degree of vitality, of mental dynamism, of a properly rational life that involves a right use of intellect and will, of human spiritual life (as opposed to spiritual death), etc.

Instead, I will chiefly investigate the object of the two Greek terms *zoee* and *bios.* These terms suggest at least two of the many meanings of "life," and in the present work I will clarify the meanings of these two terms and above all the things to which they refer. Both of these terms have many meanings in Greek, some of which will be excluded from the following considerations. What, then, are we to understand under these terms?

Under *bios* we should understand the organic life of plants, but also of animals and of human beings, and thus a life which is inseparable from a body. *Zoee*, on the other hand, refers to all kinds of life, both to the most universal essence of life and to the supreme real or even thinkable forms of it. My interpretation of *bios* in its distinction from *zoee* is arbitrary in a purely linguistic respect. For "*bios*" can also refer, not to the opposite of death (as *zoee*) but to a "form of life," in relation to "ethos" or political life.[2] But I will use *bios* as a technical term referring to the (biological) life of organisms as it is inseparable from the body. In this sense of the term, *bios* stands in contrast to the immortal life of a soul separated from the body, as Plato defends it in the *Phaedo.*[3] Hans Jonas seems to regard this kind of *bios*-life as the only one in the human being as well. This is probably also the reason why Jonas – besides the "eternal image of the self" and some form of "eternal fame" – does not recognize any real life after death.[4] Later I will give a more complete list of the properties of biological life and get at the very essence of it.

2. "Being in Itself" and "Self-Motion" as Universal Properties of All Life – The Analogous Meaning of Self-Motion and Freedom

The terms *bios* and *zoee* have some elements in common which should be explored. Both *bios* and *zoee* in their strict sense refer to that actuality and dynamism which only real beings can possess. Fictions, irreal or abstract objects can never possess life, but only beings that are real in the full sense of the term, as Hans Jonas points out well:

> The abstractions themselves do not live ....[5]

While fictitious objects or pure intentional objects of consciousness may be *given to us* as living objects and may *appear to live*, purely intentional objects *can never actually* live.[6] The first ontological condition of life is the autonomous being in itself of an object. Only *things in themselves can* live, never appearances that can only appear to live. For this reason, not only Immanuel Kant's negation of the possibility of knowing things in themselves but also Edmund Husserl's position according to which we can only reach intentional objects and *noemata* of consciousness cuts off a real way to the knowledge of life. This can only be provided by a realist philosophy which recognizes the transcendence of the human person in knowledge that allows him or her access to beings in themselves.[7] Husserl, after his turn to the transcendental phenomenological standpoint, in *Cartesian Meditations* and other works, lays emphasis on the idea of life, insisting on the life of this *ego.* But this either constitutes a contradiction to his position which denies of the transcendental ego the concrete, individual reality which is necessarily presupposed for life, or it asserts an intrinsic impossibility, which is precisely what Jonas rejects in the above passage: namely, that a non-real, non-individual entity lives. Not only autonomous reality and being are required for a being to live, as we shall see, but also the possession of a real principle of soul or *entelechy.*

What, besides an autonomous being in itself, are the essential characteristics of life in all its forms? Plato saw one of the most prominent marks of life in self-motion, in a motility which has its source in the living being itself and not outside of it. Plato writes about this essential feature of life:

> ... we shall not be disgraced if we declare that this ... self motion is the essence, the very definition of the soul. For every body that is moved

> from without is soulless; and every body that derives its motion from within itself has a soul, since that is indeed the soul's nature.[8]

Plato bases an argument for the immortality and eternity of the soul on this feature of self-motion.[9] While he insists that the soul possesses self-motion, he does not imply that the soul is in some form of "physical motion." Aristotle adds with greater precision that life and soul are what originates movement but not what is itself in motion. He rejects the respective Presocratic views of life and soul:

> This implies the view that the soul is identical with what produces movement in animals. That is why, further, they regard respiration as the characteristic mark of life.[10]

Aristotle rejects the materialist interpretation of soul in relationship to self-movement; the soul is not itself in motion but a transcendent cause of self-motion *in living things*:

> for, doubtless, not only is it false that the essence of soul is correctly described by those who say that it is what moves (or is capable of moving) itself, but it is an impossibility that movement should be even an attribute of it.
>
> We have already pointed out that there is no necessity that what originates movement should itself be moved.[11]

However, this observation can only refer to physical motion which must not be attributed to the living soul itself. In another sense, as we shall see, self-motion can certainly be attributed to life itself, especially to the free living subject. Thomas Aquinas also held the view that life is essentially characterized by bestowing the ability of self-motion to living things:

> We say then that an animal begins to live when it begins to move of itself: and as long as such motion appears in it, so long is it considered to be alive. When it has no longer any movement of itself, but is only moved by another power, then its life is said to fail, and the animal to be dead. Whereby it is clear that those things are properly called living that move themselves by some kind of motion .... Accordingly all things are said to be alive that determine themselves to motion or operation of any kind: whereas those things that cannot by their nature do so, cannot be called living, unless by a similitude.[12]

The modern term "endogen motility" has a similar, although more limited, meaning and is intended to distinguish the organism not only from inorganic matter moved from an external source, but also from the type of self-movement found in the sub-atomic structure or in the motor. Max Scheler also recognizes this essential mark of life but extends it beyond self-motion and calls the objective essential phenomena of life: self-motion, self-formation, self-differentiation, and self-limitation. When we think of this kind of self-motion in dead matter, we recognize need to resolve the following difficulty: What, if anything, distinguishes the self-motion characteristic of life, from phenomena of auto-motion in the purely physical universe?[13] In order to do justice to the new phenomenon of the self-movement of the living being, Max Scheler declares that a necessary essential law is that the movement of living beings which is specific for life is always the consequence of a vital tendency.[14] He adds that the vital movement does not fall under some of the laws of the inanimate physical universe, as, for example, the law of inertia; instead, this movement is the immediate consequence of an inner force and activity of the living being.[15] Scheler brilliantly observes that the law of inertia can only dominate completely a world in which there would be no life. He offers fascinating analyses of the changes of states specific to living beings and of the animal movements dominated by instincts. He sees the principle "live is what moves itself" culminate in freedom.[16]

The self-movement, more precisely the originating of a dynamism or movement from within oneself, which is an essential mark of life, must be distinguished from the purely material "self-movement" of sub-atomic particles, pendulums, or planets. The closest to self-movement in physical reality is the motion of sub-atomic particles, in particular, Brawns movement, which exists even at around the temperature of absolute zero and which, in principle, cannot be stopped. These forms of self-motion cannot be regarded as forms of self-movement in the proper sense of the word. They depend on the laws of the sub-atomic world or on the laws of mechanics and on other material events in bodies, and lack the true origin from a vital tendency or a spontaneous and living center in the being that moves itself in the way of living things. "Self-motion" applied to both of these phenomena is a merely analogous and even a misleading use of terms.

In view of the essentially different form of "self-motion" characteristic of all living things, Plato, Augustine, Descartes, Kant, and many other philosophers see the highest forms of life linked to freedom. When Kant says: "For all life rests on the inner faculty to determine oneself at will,"[17] he seems to have in mind already the highest form of this self-movement and thus of efficient causality, namely, freedom. Freedom allows for a spontaneous and rational self-determination and for a movement which has its source in the agent and not outside of the subject of free acts. This free life, Kant emphasizes, embodies life preeminently.

It would be interesting to compare the texts from Plato's *Phaedrus* and from Kant's discussion of life in *Träume eines Geistersehers* and elsewhere with Augustine's discussion of the order of efficient causes in *The City of God*, where Augustine sees in the "making without being made" the highest form of freedom and of efficient causality which must be attributed solely to God. This highest free causality is also linked to life in the supreme form. However, "both making (*facere*) and being made" are characteristic for contingent free agents. We can say, according to Augustine, that "making (acting) in a way that exceeds being acted upon or happening (*fieri*)" is a characteristic of freedom and a sign of higher life and efficient causality which only belong to free beings.[18] In view of this "order of efficient causes," as seen by Augustine, material causes are not even properly causes of anything: "Material causes, therefore, which may rather be said to be made than to make, are not to be reckoned among efficient causes, because they can only do what the wills of spirits do by them."[19]

Because of this character of life as "self-motion" – which Gottfried Wilhelm Leibniz attributes to all substances (monads) – and in view of the free self-determination in which self-motion culminates and which we discover in our own life, Plato[20] regards life as immortal. What moves itself from within cannot be deserted by the principle of its motion.

In all of these conceptions from Plato to Kant, the self-motion of life is interpreted more or less explicitly in terms of freedom because in freedom alone the self-movement characteristic of all life culminates. This thesis is also contained in Hans Jonas's philosophy of life. Jonas follows a similar path and even sees metabolism as a first manifestation of freedom.[21] To the degrees of freedom (understood in a way analogous to the degrees of spontaneity distinguished by various ancient philosophers) as a mark of life, he adds the reference to awareness, consciousness, and knowledge as another fundamental characteristic of life:

> One way of interpreting this scale is in terms of scope and distinctness of experience, of rising degrees of world perception which move toward the widest and freest objectification of the sum of being in individual percipients. Another way, concurrent with the grades of perception, is in terms of progressive freedom of action. The correlation and interpenetration of these two aspects – of perceiving and acting ... is a constant theme for the empathic study of the many forms of life.

In both of these respects, Jonas appears to conceive of life completely in terms of its first inner-worldly analogue, personal life, and possibly in terms of animal awareness and spontaneity of action, and thus to reduce somehow anthropomorphically the vegetative life of plants to conscious and free life. Yet, Jonas, in spite of many critical notes on Darwinistic evolutionism, appears to embrace a monism, and he speaks of "the first feat of matter's organizing itself for life, ... actuated by a tendency in the depth of being toward the very modes of freedom to which this transition opened the gate."[22] Concomitantly with this monism, Jonas rejects any form of "dualism,"[23] a term which Jonas fails to analyze, and consequently sees the prime manifestation of life in organic life, thus reducing personal life to an emergent property of biological life, a position he rejects in his later *Macht oder Ohnmacht der Subjektivität*.[24] I see here contradictions in Jonas's philosophy of life. Helmuth Plessner criticizes "dualism" in another sense: of a *divisio mundi* into physical and psychic objects. This dualism would not provide any category for life below rational life.[25]

Linked to Jonas's all too literal interpretation of all life, including the purely vegetative life of plants, in terms of freedom, is a type of evolutionism in Jonas's philosophy. Jonas certainly does not proceed far in the direction of evolutionist monism. For example, he criticizes Alfred North Whitehead's metaphysics of the organism for blurring the distinction between life and non-life, and for its immanentistic metaphysics which divinizes the world and has no room for death or evil.[26]

To reject any evolutionism which denies the fundamental and unbridgeable differences between the different forms of life, especially between human and animal life, should not lead us to deny some good meaning in the thesis that self-motion is linked to freedom. If the essence of *bios*, of organic life, is interpreted in terms of freedom, because the organism possesses an inner principle of motility which foreshadows freedom, we can, though we deplore any confusion between the essentially different levels of life, also learn something important from the interpretation of the self-motion of all life in terms of freedom. For in analyzing cautiously biological life and the idea of self-motion, we transcend – by the very characterization of life with reference to freedom – the level of mere biological life, *bios*-life. Who could deny that freedom constitutes the clearest example of self-motion and presupposes necessarily the life of its subject? Through a reflection on the organism's having a principle of action within itself, we arrive at freedom as the prime example of this automotion, and thus at the more universal meaning of life: *zoee*. *Zoee*, in contrast to *bios*, refers to an essential moment of all living things and does not imply any restrictions of life to bodily beings. The life of a soul, of a pure spirit or an absolutely perfect personal being would have to be characterized by self-motion even more so than biological bodily life.

Jonas's opinion that only bodily beings live and that "the abstractions themselves do not live," while being true about abstractions, overlooks that the idea of a perfect life which is not bound to matter has nothing to do with the life of abstractions. Therefore, he cannot validly conclude from his insight that abstractions cannot live and that only bodily or biological life is life. The *haecceitas* and concrete individuality is as much a property of an absolute person, if there is a living God, as it is a property of a human person, nay even much more. The idea inherited by Aristotle that pure spirits not bound to matter are abstract entities, and the correlated assumption that matter is the principle of individuation, have to be criticized by a truly personalistic metaphysics which shows Jonas's statement that "pure consciousness is as little alive as the pure matter standing over against it ..."[27] to be quite false if it does not only refer to abstractions but excludes any life which is not bound to corporeity.[28]

Thus we attain a new insight: This self-motion which is characteristic of life is not restricted to *bios* but characterizes all forms of *zoee*, even in their supreme form. This is expressed with clarity by Thomas Aquinas:

> Hence a more perfect degree of life is that of intelligent beings; for their power of self-movement is more perfect .... Wherefore that being whose act of understanding is its very nature, and which, in what it naturally possesses, is not determined by another, must have life in the most perfect degree. Such is God; and hence in Him principally is life. From this the Philosopher concludes (*Metaph.* XII 51), after showing God to be intelligent, that God has life most perfect and eternal, since His intellect is most perfect and always in act.[29]

As Thomas says, Aristotle clearly ascribes *zoee* to God, saying, for example:

> Moreover, life belongs to God. For the actuality of thought is life (*zoee*), and God is that actuality (*energeia*); and the essential actuality of God is life most good and eternal. We hold, then, that God is a living being, eternal, most good; and therefore life and a continuous eternal existence belong to God; for that is what God is.[30]

3. Can Life be Sufficiently Identified by Means of Self-Motion or Intrinsic Teleology, etc.? On the Character of Life as an *Urphenomenon*

But are self-motion and freedom adequate or sufficient categories to capture the essence of life? They seem to contain too much and too little at the same time to be properly regarded as essential features of all life. Certainly, not all living beings are free, and Jonas uses this term quite ambiguously, or at least analogously, when he attributes some freedom to all living things. Yet, many beings live that are not free. Besides, even free beings do not only live *inasmuch as they are free.* The vegetative life of plants, the sensitive life of animals, and the higher mental life of human beings can in no way be reduced to the notion of self-motion which culminates in freedom. Mental life includes many forms of affective experiences and emotions which are not free, and it includes the cognitive life which is completely misconstrued if conceived as a self-motion or spontaneous active synthesis, or a *Tathandlung* of the mind, as Johann Gottlieb Fichte conceives intellectual intuition. Instead, cognition is characterized by a "receptive transcendence," that is, by a mental discovery of what is the case and by a conscious "taking in" and possessing objects and states of affairs as they are independently of the act of knowing.[31] But inasmuch as a rational subject lives just as much in knowing as in acting freely, life cannot correctly and sufficiently be characterized simply in terms of self-motion or of freedom as its supreme form. *Zoee* in the broad sense of life as such includes a unique and irreducible dynamism of being which manifests itself in the human being just as much in knowledge or in the affective life as in freedom. Therefore, it cannot be reduced to self-motion in any sense of this term.

If we recognize that life cannot be simply reduced to self-motion nor be defined in terms of it, we could ask: Can it be defined in terms of another property distinct from life itself? When we ponder the answer to this question, we see that life cannot be defined exhaustively by means of any other property either. Life is an ultimate and irreducible datum. That life is, ultimately, undefinable, is not due to a weakness of our minds but to the originality and irreducible simplicity that are characteristic of all first principles and pure perfections, as well as of many other essences. The term of "simple" (or ultimate) simplicity, of the *simpliciter simplex*, introduced by Duns Scotus to designate the "pure perfections," could be applied to all fundamental and ultimate (irreducible) data as, for example, red or blue, numbers, being, knowledge, etc.

The widespread opinion that what is absolutely undefinable is also unknowable is completely mistaken. On the contrary, the intelligibility of the first undefinable essences and principles is the supreme intelligibility which is already presupposed for the derivative intelligibility of essences defined in terms of more primary elements. But undefinability through something else does not mean that we cannot analyze essential characteristics and thus arrive at something like a non-reductive "essential definition." This is overlooked by George Edward Moore who concludes[32] from his excellent analysis of the impossibility of defining the "good" in terms of something else that we cannot say more than "the good is the good."[33]

We should also not say that Plato fails in his definitions of knowledge, friendship, etc. but that he arrives at the recognition of the impossibility of defining them in terms of something else. Also Aristotle does not fail to define the soul and life, but he recognizes, even though without sufficient clarity, their irreducibility.[34] In the passages from *Posterior Analytics* quoted in the following notes, Aristotle provides an excellent theoretical explanation for the superior knowledge we possess with regard to undefinable and irreducible data when compared with definable data.

Phenomenological realism has shown that Aristotle's notion of these irreducible data is far too limited and that he – as later Kant with his twelve categories – impoverished the *a priori*. The first and most abstract principles –

as, for example, being – and many more specific ones (such as love, hope, despair, knowledge, sight) have their own irreducible essences. These essences are intelligible and their elements are analyzable, although they are not reducible to anything else. Moreover, intuitions of first principles are not unreliable or vague but most reliable and rational. Besides, what is given in them can often be formulated with utmost clarity, as, for example, the principle of contradiction both in its metaphysical and its logical sense, as Aristotle and, more clearly Husserl in his *Logical Investigations*, have shown. The individual colors likewise cannot be defined in terms of anything else. Aristotle has well shown that the quest to define everything through something else is just as irrational as the desire to prove everything. For all definitions and all syllogisms rest on foundations that are prior to them and cannot be defined or proven but must be understood in their own right and by means of some immediate understanding or perception. The experience and knowledge in which these undefinable and irreducible data are given to us are in no way irrational. On the contrary, the supreme form of reason and rational knowledge consists precisely in the rational intuition into these arch-phenomena, a fact on which Aristotle insisted.[35] This truth is also a central point of any phenomenological method.[36]

Let me explain this further. Life is one of those ultimate data, like being or the good, which are undefinable through something else, and our labor is doomed to failure if we undertake an effort to define these data in terms of other known entities, as Moore and Dietrich von Hildebrand have shown so convincingly for the good and for value.[37] Any definition and explanation of this kind is impossible and inadequate with respect to the first principles and first things, as, for example, being, as Aristotle noted, or value, or life. Any attempt to define everything in terms of something else or of other elements is just as circular as any effort to prove everything. For as each definition requires first undefinable essences, so each argument presupposes first premises and laws of correct inference that cannot be further proven without falling into circular argument or begging the question.

Any effort to define irreducible essences through their parts, or by proximate genus and specific difference, already presupposes preceding notions of other essences that cannot be endlessly defined. It also requires the notion itself which we are seeking to explain. What is more important, any attempt at a definition in terms of something else is inadequate with reference to each original essence. Aristotle conceives original and undefinable elements and essences in terms of a few first principles and categories (*archai*), but in reality these “first principles” comprise an enormous variety of irreducible arch-data. This is not to deny that Aristotle’s practice, especially in his ethics, contradicts this restriction, nor that the Aristotelian notion of immediately known propositions spreads much more widely than it does in the theories of many of his professed followers. In fact, the epistemological features of irreducible propositions according to Aristotle presuppose many irreducibilia.

The irreducible character of life, which resists its reduction to other notions (even if these are so closely related to life as self-motion) – and the irreducibility of similar phenomena – was seen clearly by Johann Wolfgang von Goethe in his *Farbenlehre*. Goethe insists that when we encounter an ultimate *Urphenomenon*, we must not seek to explain it any further by other things. Instead, we have important work to do in clarifying and elucidating these arch-phenomena. He complains that authors normally fail to do just that; and hence, they distort these phenomena by their futile attempts at reductionist explanations. Thus, he writes:

> Even if one were to encounter such an *Urphenomenon*, there remains the evil that one does not want to acknowledge it as such, and that one is looking behind it and above it for some other thing, whereas we should confess here that we have reached the endpoint of such looking.[38]

And elsewhere he adds:

> The highest thing at which man can arrive ... is the sense of wonder, and when an *Urphenomenon* provokes wonder in him, he should be content; for it cannot accord him anything higher than that, and he should not look for anything higher behind it; for here is the limit. But to humans the sight of an *Urphenomenon* is normally not sufficient, they think, one has to go farther than that, and they resemble children, who, when they have looked into the mirror, turn it right away around, in order so see what is on the other side.[39]

The formulation of the character of arch-phenomena (*Urphänomene*), which cannot be explained by anything outside themselves, which the scientist "should allow to stand there in their eternal tranquillity and glory," and "which the philosopher should let enter into his region,"[40] makes Goethe a forerunner of the phenomenological method of returning to things themselves.[41] In writing the following things, he sets up for us a high ideal of a philosophy that is faithful to ultimate data, as, for example, life, without attempting to reduce the irreducible phenomenon to anything else:

> We believe to deserve the thankfulness of the philosopher for having attempted to pursue the phenomena up till their original sources (*Urquellen*), up till the point where they do nothing but manifest themselves and are, and where it is impossible to explain anything beyond in them ...[42]

> He [the philosopher] ought to form for himself a method which is adequate to intuition (*eine Methode, die dem Anschauen gemäß ist*); he should avoid carefully to transform the intuition into concepts, and the

concept into words, and then to operate with these words as if they were things ... (no. 720).

If on the other hand the physicist is able to arrive at the cognition of that which we have called an *Urphenomenon* (*Urphänomen*), he is well sheltered [as it were, he has arrived at home] and the philosopher is sheltered with him ... the philosopher accepts from the physicist's hands some last thing which with him now becomes a first thing.[43]

Elsewhere in his *Theory of Colors*,[44] Goethe speaks of the *Urphänomene*, saying that they reveal themselves only to an intuitive knowledge and that "nothing on the order of their [self-]appearing lies above them."[45] To use a felicitous expression in Heidegger's *Being and Time*, § 7, we may say that they can only "show themselves from themselves." It becomes quickly clear that – in spite of the magnificent things Goethe says about the arch-phenomena that lend themselves to philosophical analysis – for Goethe many phenomena in nature, as, for example, the *Granit* or the *magnet*, are arch-phenomena which in the strict philosophical sense of necessary intelligible essences are not irreducible arch-phenomena.[46]

But Goethe also insists on the same fundamental feature of the phenomenological method upon which Adolf Reinach insists: hardly anything is a greater labor than to elucidate these arch-phenomena such as life, without reducing them to something else. And it is hard work to identify the essential marks of these irreducible phenomena.[47]

In the spirit of these texts of Goethe, some phenomenologists and philosophers in our century, as, for example, Moore, have pointed out the irreducible character of value, of the good, of being, of promises, of love, and of countless other irreducible data.

Life, both as *zoee* and as *bios*, is an irreducible datum, which Goethe also designates as something "incommensurable" that cannot be captured by mathematical formulas and ratios.[48] He says that many explanations of it risk "to transform the living into something dead,"[49] "covering it up and obscuring it," instead of "elucidating it and bringing it closer to us."[50] Not by accident Goethe refers to a famous passage in Kant's *Critique of Pure Reason* on the "*anschauende Urteilskraft*" (the intuitive power of judgment), where Kant speaks of the possibility of an intuitive knowledge of essences which he denies to humans. Even less of an accident is that Goethe sees precisely those passages in which Kant speaks of an *intellectus archetypicus* who would be capable of intuitive knowledge of essences, as exemplifying what also, at least to some extent, a human person is capable of: to intuit irreducible essences and forms.[51]

Some other philosophers, as, for example, Plessner, have attempted to combine an anti-reductionism which insists on the character of life as an irreducible phenomenon with a reductionism. Plessner holds that life and its modals (*Modale*)[52] are in their quality "absolutely undissectable and irreducible." He implied that the ultimate phenomena of life cannot be dissolved into the totality of their physico-electrical-chemical conditions, and yet claimed a total reducibility of all organic modalities to physical-chemical conditions. The term *zoee* designates an arch-phenomenon (an *Urphänomen*), the nature of which I am going to discuss later. Goethe recognizes life as an *Urphänomen* in which even God reveals Himself, operating and manifesting Himself only in the *Urphenomenon* of the living, not in the dead.[53] Goethe goes on to claim that the pure analyzing intellect can grasp the dead, whereas higher reason (*Vernunft*) alone is capable of grasping the higher *Urphenomenon* of the living.[54]

Zoee designates that unique and irreducible actuality and source of the internal dynamic activity and self-movement which we call "life" and which to elucidate and clarify is the purpose of this book. Let us heed the excellent warning Goethe gives us with regard to treating these arch-phenomena:

> How hard is it, however, not to put the sign in the place of the thing, to keep always alive before oneself the essence and not to kill it through the word.[55]

4. Life as a "Transcendental" in the Medieval Sense and as a Pure Perfection

Life is also a "transcendental" in the medieval sense of a pure perfection.[56] This *Urphenomenon* of life manifests itself in cognition, in all rational activity, including meaningful affective experiences, and in freedom, as well as in animals and plants. For the reason of its presence in a wide multitude of phenomena and on so many levels of being, *zoee* in the universal sense of "life as such" (unlike *bios*) can be attributed also to the highest imaginable forms of the irreducible dynamic form of being which we call life.

Zoee in this respect is similar to the Scholastic "transcendentals" which constitute characteristics of everything that is, except that life only refers to all *living* beings, not to *all* beings. The so-called "transcendentals" include properties as *being* itself, *essence*, *unity*, the being *something* as opposed to nothing or something else, *intelligibility*, and – in a restricted sense not related to all acts and evil in beings[57] – *value* or the *good* (*bonum*), and *beauty* (*pulchrum*). This restricted sense of "transcendentality" means that *in all beings* must exist some value in the sense of intrinsic positive importance and some beauty, but that not all acts and abuses of freedom or sufferings or concentration camps – which possess being – are *eo ipso* beautiful or good. Not all things, and not all respects in which they are real, are bearers of value in the sense of an intrinsic positive importance (preciousness), which can neither be reduced to that which is good for us nor to the merely subjectively important.[58]

If Thomists consider as "transcendental" all properties which belong to all beings, *zoee*-"life" is certainly not a "transcendental" in this sense, because not all beings live. Some bio-monists, including Erwin Schrödinger, would object that the whole cosmos should be considered as a huge organism. But this view denies the obvious datum and evident possibility of lifeless material substances. At the same time, contradicting himself, Schrödinger reduces this universal "life" of the entire cosmos to some inanimate form of being.

Though we should recognize that not all beings live and that therefore life is not a transcendental property of all entities, *zoee*-life bears a similarity to the transcendentals inasmuch as it is not restricted, as *bios*, to a specific form of life bound to matter but applies to *all living* beings. *Zoee* is, as it were, a peculiarly restricted "transcendental for all living beings." It is found in all orders of life and binds together biological life with the highest forms of spiritual life, whose distinctness from *bios*-life I will discuss in detail.

But if life can be called a "transcendental" – when this term means characteristics that are coextensive with being – only in a restricted sense of properties which do not belong to *all* beings but to an extremely large and diversified class of entities, it definitely is a transcendental property in another and more significant sense, introduced by Duns Scotus. This meaning of transcendental coincides with those "*pure perfections*" which are not essentially limited and therefore not restricted to a limited sphere of being. Elaborating on Anselm of Canterbury's discovery,[59] which in my judgment is one of the greatest in the history of thought, Scotus characterizes these transcendental pure perfections by the following five marks.[60] (1) It is absolutely better to have or to be them rather than not to possess or not to be them, in whatever reason their non-possession may be grounded. In this sense, being or wisdom are pure perfections, whereas silver, all species of animals, as well as human nature, are not pure or absolute perfections, but "mixed perfections." For, in virtue of their *ratio formalis*, that is, because of what formally constitutes their essence, they are necessarily limited and limiting. A being can be more perfect than gold, for example, or nobler than any of the plants and animals and even than human beings, without being them or possessing any of their natures. Mixed perfections, by their necessary limitations, differ from pure perfections such as life. Of pure perfections we gain the insight that their possession is absolutely better than their non-possession because they are not surpassable, except in their limited manifestations and by a being possessing their form in a higher mode. These pure perfections play a central role in metaphysics and are the condition of the possibility of any knowledge of God. (2) Pure perfections must all be compatible with one another, which follows logically from their first characteristic. Otherwise, the same thing could both (as pure perfection) be better to be than not to be, and not be better to possess than not to possess (as contradicting another pure perfection). (3) All pure perfections "can be infinite in something" and are only fully themselves when they are infinite. Any limit of life, for example, implies that a being does not fully possess the *ratio* and the *logos* of life and is in some ways half-living or deprived of the fullness of life. The same is true of goodness, knowledge, justice, being, wisdom, mercy, freedom, and all pure perfections: they all are not fully themselves when they are limited. (4) Pure perfections are all irreducibly simple and consequently not composite, deducible, or derived from something else – and thus in a sense undefinable through something else. This irreducible originality as a characteristic of pure perfections is also found in the irreducible essence of life. (5) All pure perfections are communicable to more than one subject. Therefore, it is a pure perfection to be a person, but the incommunicable existence of "being me" rather than "being you" can never be an absolute perfection.[61]

The last two characteristics Scotus lists are also found in many mixed perfections. Irreducibility, for instance, belongs to irreducible data as color, prime colors, motion, the mathematical point or line, as well as to guilt and contingency, which are not pure perfections. The same applies to the communicability to more than one subject which is also found in all universals that belong to the order of mixed perfections, for example, in human nature or animal species. Of the two last characteristics of pure perfections it is more difficult to show that they belong to pure perfections than to show that they are characteristics of mixed ones.

With respect to the first through the third of these characteristics, pure perfections differ from mixed perfections or from those perfections which are good only from a certain point of view and in comparison with lower beings. These characteristics which are good in many respects but include essential limitations, such as being a lion or a human being, can be surpassed by higher perfections, are not compatible with all pure perfections, and cannot be infinite.

Pure perfections encompass three distinct classes:

1. Being itself and all those properties which are coextensive with it are *eo ipso* pure perfections because they evidently are the ontic condition of the possibility of any perfection whatsoever, and nothing, including the absolute being, can be without them. These absolutely universal transcendentals include, besides being itself, *res* (essence), being *something* (*aliquid*) in the sense of distinctness and in that of being something rather than nothing, having some unity (*unum*), being intelligible (*verum*), and also goodness (*bonum*) and beauty (*pulchrum*) of which no being whatsoever can be entirely deprived.

2. Some other pure perfections, as, for example, being alive or being a person, are pure perfections yet are not found in all entities but only in some

beings. Nevertheless, these are also "transcendental" in the Scotistic sense of the term, which signifies, in contradistinction to the use of this term by Aquinas and other Medievals, the character of pure perfections *per se*, the absence of any essential limitations and of any restriction to a limited category of being.

3. Some divine attributes, as, for example, omnipotence, necessary real existence, absolute and unsurpassable perfection, constitute a third class of pure perfections: the exclusively divine attributes. Since these are not only compatible with absolute infinity but are essentially infinite, they are also "transcendental" in Duns Scotus's sense of this term; in fact they are so in the supreme mode.

All pure perfections of all three classes are not restricted to a finite category or kind of being, are in this very sense "transcendental," and must exist in an infinite divine being if God exists at all. This is obvious for the third class, the exclusively divine transcendentals, but it also applies to the first two groups of transcendental properties because they admit of absolute infinity and are only fully themselves in the infinitely perfect. In addition, they cannot be surpassed by anything in perfection that does not possess them in their *ratio formalis* (in what formally constitutes them). In this Scotistic sense, life, falling in the second class of pure perfections, is not only analogous to the transcendentals but is itself a transcendental property of being.[62]

The notion of *zoee*-life encompasses *all conceivable forms of life.* But, by not being restricted to the physical life linked to a body, *zoee*-life allows us to mean the *pure perfection of life. Zoee* refers to the pure positivity of life, of which Anselm says that to possess it is absolutely better than not to possess it, and which can exist in a perfect form:

> Therefore it is necessary that it [the supreme nature: God] be alive, be wise, powerful and omnipotent, true, just, blessed, eternal, and whatever in a similar way is absolutely better than its lack [literally: than not it].[63]

Also Bonaventure says of absolute life that "as it is the first act, it is an absolute perfection."[64] One cannot surpass any limited form of life in perfection without living, whereas it is possible to surpass all those mixed perfections which are essentially limited, as, for example, all natural species of material substances, plants, and animals on earth, without being any of them.

Zoee in the highest sense, because of its character as pure perfection, was attributed by Aristotle (and by Plato[65]) to God, to the Demiurge, to "the unmoved mover," and to the activity of the highest intellectual contemplation, or rather to its subject, of whom Aristotle says that *zoee* belongs to God and that "the actuality (*energeia*) of the *nous* is life" and "eternal life."[66] Plato speaks extensively of God (as the Princeton Edition translates the "Demiurge") and calls him in his *Timaeus* (for example, 37 c) the "creator and father of the universe." Giovanni Reale has shown in his book on Plato that this Demiurge is not a mere mythological figure but a central reality in the Platonic metaphysics. This position, originally developed in contrast to the Tübingen school of Plato-research, has overthrown the common scholarly opinion that Plato considered his "God" as a mere mythological symbolic figure. Reale shows, in his balanced interpretation of Plato, both the essential difference between the Demiurge and God in the Jewish-Christian-Islamic understanding, and the astonishing closeness of Plato's Creationism to the later Christian one. Thinking of the supreme form of life, we remember also the famous definition offered by Boethius of the eternity of God in terms of life: eternity is "the wholly simultaneous and perfect possession of interminable life" (*interminabilis vitae tota simul et perfecta possessio*).[67] Thus, the term *zoee* can refer to all lower and higher forms of life, and even to the supreme mode of living.

5. The Fundamentally Different Forms and Phenomena of Life

If we descend from a lofty transcendental (not in Kant's but in the Scholastic sense explained above) and metaphysical consideration of life to the world of our immediate experience, we encounter life originally in three fundamental kinds of being, we get acquainted with it in two experiential ways, and we understand it by means of two chief methods which also allow us to gain access to a form of life and a living being above human life.

We know from two fundamentally different kinds of immediate experience, the nature of which I will discuss in the next section, three kinds of being which are alive and in whom we find fundamentally different "types" or "degrees" of life: (1) plants, which show only the marks of vegetative or "purely biological" life; (2) animals, which possess in addition many other features such as perceptions, drives, instincts, feelings, etc.; and (3) human beings who are endowed, above and beyond this, with reason, knowledge, language, the ability of logical thinking, and moral qualities, religion, and who differ in countless other ways from animals.

Whereas only these three living beings are immediately known to us from experience, we are also able, through different arguments and methods of understanding, to reach a sure philosophical knowledge of another, fourth, type of life as the most perfect one. (4) For we can understand that living beings who exist contingently (non-necessarily) and imperfectly cannot account for their own life[68] and that their life must derive from an absolute being. Thus, we understand that human life requires a supremely and eternally living divine being as the cause of all other life.[69] There is also a more direct form of knowing this absolute life by means of the ontological argument.[70] (5) Further, we can form a concept of purely spiritual finite beings (pure spirits or angels), of whose existence we have no absolute philosophical proof but whose fundamental nature and possibility we can understand philosophically and in whose existence we can believe on the basis of empirical evidence, aesthetic considerations, philosophical arguments, or religious reasons.

The empirical and the philosophical grounds for assuming pure spirits may be insufficient, epistemologically speaking, except for the arguments for the immortality of the human soul. Therefore, a firm assertion of the existence of pure spirits appears to have its origin in religious faith only. Nevertheless, one might cite some empirical and philosophical arguments for the existence of angels. Many empirical experiences of appearances and visions of "pure spirits" are reported (some of these are recorded by Plato, others by Jewish prophets, Moslems, and Christians, and still others are written about in contemporary books). Aesthetic reasons for assuming pure spirits are found in poetry (for example, in Dante Alighieri's detailed angelology) but also in philosophers, like Aristotle and medieval thinkers, who held that creation would not be complete if there were a "disturbing hole" within the world of living beings that can only be filled by pure spirits. This argument from the "golden chain of being" is one of the arguments which prompted Aristotle to assume his 44 movers in the *Metaphysics.* More philosophical arguments for the existence of pure spirits abound in medieval "angelologies." Christians, Jews, and Moslems believe in the existence of angels also as tenets of religious faith and because of the vast role they play in Sacred Writings.

The distinction of five different classes of living beings does not exhaust the complexity of the datum of life. Human life, and in part the life of plants and animals, involves five distinct phenomena which all can be designated as "life": (1) The partial life-processes in individual cells and cell-cultures, which in multi-cellular organisms can continue after the death of the organism. In multi-cellular organisms, these processes are life only in a weak sense. (2) The biological life of the organism as a whole, which many defenders of brain-death today believe to continue even after the mental life in the human body disappears.[71] This life constitutes a far more significant sense of *bios*-life than the partial life-phenomena in single cells. In single-cellular beings, the life of the organism as a whole coincides with the life of the single cell which is simultaneously the life of the organism as a whole. But in multi-cellular plants and animals, and most of all in human beings, life in the second "holistic" sense is utterly different and much more significant. (3) Moving beyond the level of the vegetative life, we arrive at the sensitive life of animals who can feel pleasure and pain, and have instincts, drives, etc. Here we encounter an entirely new phenomenon of life which manifests itself in the essential difference of animals from plants.[72] In human beings, this level of life is inseparably interwoven with the next two senses of the life that we encounter in humankind. (4) The rational life of the mind *per se*, which many philosophers, the Jewish sect of the Pharisees, Christians, and others hold to originate in a soul and to continue after death, and which we find in each person. The death which wipes out this life would be a total annihilation of the soul or its final privation of any rational and conscious life. This rational life of the rational human soul, or of a spiritual person, is the archetypal form of life, as far as inner-worldly beings are concerned. The attempt to understand it will occupy us at length in the third chapter. (5) A fifth sense of life, the one most frequently used when we speak of human beings, refers to the union of mind and body.[73] In this last concept of human life, which is distinct from the fourth but depends on it, we regard human death as opposite – when death is considered, as does Plato, not as the annihilation of soul and life but as the separation of the soul from the body.

The first two senses of life apply likewise to the life of animals and – to a lesser degree – of plants, the fourth exclusively to the human being and only analogously to animals, the third to all personal beings. For humanity the most significant of these meanings of life are the second (the biological life of an organism as a whole) and the fourth (the life of the human mind which also constitutes the ultimate source of life in the fifth sense, being itself the deepest level of the life which animates the human body from within).

Between these different phenomena of life, and even within them, particularly within the fourth one, we find a well-nigh infinite gradation and many hierarchically ordered levels of life, such that "life" is not a univocal term but an analogous term. The differences between life on the different orders of being are so great that they far outweigh the commonalities. Even the "common features of all life," as, for example, a type of auto-motion (*zoee* in the encompassing "transcendental sense" that can be applied to all living things) are present in all living entities only in an analogous sense which involves a similarity but simultaneously a fundamental dissimilarity in the kind of life proper to different living beings. The topic of analogy and its types was treated from Aristotle to Thomas Aquinas and Cajetan up to the present by many thinkers.

For this reason, we cannot comprehend life simply on this general analogous level but have to comprehend it also in terms of the most significant being and form of life on earth: the life of the human being and of the human soul which will constitute the topic of the third chapter of this book. A fuller treatment of life would also require a clear delineation of vegetative life (found also in plants) from sensitive life (only present in animals and in human beings) as well as a speculative metaphysical investigation into the supreme and ultimate archetypal form of life: divine eternal life. Indirectly, by discussing the way from temporal to eternal being, I attempted such an analysis of life in *Essere e persona* in a chapter on time and eternity.[74] Some of us who admit mysterious sides of life that are not accessible to philosophical or scientific knowledge will also recognize aspects and origins of life that only Divine Revelation can reveal and theology explore. For this reason, the exploration of life is an interdisciplinary or transdisciplinary task.

In this book, I will deal almost exclusively with life in plants, animals, and in human beings, and I will deal with life only from a philosophical point of view.

A. The First Experiential Way in which We Get to Know Vegetative, Animal, and Human Life, and Its Different Dimensions of Sense and Understanding

The first experiential way in which we know vegetative life and animal life consists in the combination between the immediate experience of data associated with life and a pre-philosophical understanding of the principles that underlie these phenomena. We observe the biological life of animals and plants, *bios*, from without, inasmuch as we do not immediately experience biological life itself but only its observable and visible essential signs, as, for example, nutrition, growth, propagation, regeneration, and integrated wholeness. Mortality, the possibility in principle of death, could be regarded as also an essential characteristic of *bios*.[75]

The biologist, botanist, zoologist, and the medical researcher or doctor observe the described phenomena of life in many different forms and manifestations. Life is not directly observed by them but grasped in and through effects and appearances in which it manifests itself. This thesis of the indirect mode of givenness of biological life is even more true with respect to those facts of life which have become accessible exclusively through scientific research, as, for example, the highly complex proteins in living organisms, DNA and RNA structures, and oxygen transfer. The life in animals and plants, though given from without, is not merely deduced from syllogisms but manifests itself more immediately in the described phenomena, in particular in those phenomena which appeal to our prescientific knowledge and give rise to the immediate common-sense experience of plants or dogs as living. In spite of this immediacy, as opposed to the indirectness of mere inferences, in grasping plants and especially animals as living, we do not observe biological life as an immediate object of knowledge in the proper sense of this term. We grasp biological life in some form of indirect immediacy or mediated immediacy in and through its manifestations and effects. Even our own vegetative life we know in a way from without. This is true, although we live our body consciously and feel its life and the signs of its life, like breathing or our heartbeat, from within our body.

While these phenomena of life and death are partly accessible to us through sense-perception, other phenomena become accessible only through our intellectual understanding. The experience of life also involves an understanding of causality (for example, when we speak of reproduction or propagation), of the unity of form (which allows us to speak of one organism distinct from others) and integrated wholeness, and of finality (which allows us to speak of functions and purposes of genetic codes, of the teleology in organs, or of respiration). Reviving great Aristotelian and Hegelian insights, Robert Spaemann reintroduces the category of finality and teleology, as the "*aus-sein-auf*" (the being aimed at) as a central category for life. He also distinguishes an external finality since it can likewise be found in a machine (*teleonomy*), a concept introduced in 1958 by Colin Pittendrigh, from authentic teleology which is characteristic for life.[76]Georg Friedrich Wilhelm Hegel says in a similar fashion in his *Science of Logic:* "thus the finality of the living being has to be conceived as an *internal* one."[77]

The getting acquainted experientially with the specifically sensitive dimensions of animal life involves still more complex modes of understanding and interpreting signs, expressions, and movements of animals, a key topic which I largely exclude from consideration in this book.

The type of immediate experience in which we first get acquainted with the external, visible, and audible signs and expressions of life and move from them to the grasp of the life that is their source, is also the experiential contact we have with the human life of others. Here, the acts of understanding by means of which we proceed to the grasping of specifically human life transcend the sense experience *per se.* We do not just hear voices but understand the meaning of human language; we do not just see colors but recognize shapes and artistic creations; we do not just witness external bodily behavior of human body-machines, but understand the motives, intentions, and actions of human beings. When we experience their laughter and crying, their mourning and loving, we go infinitely beyond the sense experience of the external manifestations of these specifically human dimensions of life.

Animal life, and even more human bodily life, shows that *bios*, as a life connected with the body, cannot be identified with purely vegetative or "biological" life, and that the experiential contact with this life is not restricted to vegetative life as its object. The sensations, feelings of pleasure and pain, and perceptions of animals, which we experience starting from acts of perception and understanding, transcend entirely the level of plant life and of vegetative life. This is especially true for the human life which we grasp starting from the experience of the sensible expressions of human life and their understanding and interpretation which leads us to the recognition of specifically human life in others. In getting acquainted with the intellectual or artistic life of human beings, we grasp not only *bios* but purely spiritual dimensions of life. Thus, this first and "external" experiential contact with life is an extremely rich and extraordinarily complex whole of acts of perceiving and understanding. While sense perceptions lie at its roots, the contents and objects of this experience, vegetative, animal, and human life are not simply perceived by the senses. Nevertheless, we can speak here of an original givenness and experience of life, an experience which encompasses innumerable perceptions, interpretations, and acts of understanding, and is thus, even in the simplest child, a deeply intellectual or rationally formed experience. I do not exclude that in still other experiences of life, for example, specifically religious experience, we get acquainted not only with animal and human life but also with living beings above human beings.

B. A Second and More Immediate Experiential Way of Gaining Access to the Datum of Life: The Direct Access to Conscious Life in the *Cogito*

The second experiential way in which we encounter life is the truly immediate inner experience of our own life in the living of our conscious life, a unique phenomenon to which I will return in Chapter Three of this book. Here we no longer observe phenomena which reveal to our understanding life as their only appropriate source, as in the case of vegetative and animal life, but we gain a direct and intimate conscious and cognitive access to life. In the very performance of consciousness and of conscious acts, life itself, which is the condition and element of consciousness, becomes accessible to us. We live life from within and get acquainted with it from within: in performing conscious acts and in consciously living. In the *cogito* our life becomes immediately given to our experience and intellect as our being itself, wherefore Augustine regards the *vivere me* (my living) as equally evident as the *esse me* and both as indubitably certain.[78]

While in terms of the focusing of our attention, the experience of the life of others may temporally precede the child's experience of its own life, no experience of anything and of any other life is possible which would not be accompanied by this unique inner and immediate experience of life in our consciousness and perceptions. No other experience can absolutely precede this experience in time, and no other experience of life is more immediate. This fact that our immediate inner experience of our life in consciousness is the primary, most indubitable, and archetypal form of the original experience of life leads Heidegger to the thesis that all other forms of life are only known "privatively":

> The ontology of life is accomplished by means of a privative interpretation: it identifies that which must be in order that something like "only

life" may exist. Life is neither purely objectual being nor *Dasein* (human being). *Dasein* on the other hand is to be identified as alive.[79]

Starting from a similar observation regarding the primacy and immediacy of the inner experience of our life but also of other life, especially human life, and based on empirical observations of children, Balduin Schwarz argues that the child experiences life first and that the child takes a long process of becoming aware that things exist which do not live.[80]

C. Two Chief Methods of Theoretically Understanding Life

The two chief forms and methods of theoretically cognizing life are: (1) empirical methods and (2) philosophical methods. These differ not only from the two mentioned forms of experiencing life but also from naive common sense knowledge of life which contains many philosophical and empirical cognitions of life, but in a prephilosophical and prescientific mode.[81]

(1) The empirical methods entail sophisticated scientific observations, often by means of instruments, lab-tests, psychological self-observation, etc. Empirical methods also include theoretical explanations of the observed phenomena by means of induction, corroboration or falsification of theories by trial and error, the development and use of models and paradigms in terms of which the pieces of the scientific puzzles of the observed world are interpreted. An explanation and justification of these methods of empirical scientific knowledge I have given elsewhere.[82]

In addition to the empirical methods of investigating life, we also have to use: (2) philosophical methods. They consist first of all in rational intuitions into the essence of life and into the intelligible causes of the observed phenomena, and in the analysis of life's highly intelligible and necessary essence and irreducible character. Philosophy requires as well a rigorous analysis of the essential marks of life and of related data. The methods of philosophical investigations into life include dialectical and deductive methods based on self-evident premises and on equally evident logical laws of correct inference. Philosophical intuition, analysis, and deduction are forms of *a priori* knowledge not based on experience in the sense of observation of facts.

By "*a priori*" knowledge I mean a knowledge independent of observation of contingent facts and of induction, but characterized by apodictic certainty and, in its object, by strict necessity. I do not include in my notion of the *a priori* any of the subjectivistic conceptions included in Kant's notion of the *a priori* – as that which "lies ready-made in the subject" (*im Gemüthe bereitliegt*), or any innatism – but I see in this knowledge the height of objectivity: the discovery of absolutely necessary essences and essentially necessary states of affairs rooted in them.

Like Scheler, Reinach, Hildebrand, and other realist phenomenologists, I do not hold this knowledge to be independent of such-being experience or of becoming acquainted with an essence in concretely existing or imagined instances. Since the supremely intelligible and necessary essences which alone can justify this objective *a priori* knowledge stand completely on their own feet in their necessity, knowledge of them (rational intuition and deduction) does not depend on repeated observation and induction.[83]

This *a priori* knowledge is not entirely independent of experience, as Kant thought. Instead, it is based on a such-being experience in which we become acquainted with the intelligible essences of things. It can proceed from the external experience of biological life or from the immediate inner perception or experience of our life. In both cases, this kind of experience allows philosophical knowledge only when it reaches absolutely necessary essences and essentially necessary states of affairs grounded in them. We find essences in our sense on the level of species (like humanity, bacteria), of genus (like animal as opposed to plants), and even on the level of the most universal abstract data, as, for example, being itself, life itself, etc. The term "necessary essence" is no synonym for intelligibility or essence. Instead, it refers to a type of essence the elements of which are held together by absolute and intrinsic necessity. Examples are motion, color, number (including all individual natural numbers and mathematical operations), matter, life, intellect, knowledge, will, promise, moral values, etc. Necessary essences differ from contingent essences which, as essences (and not only with respect to their existence), are not necessary. The elements of contingent essences are linked in non-necessary ways. To this group of contingent essences belong all species of animals and plants, or the human body, whose elements and parts we can get to know only by observations and understanding of meaningful but contingent facts, and through inductive inferences based on repeated observations, experiments, etc.[84]

As long as experience brings us into contact only with meaningful but non-necessary unities of elements and natures, only empirical observation and experimental or similar, for example, historical, methods based on the observation of facts are possible. Without a method of exploring absolutely necessary essences and essential states of affairs, an objective knowledge of the essence of life and a philosophy of life would be impossible. I will not repeat here what was expounded elsewhere in detail concerning this method and the rehabilitation of a classical concept of philosophy rendered possible through it.[85] Each of these two methods has many parts and involves further differentiated forms of knowledge.

6. The Purpose of the Following Chapters

What, then, in the light of the preceding distinctions, is my plan for the remaining portions of this book? The second chapter will be devoted to the irreducible essence of life in the sense of *bios*, whereas the third chapter will be dedicated to the much more clearly given datum of the irreducible life of the person (mind, soul), in the light of which the radical impossibility of the reduction of life to physical systems themselves or to their properties will become even more evident. I will omit an investigation into the life-principle (or soul) of animals. In view of the specific characteristics of animals – sensation, perception, locomotion, learning, etc. – the task of showing the irreducibility of their life to physical systems would be far more easily fulfilled than the attempt to be undertaken in Chapter Two of showing the irreducibility of organic life, which exists even in plants, to physical systems. If we can show the irreducibility of plant-life to matter, the irreducibility of animal-life to matter follows immediately. (We could not replace the term "matter" here by "non-living corporeal beings." To say that life cannot be reduced to non-living beings would be a tautology. For whatever life is and means, it cannot coincide with its own opposite. Matter, i. e., bodily being, has an essence of its own, including spatial extension and many other attributes as, for example, composition of non-identical parts and a non-simplicity which even the "simple atomic parts" and micro-particles possess. Life is irreducible to matter and to any chaotic or non-chaotic physical system.) Therefore, we can content ourselves here with the solution of the far more difficult problem whether all life, including that of plants, is irreducible to physical, material reality, regardless of whether material reality obeys chaotic or non-chaotic laws. Yet, the irreducibility of mental human life is more evident and more important for us.

The task of the third chapter of demonstrating the irreducibility of human rational life to physical systems is easier to accomplish than the other two tasks, partly because we experience our conscious life immediately and indubitably from within, and partly because the essential marks of its rationality reveal more clearly than vegetative or purely sensitive life its radical irreducibility to physical systems or to properties of brains.

Two

WHAT IS BIOLOGICAL LIFE? THE IRREDUCIBILITY OF VEGETATIVE LIFE (*BIOS*) TO ORDERED AND CHAOTIC PHYSICAL SYSTEMS

1. Irreducibility and Undefinability of Organic Life, yet Possibility of Its Essential Definition through Its Various Marks

What, then, is organic life? I am using here the terms "*bios*," "biological life," "vegetative life," and "organic life" as synonyms which indicate the kind of life which we find in all living entities on earth, including plants. The term "sensitive life" refers to animals (and human beings), "mental or rational life" to persons only.

Bios is an astonishing phenomenon. Like all absolutely original and ultimate data, for example, being, *bios* defies our attempts to define it. We realize that all the complex protein, nucleotide-structures, and the most diverse phenomena linked to life, as, for example, genetic codes, cannot explain what life itself is though it presupposes or originates these or similar phenomena. Apart from life (proteins in an organism at the moment of its death or genetic codes stored on a computer), all these elements would be part of a dead thing and not constitute life.

Max Scheler calls life a "genuine essence" (*eine echte Wesenheit*), a "fundamental phenomenon" (*ein Grundphänomen*), an "underivable archphenomenon" (*ein unableitbares Urphänomen*), in order to point at this irreducible and original identity of life with respect to which all forms of reductionism must fail.[1] Following some authors, we can render in the following "*Urphänomen*" also as "*Urphenomenon*" (instead of arch-phenomenon). Viktor Frankl, in his "Der Mensch auf der Suche nach Sinn: Anthropologische Grundlagen der Psychotherapie," gives a striking example of a reductionism, which he calls, jokingly, "oxidationism." His teacher of biology explained that life is nothing but processes of combustion or oxidation, a statement to which the young boy Frankl retorted: "But what then, professor, is the meaning of life?" Frankl observes convincingly that it might not be by chance that this teacher later became a fanatic Nazi because Nazism is based on a reductionistic and meaningless concept of life.[2]

In a sense, life allows us only to say what George Edward Moore said about the good: Life is life. Note the striking text of Moore:

> If I am asked "What is good?" my answer is that good is good, and that is the end of the matter. Or if I am asked "How is good to be defined?" my answer is that it cannot be defined, and that is all I have to say about it. But disappointing as these answers may appear, they are of the very last importance.[3]

In spite of life's undefinability in terms of anything else, we can approach life itself by analyzing its essential marks or by giving an essential definition of it, as we shall see, a fact which Moore overlooks, which makes his analysis of the good (especially of the moral good) insufficient. This had grave consequences for his ethics in which the notion of the good is not further explained, and the distinctions between the irreducible essences of moral goodness and extramoral values are not made.

By essential definition, I do not mean a definition of life through something else, which is impossible with any ultimate and simple arch-data, but I mean the delineation of a given essence from other natures by reference to its essential marks, characteristics, relationships, etc.

If we admit with Aristotle, Goethe, Moore, or phenomenology that these data cannot be defined through anything else, and if we admit their enormous number, we can nevertheless attempt, as Moore failed to see, an essential analysis and an "essential definition" that aims at unfolding distinctive marks and characteristics of these data without explaining the given essence through another thing or through its elements, and without reducing it to its elements or characteristics.[4] If this is so, what can we say about the essential marks of life that characterize its essence?

Even when we are unable to explain a nature to someone who does not know it, or to define it in terms of its generic features and its specific differences in such a way that someone who does not already know it can be led to understand it through our definition, we still can bring this essence to further evidence through analysis and we can unfold its different marks and express the results of the analysis of an irreducible datum in an essential definition.[5] We can certainly describe *bios*-life, in spite of its mysterious character, in terms of phenomena as, for example, nutrition, growth, regeneration, propagation, complex DNA-RNA structures, and genetic codes,[6] but also in terms of deeper philosophical marks which I am going to discuss in this chapter. I have treated elsewhere the role of genetic codes for life, and the irreducibility of the individual person to the uniqueness of genetic codes.

Bios-life is precisely that irreducible power and actuality of which we comprehend that it must lie at the root of all the activities and marks of living organisms. Just as we can understand the nature and existence of material substances by an intellectual act in which we understand that extension, color, shape, form, etc. cannot "stand in themselves" but demand a subject which does exist in itself, so we comprehend also that the many astonishing traits and actions of living organisms proceed from something beyond these qualities and actions which we call life. We understand that these qualities and features of living organisms do not find a proper explanation either in themselves or in a material substance or machine. But an irreducible phenomenon discloses itself to our intellect as the only appropriate cause and actuality in terms of which these phenomena become intelligible and find their root and origin. This irreducible phenomenon we call life, comprehending its irreducibility to the entirety of its effects. This *bios*-life as the principle from which many phenomena in living things proceed was designated by Aristotle as *entelecheia*, which is characterized by nutrition, growth, etc., and brings forth these effects. Therefore, when the same entity that just showed the signs of life, dies, the highly complex structures of the organism disintegrate and its activities cease. Let us examine more closely both the undefinability and the analyzability of biological life.

I should mention immediately, by way of introduction to a discussion of some essential marks of life, that life has essentially necessary and intelligible features which only philosophical knowledge can explore, as well as contingent (non-necessary) morphic sides which only observation and common sense or, in other respects, natural science can verify.

The necessary and philosophically intelligible sides and the contingent morphic and only empirically accessible aspects of life are found as well in some quite universal features of biological life and in more specific forms of life in which the non-necessary elements abound to a greater degree. For example, many of the universal features of life, such as the cellular structure and the role of nutrition, are open only or mainly to empirical knowledge, not to philosophy. Other universal features of life and many specific ones are solely knowable by means of philosophical methods, as we shall see.

Philosophy is not restricted to the most universal essence of life. The essences of plants, animals, and human beings are also accessible to philosophy. Yet again, most aspects of the concrete species of plants and animals, because of their non-necessity, are only accessible to empirical observational methods. Let us first turn to the investigation of the empirical marks of life. Some of them also constitute the experiential starting point for the following analysis of the essential marks of life and may, at least in their bare outline, partake in the necessary essence of *bios*.

2. The Empirical Marks of Biological Life and Two Scientific Attempts to Define Life through Them

Biological life is, empirically speaking and referring to obvious notes of organic life, characterized by nutrition, growth (the more technical scientific term is "morphogenesis"), regeneration, propagation, endogen motility, adaptability, and further features.

As we shall see, "metabolism" is only part of nutrition. "Dynamogenesis" may replace the ordinary-language term of "nutrition," which, however, is more suitable to philosophical discussion.

Other characteristics of living beings, as, for example, the cellular structure of organisms, the parts of cells and their functions, DNA and RNA, are hidden from our ordinary experience and require the use of special instruments to be discovered.

Biology largely concurs with the understanding of life of the ordinary person and of the philosopher and seeks to "define" or to delineate the essence of life by establishing a thorough empirical list of obvious and hidden vital functions. The two chief methods of science in characterizing life proceed either (1) by an exhaustive enumeration of the main characteristics and biological functions of living organisms (with the problem that not every living organism shows all these functions); or (2) by identifying among these functions those which are present in *all* living individuals (with the danger of losing the wealth of phenomena that pertain to life).

Following the first method, we could give the following list of properties of living beings:[7] 1. Nutrition (which, in its wide sense, includes ingestion [feeding],[8] digestion, absorption, transport [which includes the circulatory and respiratory systems], metabolism, exchange of gases [which includes respiration], excretion); 2. Regeneration, 3. Reproduction, 4. Endogen motility, 5. Irritability, 6. Adaptive capacity.

Some authors, for example, Carroll Lane Fenton, wish to introduce seven marks of life and to separate "feeding" (ingestion) as a distinct characteristic of living things, distinguishing it from nutrition. But the classification in which ingestion is an essential part and the beginning of one single nutritive system is more convincing. Otherwise, metabolism and other parts of the nutritive system (for example, digestion and excretion) would also have to be distinct marks of life. Fenton does not consider adaptive capacity as a mark of life but introduces, besides feeding, excretion as a separate characteristic of living things. But the unitary character and purpose of all of the elements and structures of nutrition, starting with ingestion and ending with excretion, suggests that we regard them all as parts of one (nutritive) system.

Following the second type of scientific "definition" of life, we identify some properties or even one property present in all living entities, for example, "nutrition" in a wide sense of the term as an exchange of matter and energy which the organism establishes with the surrounding environment or "medium." Nutrition in this wide sense can be considered biologically as the basic function of the organism in three senses: 1. as empirical *conditio sine qua non* for the existence of living organisms and of all their other functions; 2. as a "total function" exercised by each of the parts of an organism (cells, organs) as well as by the organism as a whole; 3. as a "permanent function" during life (from the very beginning until the end of the organism's existence). We shall see that the ideas contained in this attempt of a biological definition of life are partly erroneous. They go back to Aristotle:

> The nutritive soul then must be possessed by everything that is alive, and every such thing is endowed with soul from birth to death. For what has been born must grow, reach maturity, and decay – all of which are impossible without nutrition. Therefore the nutritive faculty must be found in everything that grows and decays.[9]

Another attempt to identify one single property present in all living organisms is the theory that the possession of genetic information (to have a genetic code) and ability to transmit it constitute the essence of organic life. But this position cannot be defended successfully. The same genetic "information" is stored in the body cells immediately after the death of the organism and could be stored even on a computer disk. But this "pure information" is entirely different from life or from thinking (as I will discuss more in depth in Chapter Five in answer to Question 4). Elsewhere,[10] I tried to distinguish many meanings of information: (1) in an exclusively personal sense, as acts of informing; (2) in the sense of objective thoughts, meaning-units, propositions, and symbolic expression of information, which can only be addressed to persons who alone can understand them; (3) as physical language in which this objective information may be transmitted; (4) as mere "body" of information which can be handled and exert influence without being understood by its recipient in the form of language-games, computer-manipulation of symbols, etc.; (5) as causally effective physical languages (in the fourth sense); (6) as these languages giving rise to conscious experiences, for example, in the relationship between brain and perception (but without any conveying or personally receiving of information); (7) in each immediate perception and knowledge of an object (self-information of the object about itself). Only "information" which is causally active and requires for its causal effectiveness to be executed through life-principles (souls) and to be "interpreted" by the living organism (4 and 5) is essential for life.

Another attempt to identify one single property of living beings which would constitute the core of the essence of organic life proceeds more materialistically and more statically. It does not identify one function of living things with life but identifies the presence of protoplasm with the essence of *bios*-life. But this effort to get at the core of the essence of life is not persuasive. While all living organisms and cells, even the one-celled amoeba or protococcus, contain protoplasm, we cannot identify life with the presence of protoplasm. This identification contradicts the facts that protoplasm is also found in cells after the death of the organism and that this chemical substance, peculiarly related to life as it is, cannot constitute the essence of life because life does not *consist* in a particular type of matter. Similar problems arise when other material properties of living things (having a cell, a nucleus of a cell, etc.) are identified with life or with the indispensable core of its essence.[11] These characteristics of organisms are also preserved in dead organisms, even if they do not function properly in them. In addition, they cannot *constitute* life because their significance for life evidently in no way is the core of the essence of life.

A more general problem with the second type of scientific "definition" through one central property is that, while this definition seeks to get at the core of the essence of life, it loses the fullness of the content of life and the sense for the polymorphism of the appearances of life. If we seek one central essential mark of life, we should do so in a more philosophical manner along the lines to be developed below.

Both of these methods used in biology to "define" or to characterize life are seriously deficient as attempts to tell us what life is. They should be complemented by a philosophical grasp of the intelligible marks and essence of life. Such an analysis of life goes beyond an empirical description of the factual properties of living organisms, which could be imitated by an automaton, as Descartes pointed out. The analysis should penetrate into the intelligible essence of life. Robert Spaemann rightly points out that today we witness a great ability to imitate and to simulate both life and thinking, and then to forget that we are just dealing with simulations of life and thought. This gives rise to a growing tendency to identify the original data with their simulations which was well expressed by Spaemann:

> Modern biology ... can only attempt to approach the living by simulating it. Its mistake consists in believing that the simulation is the original.[12]

3. The Essentially Necessary (*A Priori*) Characteristics of Biological Life Open to Philosophical Knowledge

Can we only refer to distinct empirically given properties of organisms such as to the concrete properties of nutrition, growth, regeneration, and propagation, or is there a deeper unified essential core[13] of biological life, such as the *entelechy* of which Aristotle and Hans Driesch have spoken and which implies the organism's dynamic and teleological building itself up?[14] (The notion of "essential core" has been introduced by Jean Hering and Roman Ingarden and signifies the inner principle of unity of an essence.)

Driesch offers many arguments for his position that no chemical or mechanical explanation of the morphogenesis of organisms is tenable. He also presents different proofs for the existence of entelechy: the first one is taken from the autonomy of vital morphogenesis, the laws of which are not derivable from chemistry and physics but show that biology is a new fundamental science, the object and methods of which cannot be reduced to those of other natural sciences.[15] This argument is continued by a consideration of various modes of regeneration, regulation, and adaptation.[16] The second argument is taken from the hereditary laws[17] which Driesch sees as inexplicable without the vitalistic assumption of an entelechy which is irreducible to material systems and functions of any kind which do not include this entirely new element of entelechy or soul. We could give to Driesch's Gifford Lectures an importance for biology similar to the importance of Edmund Husserl's *Logical Investigations* for logic. Remarkable similarities occur between Driesch's method in biology and philosophy of nature and Husserl's method (whom Driesch quotes in this respect, *ibid.*, p. 369). The autonomy and irreducibility of the subject-matter and methods of biology are spelled out by Driesch with admirable clarity.[18]

The irreducibility of life to the mentioned features of living things is suggested not only by the philosophical quest for an underlying unity and core in each essence and for an intelligible origin of the striking phenomena of *bios*, but also by the fact that none of these single features of life is absolutely necessary for biological life. Organisms live which no longer grow, which no longer have any ability of regeneration, and which are sterile and unable to propagate. Even nutrition can stop, for an extended time, while life continues, although in one sense nutrition can be regarded, with some justification, as an empirically universal feature of all biological life, at least in life's actualized state.[19] An exception to this is the entirely dormant state of life in a seed, for example, a stonepine seed, which behaves like a lifeless thing and in a way has to abandon all organic activity before it awakens to new life when it is planted, properly nourished, and taken care of. Empirically speaking, a living organism that is not nourished uses progressively all its different storage resources of energy, and after that it will die if it does not receive other nutrients. Philosophically speaking, nevertheless, *zoee* and also *bios* is not absolutely – but only contingently – dependent on nutrition and can be easily understood to be able in principle to continue after a total collapse or paralysis of the nutritive system. The diverse aspects of nutrition explained above could cease, yet life could continue, which is one of the reasons why the endeavor of defining life scientifically mentioned above – through nutrition – appears insufficient.

Let us consider more closely empirical evidence for this. The reader will pardon a brief interruption of the strictly philosophical content of this book. Empirical experience confirms that life can continue, for example, in a seed or in a frozen state, without the continuation of nutrition, in the usual sense of the term. This does not exclude that for cryo-conservation a special "nourishing medium" is needed, as well as the preservation of the cells, and that metabolism is not reduced absolutely to zero, although it comes close to that. Kenneth B. Storey and Janet M. Storey show[20] that the temperatures of frozen live organisms can drop below -50°C and that an enormous variety of animals (from insects through reptiles) can continue to live in a frozen state, with up to 65 percent or more of the body fluids being frozen. Different strategies of living organisms exist to deal with sub-zero temperatures:

> The first ... is to avoid exposure to temperatures below the freezing point of body fluids. Animals simply "choose" relatively warm hibernation sites ... .
>
> The second alternative to freezing is to use specific adaptations that stabilize the liquid state at sub-zero temperatures ... all water solutions can also be supercooled – ... they can be chilled well below the equilibrium freezing point before the water crystallizes spontaneously into ice. Human plasma, for example, has a freezing point of -8 degree C but, if chilled in a controlled manner, can be supercooled to -16 degrees C.[21]

Sometimes this happens by antifreeze proteins in the body fluids of, for example, polar fish. Even more effective is a second method to reach antifreeze effects. It is found in those insects which "load their body fluids with an antifreeze made of low molecular weight polyhydroxy (sugar) alcohols ... ."[22]

Yet a third method of dealing with sub-zero temperatures is survival in spite of the freezing of body-fluids, which we find in some animals. Presupposed here is "a slow and controlled freezing that, if done properly, is readily survivable." For example, gallfly larvae "choose" this third method of surviving cold temperatures. The cytoplasm in the cells still needs to remain liquid, which is accomplished by spectacular methods of combining proteins which further the freezing of some external body-fluids while preventing the freezing of intra-cellular cytoplasm. Also cell structure and function need to be protected. The Storeys rightly call these highly sophisticated processes "marvelous."

A state of life in which nutrition in the usual sense is absent happens quite regularly in plants, as we shall see, and, under exceptional circumstances, also in animals and human beings, for example, in a cryo-conserved state in which no nutrition and no gas-exchange through breathing take place. The normal process of breathing does not take place any more. In the wide sense of "oxido-reduction processes" in the chemical structures of cells, "respiration of cells" might still take place. Sometimes, these processes might only occur in sub-cellular structures, as I suspect but as non-scientist cannot verify. That respiration and oxygen-supply can stop in frozen animals is a well-documented scientific fact. In some frogs, "high glucose levels may help arrest the metabolism of frozen organs, limiting cellular energy needs and thereby enhancing long-term survival."[23]

> ... freeze-tolerant animals must have a well-developed ability to survive without oxygen, without access to blood-borne fuels and without being poisoned by a buildup of the metabolic end-products that are normally carried away by the blood .... Such animals must continue to generate cellular energy in the absence of oxygen.[24]

Metabolism drops down to about 1 to 10 percent of normal resting rate. "While frozen, all these animals show no movement, respiration, heart beat or blood circulation, and ... barely detectable neurological activity."[25]

More clearly, nutrition is not necessary for all states of vegetative life in plants. Certainly, the "sleeping life" in live seeds does not require any nourishment. Although nutrition (the drawing on sources of energy acquired by nutrients) seems necessary for all actualized states of biological human life, this is perhaps not so in the unique cases of phenomena described and empirically verified in some mystics who lived for years without taking any food. Although the believer will explain these phenomena as miracles or as supernatural events, their *occurrence* is an empirical fact and – just as the imagination of it – may be helpful for the philosopher to distinguish the essence of life from what is accidental to it, or not essentially necessary and absolutely indispensable for it.

Insights into essentially necessary facts can also be gained on the basis of imagination, as they are presented in literature or in examples invented by our fantasy. This is so because the necessary essences are so filled with meaning and are to such a degree autonomous objects of knowledge that they do not have to be instantiated in order to prove their objective validity. This is absolutely crucial for ethics, which deals with an order of essence, value, and oughtness never fully realized in our lives yet totally objective and valid. I am able to judge my life as good or bad, yet not in the light of empirical "facts."[26]

These empirical and philosophical considerations prompt us to look for a deeper core of the essence of biological life.[27] The existence of a unified essential core of life is also suggested by the fact that we understand clearly that even the potentiality to produce all the effects of life – including self-motion – *is not* yet life. We know that if the essential marks of *bios*, namely, nourishment, growth, etc. were found in an artfully constructed puppet as, for example, in the Marionette Olympia in Ernst Theodor Amadeus Hoffmann's tale *The Sandman*, and if they were produced by complicated machines or by mechanical or physical processes and devices, as Julien Offray de LaMettrie and René Descartes assumed,[28] none of these dead entities which could be imagined to show signs as those which we observe in living things would *be* living organisms. This conclusion is likewise reached by Josef Simon regarding Descartes's concept of life-machine: "Life is in this context a mere lingering concept from traditional metaphysics without objective meaning. Organisms are supposed to be understood in purely mechanistic terms fashioned after the model of machines."[29] This is precisely the thesis of Descartes and of many philosophers and scientists today: all of these entities, with the exception of the human mind, *are machines* and *therefore not living.*

Consider the following texts from Descartes's correspondence:

> We are so accustomed to persuade ourselves that the brute beasts feel as we do that it is difficult for us to rid ourselves of this opinion. But if we were as accustomed to see automata which imitate perfectly all those of our actions which they can imitate, and to taking them for automata only, we should have no doubt at all that all the irrational animals are automata too.[30]

This last remark is, however, not true, because nobody takes a speaking chess-computer which "imitates our actions" to be a living being. I am inclined to think that a perfect simulation of animal behavior or human action through automata is naturally speaking impossible and could only be imagined to occur by some supranaturally powerful being endowing inorganic matter with these faculties from without.

Whether a perfect simulation of life is possible or not, we do distinguish, on the basis of many evident differences, between any simulations of life or of our actions, and real life and real actions. The first part of Descartes's cited text expresses the opinion that animals are really not alive and do not possess souls but are complicated machines. This opinion is also expressed by Descartes in the following passage:

> I do not explain the feeling of pain without recourse to the soul ... but I do so explain all the external motions which in us accompany that feeling: these alone are found in the beasts, and not pain properly speaking.[31]

By making the above-mentioned statements, Descartes presupposes an intuition into an essence of life that is irreducible to a machine or to physical systems: therefore, according to him, animals do not live. Thus, biological life essentially and necessarily is an actuality that lies deeper than the phenomena in which it is manifested.

Philosophers have approached the quest for an underlying core of the essence of biological life chiefly in eight manners, of which four seek to identify the most universal and central essential marks of life, one seeks to identify the ontological origin of all properties of living things, while the remaining three connect the analysis of life to general metaphysics, inquiring into the relationship between life, essence, actuality, existence, substance, and value. In the Introduction, I have spoken of a more general metaphysical philosophy of life which considers life in its most universal features which encompass all forms of *zoee*, and as pure perfection. In Chapter Three, I will deal with mental life. All the essential marks of life possess evidence and supreme intelligibility, but we must avoid any confusion, committed by J. L. Mackie and many other philosophers, between evidence and easy obviousness, and we should avoid confusion between evidence and pseudo-obviousness distinguished so well by Alice von Hildebrand.[32] Some of the following essential marks of *bios* are obvious (for example, the first one), others are extremely unobvious although evident after due reflection (for example, the fifth one).

A. The Essential Link between *Bios* and Body

Life as *bios* is first of all inseparably linked to the physical sphere of some bodily being, and this link constitutes the essential difference between *bios* and *zoee* in all those forms of purely mental life which differ from *bios*. Aristotle defines *bios*-life as the *act* (or essential form) *of an organic body.*[33] This definition is to some extent reductionistic or confusing, I believe. If it refers only to the described biological phenomena and identifies life with them, it is reductionistic. If it presupposes an intuition that this "act of the organic body" – as *psyché* or *entelechy* – is transcendent to matter, to call this principle an "act of an organic body" is confusing. In that case, it says: life is a principle of the act of an organic body which is transcendent to the activities of the organic body themselves. But then the formulation of this sense of soul by Aristotle is deficient and unclear, for it amounts to saying: life is the transcendent cause of biological phenomena, or, life itself is distinct from the activation of the body in terms of which it is here defined. But then life (soul) should not be called *act* or *actuality* of a body.

That Aristotle identifies life and soul primarily with *bios*-life is evident from the following assertion: "the soul cannot be without a body, while it cannot *be* a body."[34] This sounds much too universal and should not be introduced as a statement about soul and life as such, but only as a true and brilliant assertion about *bios*-life and *bios*-soul.

We must also distinguish sharply the plant's material aspects from the animal body, and both from the human body, of which Hedwig Conrad-Martius rightly says that it alone can properly be called *Leib* in German, a term implying a "having" and a spiritual expression and possession of the body only found in human beings.

We could believe the proposition that *bios* is necessarily linked to a body is only a necessary analytical *a priori* proposition, because *bios*, in the meaning we are using, is "defined" as the life of an organism, and "organism" is defined as a living bodily being. But while it is possible to derive this proposition from the definition of the terms "organism" and "*bios*," applying to them the first logical principles of identity and contradiction, this is not the only form of understanding the necessary truth in question. Quite independently from the definition of the terms, the essence of the kind of being which "*bios*" possesses demands a bodily reality. Thus, above and beyond any definition of terms, the kind of entity in question essentially demands the relationship to a bodily being.[35]

This case is similar to a proposition which Immanuel Kant uses as classical example of analytic propositions *a priori:* "Every body is extended in space." As long as "body" is defined in terms of spatial extension, the state of affairs that all bodies are extended, and the truth of the proposition introduced by Kant as example of an analytic proposition *a prior*i, follow from the definition of "body" (and the first ontological and logical principles of identity and contradiction) and are therefore analytic. The truth of analytic propositions does not follow from definitions and the principles of identity and contradiction alone but demands the non-contradictory nature of the objects in question. The necessary truth, "bodies are extended," is still more than an analytic truth following from a definition. It cannot be compared to a truth which can be derived from the definition of "bachelor" as unmarried man. "Every bachelor is unmarried" simply follows from this definition, although nothing is in the essence of the man we call bachelor that would demand he be unmarried. Quite the contrary, the truth of the proposition, "all bodies are extended," is rooted not only in the aforesaid definition but also in the essence of the thing in question, namely, of the body. The necessity of this proposition flows from this essence quite independently of the definition of the body. This constitutes the real ontologically founded *synthetic* character *a priori* of propositions, as I have shown elsewhere.[36]

Wojciech Załaniec[37] overlooks the decisive difference between analytic and synthetic propositions *a priori.* He fails to see that criteria like "definability," "circularity of definition," and "formalizability" do not constitute the clue to understanding this difference. Instead, these criteria raise the question as to whether a necessary truth is merely derived from a definition and the first logical principles, or from necessary essences of things which ground necessary truths not derivable in this way. For this reason, Zełaniec does not see (1) that synthetic propositions *a priori* do not require the definability of their ground because they can be rooted in indefinable essences, and (2) that therefore the test of their synthetic character has nothing to do with vain attempts to first define indefinable essences and then look into the question of whether a given proposition is analytic.

B. Self-Motion and Other Essential Characteristics of Life

Another and more concrete way to characterize the essence of life consists in going more deeply into the essential characteristics of life. As we have seen, some philosophers identified the innermost property of life not as nutrition but as the mark which Plato emphasized in the *Phaedrus*:[38] self-motion. Life bestows on a being some form of self-movement (*Eigenbewegung*) which is more than "a being moved from the outside." This thought that "soul is that which imparts motion to a living thing" is also found in Aristotle.[39] Kant too characterizes the living being in terms of "the inner power to determine itself to act from an inner principle."[40] Hedwig Conrad-Martius distinguishes further between the physiological motion on its own (*physiologische Eigenbewegung*) of the plant and the spontaneous self-motion (*Selbstbewegung*) of the animal.[41]

If we seek this "essential core" of the essence of life, from which the other essential marks of life proceed, as if from a center of meaning, we should locate it in the fifth essential mark of life, described below, in the last sense of entelechy, namely, soul or principle of life. To locate it in self-movement or spontaneous movement from within overlooks activities essential to life which are more receptive than self-determining, for example, cognition. Any self-movement essential to life already presupposes the life of what can move from an internal principle of action.

The consensus of most philosophers that self-motion is an essential mark of life can hardly be rejected without becoming unfaithful to evident facts. We have already discussed this mark at some length and seen that the phenomenon of "self-motion" appears in radically different ways in nature, starting from the lowest level of the *Eigenbewegung* and ability of adaptation of plants, and going up to the spontaneous free acts by which a personal subject is the source of or "the lord over" "the being or non-being of that subject's acts," to use an Aristotelian way of speaking.

We can hardly find a stronger statement of the full metaphysical freedom of action than in Aristotle's *Eudemian Ethics*, where he asserts that the human person "is the lord over the existence or non-existence (of his actions)."[42] Here Aristotle states that human beings are the ultimate origin and cause of their own acts and have power over them. Cicero is even clearer on freedom in his thesis that the human person is an absolute origin of free action and that this is the necessary condition of the entire moral and legal order. Cicero goes so far as to deny the foreknowledge of the gods in order to save human freedom, and thus – like Aristotle – he contradicts the common prejudice that ancient philosophy did not recognize freedom in its full metaphysical implications. This could also be shown false for other champions of freedom in ancient philosophy, as, for example, Carneades or Epicurus. Thinkers like Augustine,[43] Bonaventure, Descartes, or Jean-Paul Sartre were hardly more outspoken in their recognition of freedom than these ancient philosophers. An analogous characteristic of self-motion is at work in growth, in locomotion, in adaptation to the environment, and in many other quite diverse features of living beings.

In spite of the radical differences in which life manifests itself, an analogue, an analogous universal exists, which we call "self-motion" and which we rightly ascribe to all living beings. We have seen that this self-motion as it characterizes all living beings differs from the type of mechanical self-motion of a machine or from the self-motion of subatomic particles, although it is not easy to analyze this distinction with precision.

Yet even if we agree with so many great philosophers of life and with biologists on the fundamental newness of a characteristic self-motion as essential mark of life, we must ask further: Can we capture the deeper essence of life, even its essential core, through the notion of self-motion, which Plato introduced into a philosophy of life, or do we have to look more deeply into the intelligible marks of life to discover its essence? Bonaventure saw that to identify life with motion or to reduce it to self-motion is not tenable, but that life lies deeper than self-motion which merely manifests and in a manner activates life. He said: "Life is prior to motion."[44]

At this point in the analysis, we see many philosophers turning to the essential marks of *bios*-life. I find it hard to see how some of these marks could be essential features of life *per se*, of *zoee*-life. We could consider at the starting point the history of the "organism" as a philosophical concept from the time of the Presocratics (Hippocrates and Empedocles). They and many later philosophers, like Plato, Aristotle, Augustine, Albert the Great, Thomas Aquinas, Henri Bergson, Hedwig Conrad-Martius, and Hans Driesch have characterized the organism through manifold essential marks and achievements that are irreducible to the qualities and achievements of lifeless things. Consider, for example, the moment of self-generation and in a sense "self-creation" in nutrition by means of which materials foreign to the organism are transformed into its own substance and the organism constantly produces itself anew. This applies also to growth in which the organism builds up its form from a seed or a tiny fertilized egg or embryo. Another dimension of the same self-generation takes place in the regeneration of old or lost cells or even of missing parts which grow again into their former shape, as this happens in the healing of wounds, in the restoration of health, or in the growing back of removed twigs of a tree or of the torn flesh or broken bone in a wounded animal or human being. Here a meaningful whole is restored. In procreation, this feature of organic life, a self-generation and recreation of one's form, extends to other organisms. All these phenomena (nutrition, growth, regeneration, and reproduction) are different sides of the basic trait of self-generation that leads to the recognition of another essential mark of life, *entelechy*, which will be covered in the following section of this chapter.

Besides self-motion and self-generation in nutrition, growth, regeneration, and procreation, scientists and philosophers have identified other essential marks related to these as well as to the interiority and ensouled character of the organism: irritability, sensibility, contractibility, and self-regulation. Different philosophers have insisted on the response-structure of the organism and on the fact that its reactions to the environment are never mechanical repetitions and never constitute an automatized, predetermined order but a strive to achieve one's own form. Thus, the organism separates itself from ties binding it by its surroundings or nature, and it shows an element of self-determination (Albrecht von Haller, Johann Friedrich Blumenbach, Henri Bergson), which reaches its climax in free choice, as was emphasized by Kant.

Karl Ernst von Baer adds the features of temporal Gestalt-qualities and of individual temporal rhythms according to which the growth and development of the organism take place, a special form of "organic temporality." Nicolai Hartmann puts forward the idea of holistic rhythm and consistency characteristic of the organism.

In the life of the organism (*bios*), we find a multiple or multidimensional form in which each part and organ possesses its function for the whole of the organism. We also find a different role for the whole that possesses a primacy with respect to the parts. Already in antiquity (Plato, Aristotle, and Livius' report on Menenius Agrippa's fable and speech of the stomach and the limbs that ended the Plebeian secession), this feature of the organism was used in the imagery that compared states and other human communities to the organism. Christ and the Apostle Paul (1 Cor. 12, 12-27) use the image of the organism from this point of view as image of the Church. Paul expresses this by saying: As the one organism possesses many limbs and organs, the eye cannot say to the hand: I do not need you. This indicates hierarchy and mutual dependency of all organs and parts of the organism on each other and of the whole on all of them.

Given the admirable way in which the organism and its organic unity develops according to a plan in which all previous forms and phases are as it were remembered, either literally in animals and human beings, or metaphorically in the fact of continuity and in the organic and logical development of the form of living things, some philosophers have attributed "memory," which they called also *mneme* (Eugen Bleuler, Eugenio Rignano), to the organic life as such.

In virtue of this *mnemonic* feature, the part contains within itself already the whole, an old philosophical idea, expressed by Johann Gottlieb Fichte and earlier by Gottfried Wilhelm Leibniz and ancient philosophers, but newly reconfirmed by modern genetics. Conrad-Martius says that the living organism could be compared to the miracle in which an artist would have put the artist's creative idea into materials that would paint on their own the paintings or construct the cities intended by the artist – from a plan that resides in themselves. Ludwig von Bertalanffy has spoken in a similar context of a *Stufenbau offener Systeme* (of an organized step-by-step building of open systems). This idea of a preestablished and prestabilised, preformed and efficient plan that points back to an archetype has Platonic and Aristotelian roots. It leads us to another central philosophical concept and discovery about organic life: entelechy, which is so important that it must be regarded as an entirely new essential mark of life.

C. Entelechy as Teleological Directedness of Life and Entelechy in the First Sense

The underlying essence of biological life lies even deeper than self-motion and the other essential traits of life already mentioned. Instead, as Aristotle and Kant have seen, a deeper level of the essence of the organism consists in an essential teleological direction of life toward an end residing inside the living organism. Robert Spaemann, Reinhard Löw, Johannes von Uexcüll, Hans Driesch, François Jacob, and Claude Bernard have done much to rehabilitate the notion of teleology and the dominion of the question, "For the sake of which reason?" (why?) for the biosciences.[45] Finality is a crucial essential mark of biological life, which, above and beyond all empirical evidence of teleology studied by great and philosophically minded biologists, as, for example, Johannes von Uexcüll and F. J. J. Buytendijk,[46] only philosophical insights into essential necessities can bring fully to evidence.

The attempt to identify the central mark of life in terms of finality does not rest satisfied with applying the category of purpose, end, order, organization, etc. to life. Instead, it combines finality with the self-containedness of the end in the organism, in an entelechy. This term, which comes from the Greek *en* (in), *telos* (end), and *echein* (to have), is one of the most ingenious linguistic inventions of Aristotle, reflecting one of his greatest philosophical discoveries. It designates the "having within itself its own end" characteristic of *bios*-life. "End" has to be interpreted here not only formally, as a purpose toward which means are directed, but as a meaningful and good form or goal that resides in the fully developed actuality of the organism.

D. Dynamic Self-Actualization of Teleological Directedness (Entelechy in the Second Sense)

While having one's own end within oneself, which distinguishes things which have their own end and value within themselves from mere means, could strictly speaking also be applied to works of art, in living organisms we find a further moment which involves a dynamic structure aiming at the realization of its own form. Thus, besides conceiving of biological life in terms of the self-containment of an end, yet in close connection with this, philosophers have seen the essential core of life in an active and end-oriented self-engendering. In this sense the term "entelechy" can be interpreted. This sense of entelechy is still an extremely wide notion that can be conceived with Hedwig Conrad-Martius as "*eigengesetzliche Selbstgestaltung und -erzeugung*" that we find also in plants and which comprises nutrition, growth, regeneration, and propagation, and thus is far more than "endogen motility." Kant defined life quite similarly through a *self-engendering* that could explain all fundamental vital functions, including propagation.

The key notion of the influential "General System Theory," namely, the concept of an "organized whole," or "organized totality," has also much to do with entelechy in this sense, although it rejects vehemently the notion of entelechy in the further senses that I will distinguish.[47] One problem with this theory, which was shown by Conrad-Martius and Paulina Taboada to amount to a subtle reductionism, is that it fails to account for the *inner* finality and for the *dynamically self-forming* character of this organization.[48] The deepest reason for attributing reductionism to general system-theoretical accounts of life is that this theory fails entirely to see the metaphysical necessity of life itself and of soul to explain the specific irreducible essence of the effects and activities of living organisms. This is quite understandable, given the origins of Bertalanffy in the circle of disciples of Moritz Schlick and the Vienna Circle of Neopositivism to whose descendants he ascribes himself.

Perhaps the explicit effort of this theory, which combines systems, such as computer-programs, and life and seeks their general features, must fall into a reductionism and mathematization of the essence of life which was developed in the eighteenth century but which does not do justice to the dynamic teleological self-unfolding of the organism. As Conrad-Martius observes, the transphysical phenomena of life can only be "explained" by some mathematical symbolism or theory if we do not take the pain to recognize entirely new and appropriate categories.[49]

This dynamic teleological structure of the organism involves building oneself up through nutrition and growth (turning other materials into one's own substance and "form"), preserving one's own form through nourishment and oxygen-transfer, but also recreating and transmitting it through regeneration and propagation. For this reason, Alejandro Serani prefers to speak of morphogenesis rather than of nutrition and growth when pointing at the essential characteristics of organisms. None of the mentioned features, however, is absolutely necessary for life, as we have seen.

Conrad-Martius and Kant[50] have admirably described the *mirandum* of this morphogenetic feature of biological life, which is intimately connected with the genetic code. That code, which is contained in each cell of the body, cannot produce "the work of art of the organism" without the actuality of life or without the amazing order of the organism. In the order of the organism gametes and germinal cells are distinguished from others and each cell of the body, although it has the same genetic code, receives its quite distinct place and function in the whole of the organism. Conrad-Martius compares this feature of life to the case in which the most ingenious architect who produces extraordinary and beautiful works of art would succeed in putting the architect's idea into the colors, stones, and other materials so that the work could paint and build itself.[51] This feature of organic life is not a mark of *zoee* in all of its forms, but certainly of *bios.* In an analogous and even more profound sense, the *eigengesetzliche Selbstgestaltung* is also a mark of the *zoee* of free beings, who, through their value responses and free acts, build themselves up and engender themselves. Even this feature would not be part of the essence of life *per se*, or not of the perfectly actualized life that theists attribute to God, in whom all life is eternally already in full being. This does not exclude that the essential mark of life meant here, if it is more cautiously formulated, without reference to temporal development, could also find some mysterious application to God.

This "dynamic and teleologically ordered building oneself up" constitutes an astonishing trait of life that presents the chief reason why we must attribute to organic life the following mark.

E. *Psyché* and Principle of Life: Entelechy in a Third Sense as Essential Core of *Bios*-Life

A fifth philosophical effort to identify the underlying essential core of the life of organisms gives an ontological explanation to the preceding phenomena and interprets life, in its deepest ontological ground, as entelechy or soul in the wide sense in which this term applies to all living beings and, more specifically, to all forms of *bios*. Higher forms of *zoee*, that is, purely spiritual beings, would possess the marks of soul in a preeminent fashion, but we would not speak here of *bios* any more, as our first essential characterization of biological life above shows. We would also not attribute the character of soul to purely spiritual persons, because soul is always related to a body.

Aristotle stated the insight that led philosophers to the discovery of this fifth essential mark of life which is in a sense life itself. We return to the quotation of Aristotle used in the second part of our motto:

> in everything the essence [*ousia*, which can also be translated as "substance"] is identical with the ground of its being, and here, in the case of living things, their being is to live, and of their being and their living the soul in them is the cause or source.[52]

Entelechy is here understood in a third sense, namely, as soul (*psyché*): as an active principle of its own, as a principle distinct from matter that actualizes and generates from within the form, order, and essence of the living entity. This principle is life itself.[53]

In the quoted text Aristotle uses three significant terms to refer to soul: (1) *Ground of being.* While Aristotle does not identify substance and soul (the substance of the tree, for example, also includes the tree's material elements), he attributes to soul what he elsewhere attributes to substance, namely, to be "the ground of being." Another similarity between substance and soul is that both are "ground of being." With the exception of our own soul, soul, like substance, is not directly given to our experience, but we grasp it in an act of the intellect as the *ground of the properties* which we perceive. As the form and movement of bodies are understood to be dependent on substance as the ground and subject of their being, so we understand or infer the existence of the soul (or the life-principle or "psychoid") as the ground of the being of the specific operations of living things.

(2) Aristotle calls the soul also *cause* of the living and being of organisms. We understand that purely immanent physical, chemical, or electrical causes cannot explain the specific operations and signs of living entities. They involve such a different and essentially higher order of being that their cause must lie in soul as in a principle that is irreducible to matter and yet a powerful operative reality which brings about as efficient cause the phenomena of life.

(3) Aristotle calls the soul also *source* of these phenomena which is directly given in our own conscious life but also accessible through a *Wesenseinsicht* in which what originates the phenomena of life discloses itself as soul. Depending on the type of activity of which the different species of living beings are capable, quite different kinds or parts of soul reveal themselves to be their source.

"Soul" is used here as an analogous term which includes basic similarities and at the same time fundamental differences. We can speak in general, referring to *all* living things in the world, of a principle of "interiority." The *Eigenbewegung* (spontaneous movement) of the organism which contributes to the role of the body being an "organ of the soul" is linked to an *interiority* of the organism which Franz von Baader characterized through the tension "center-periphery," and which Aristotle calls soul, distinguishing its three levels: plant soul (which Driesch calls "psychoid"), sensitive soul of animals, and human soul. For some thinkers (Leibniz, Portmann),"soul" includes not three essentially distinct orders but allows for infinitely many degrees of awakenedness, an idea which led Gustav Theodor Fechner to the conception of the cosmos as an ensouled totality, a theory already found in the Presocratic Anaxagoras and in Plato's idea of the world-soul. The idea of a world-soul is in no way given to our knowledge. Soul is given immediately and from within only to ourselves. Soul in the sense of a life-principle is given indirectly in plants and animals but certainly not in the cosmos. And when we come to the principle of *psyché* (soul), we touch insights that overthrow LaMettrie's concept of man-machine. But what is this principle of *psyché* and how do we know it?

Aristotle conceives of this principle of "*psyché*" in terms of the three parts and the three kinds of *psyché* (soul): nutritive, sensitive, and intellective soul.[54] The nutritive or vegetative soul is the cause and source of all those phenomena which we have seen to be essential properties of *bios*-life, as we encounter it also in plants. The *sensitive* soul is what discloses itself as ground and cause of the new world of operations which we find in animals, as, for example, sense-perception, memory, instinct, drive, awareness of many things, and ability to learn. The *intellective soul* is not only inferred but directly experienced in our conscious life, as I will discuss in Chapter Three. It is the self-given and intelligible ground of the being of understanding, judgment, free actions, and countless other distinguishing traits of the human person.

Even vegetative life involves soul. In modern philosophy, Hedwig Conrad-Martius and Hans Driesch defended a similar understanding of *the plant soul* as *a psychoid* or *entelechy*. I myself defended this notion in an earlier work.[55] There I dealt extensively with the difference between the (intellective) soul in the human being, the "divisible" (*verzweigbare*) soul which takes on the character of a life-stream in a plant, and the sensitive and "unified" soul in the animal which is responsible also for sensation, spontaneous locomotion, and many other phenomena.

Psyché or entelechy (soul) alone we can identify as life itself or as the ground, cause, and source of life that can exist even without exercising its mentioned operations, as we witness in the seed of a pine tree that now appears like a dead piece of wood yet soon will turn into a huge tree.

Life is not reducible to the characteristic operations of living organisms and their distinctions, and not even to their unified essence in their peculiar self-engendering quality and in the diffusion and *Verzweigbarkeit* of biological life, which Hedwig Conrad-Martius explored.[56] We grasp by a pure philosophical intuition that the observed signs of biological life and the actual power to produce them are essential manifestations of life but that they do not exhaust the essence of life. We understand, for example, that organisms that do not grow, are not nourished, do not regenerate damaged parts, and are sterile, may still live.

Permit me to refer again to empirical scientific evidence on which I am no expert but which confirm my philosophical intuition empirically. The cryo-conserved organism still lives, although all its vital functions, including nutrition in the wide sense, are temporarily paralyzed and reduced to a potential state. Frozen insects and other animals can survive at -50° C (-58° Fahrenheit), as was recently explored with great scientific rigor:

> Hundreds of species of terrestrial insects survive long periods of freezing while they overwinter. At the extreme, insects of the high Arctic, such as woolly bear caterpillars ... may spend 10 months of the year frozen solid at temperatures that descend to -50° C ... or even lower. ... But of the greatest interest ... are a group of amphibians and reptiles that survive freezing during their winter hibernation.[57]

Four common species of frogs survive freezing even if 60 percent or more of their total body water has turned into ice.[58] Young turtles survive at temperatures of -8° C of nest temperatures. Human embryos at early stages can also be frozen, even if the prospects of cryo-conserving developed human organisms appear dubious.[59] This possibility of lack of vital activity in a living organism is clearer in the case of seeming or apparent death, described by phenomena like asphyxia, cataleptic trance, or state of suspended animation. An organism in this state appears to be dead – like Juliet, in Shakespeare's *Romeo and Juliet*, after having taken the potion of the Friar. The organism, however, is only apparently and not really dead. All life's functions are laid to a state of rest, as happens in a live seed. But given the right temperature or other circumstances, the life in the organism awakens, which presupposes the existence of life and the potentiality of its operations before awakening.

David Weissmann has presented an interesting modern defense of an Aristotelian standpoint which recognizes dispositions and potencies irreducible to actions. The six phenomena Weissmann analyzes and offers as reasons to hold that potencies and dispositional properties exist are the following: (1) being a condition for the production of change, (2) being irreducible to actuality, (3) being specific, (4) depending on actuality for this specificity, (5) endurance, (6) susceptibility to change.[60]

The decisive point of this intuition is not only a general relationship between disposition (potency) and actualized state but the discovery that a material body of any kind is not sufficient to explain all phenomena of life. Even if a purely material body were endowed with the extraordinary potential to produce the phenomena we witness in live things, it would not live because life necessarily and intelligibly demands a *bios*-entelechy and soul distinct from the body.

Let me venture another formulation: the essence of *bios*-life cannot consist in the previously described vital functions. It can only lie in the very principle and subject itself that underlies all the magnificent operations of the organism: in a dynamic reality which Aristotle called *entelecheia* and *psyché* (soul).

This intuition reveals the deepest reason why the life of plants, animals, and human beings is irreducible to chaotic or non-chaotic physical systems, if it exists at all. Even if what is impossible could happen, namely, that mere material bodies would produce all signs of life, organisms would only seem to live but not really live. In reality, they would be something else than living entities, namely, complex machines.

Let me summarize this crucial result of a philosophical analysis of the necessary and intelligible essence of life. There can be no life without some *psyché* (life-principle) or life-principle that is really distinct from the physical-chemical make-up of a body. Plato expresses this in the following way:

> Then, he went on, tell me, what is that which must be in a body to make it alive?
> A soul, he replied.
> And is this always so?
> Of course, he said.
> Then the soul always brings life to whatever contains soul?
> No doubt, he answered.[61]

But while the "soul" (or psychoid as Driesch puts it) of plants and animals is given only from without, on the basis of concrete observations and universal intuitions, life and soul in us are immediately given. We have arrived at an understanding of the core of the essence of life and of living organisms as lying in their *psyché*, in a principle distinct from all the phenomena of life which we observe in the experience of *bios*. Mental life is self-given with absolute certainty and experienced most directly and intimately by us.

Though life and soul are never as clearly given in plants and animals, we understand that the necessary connection between life and soul. Soul is, in virtue of an essential necessity, the source and origin and primary seat of life. On this essential connection between life and soul, Plato bases an argument for the immortality of the human soul:[62]

Soul, especially the human soul, but also any soul that brings about *bios*, is essentially alive and the cause of life (there can be no "dead soul"), and therefore distinct from the body.

Aristotle shares the same view. He continues the text from the second book of *De Anima* I, 412 a 1-5, which I used as first part of the Motto of the present book:

> Of natural bodies some have life in them, others not ... . But since it is also a *body* of such and such a kind, viz. having life, the *body* cannot be soul ... . Hence the soul must be a substance in the sense of a form of a natural body having life potentially in it.[63]

Agreeing with Aristotle on the essential connection between soul and life, and on the fact that no body can be soul, I find his "definition" of soul in terms of "essence of a natural body" quite insufficient and incorrect, as I will point out in Chapter Three.

An empiricist could raise objections here, along the lines of J. L. Mackie,[64] starting with the idea of the "queerness" of a concept of "soul" as distinct from bodies. But John Finnis and others have well shown that notions employed by Mackie, as, for example, truth, reality, objectivity, argument, and coherence, likewise demand some intuition radically different from sense-perception or from what can be verified or falsified through sense-observations. Mackie admits that for a variety of phenomena, he, too, requires modes of knowledge that could be regarded as "queer," namely, for:

> essence, number, identity, diversity, solidity, inertia, substance, the necessary existence and infinite extension of time and space, necessity and possibility in general, power, and causation.[65]

I am not convinced when Mackie retorts that most of these terms can be explained by empirical modes of knowledge, and if any of them could not so be accounted for, we would have to argue against it as against an objective right and wrong.[66] Finnis points out that all the visible marks in Mackie's book mean propositions and that, if we take as the only kind of non-queer entities, qualities, and relations just those to which we refer in chemical or other scientific theories, then we:

> will be inclined to say that intentions, meanings and truth are utterly queer, and that the understanding of intentions and meanings and the adjudging of truth or falsity are so different from observing, inspecting, surveying, measuring and comparing that one had better give that understanding and adjudging the label "special faculty of intuition," that is, fishy.[67]

Apart from this necessary self-contradiction which Finnis pointed out, the application of Mackie's argument from queerness, when leveled against the intuition into the necessity that life-phenomena are grounded in some life-principle and soul distinct from bodies, is overcome as soon as we recognize insights into necessary essences and essential states of affairs as the most foundational form of rational knowledge. I have pointed out, with Aristotle, the existence of an immediate intellectual knowledge and its features in the introduction to this book, and I have explained them in detail elsewhere.[68]

F. Life as Existence (to Be) and Actuality of Living Things, and as Part of Their Essence: Toward a Metaphysics of Living Beings

After having reached these results, a more general metaphysical question poses itself: What exactly is life? How is it related to the nature (essence) and to the real being of the living organism?

At a first glance, what we mean by the life of an organism appears identical with its existence. Whether Orpheus in Gluck's opera of the same name says, "Euridice is no more," or "Euridice no longer lives," seems to amount to the same thing. In these contexts, to live and to be real appear to merge and to possess almost the same reality. The statement that a thing lives and that it exists appears to have almost the same meaning. For only real beings can actually live, while pure objects of imagination and dream, possible objects, or abstract ideas cannot themselves live, even if they are imaginations, ideas, etc. *of life* or *of living things*. The actual life of living organisms is inseparable from the very being and real existence of individual entities that alone can live. And vice versa, these beings, in virtue of their nature, could not exist without living.

When the beings capable of life no longer live but exist only as corpses, they do not exist in the mode of existence proper to living beings, a mode of existence far superior to the existence of lifeless things. Bonaventure expresses this by saying: "*nobilius et verius est esse vitae quam non viventis*" (the being of the living entity is more nobly and more truly being than the being of that which is lifeless).[69] Bonaventure also says that the "*substantia vivens*" is "*nobilior non vivente, carente vita simpliciter*" (the living substance ranks higher than the non-living one, which simply lacks life).[70] From these observations we could easily conclude with Aristotle and Thomas Aquinas that *to live* belongs to living things not accidentally but substantially, that *to live* is just the *to be* of living things: *"vivere viventibus est esse."*[71]

> The name is given from a certain external appearance, namely, self-movement, yet not precisely to signify this, but rather a substance to which self-movement and the application of itself to any kind of opera-

tion, belong naturally. To live, accordingly, is nothing else than to exist in this or that nature. ... Hence *living* is not an accidental but an essential predicate.[72]

This view points to the indubitable fact that no living organism can possess its proper *esse* as organism without living. And to live in a certain way refers to that unique mode of *esse*, of the actuality of being which pertains to organisms and to any living entity. Applying an idea of Edith Stein's *Eternal and Finite Being*, we can say that a "metaphysical ordination between essence and existence" exists so that to live is a unique mode of existing proper to living things. Taken in this sense, saying of an entity that it lives signifies that it possesses this form of existing uniquely found only in living entities. Therefore, for an organism to die means that it loses its existential identity, even though many material parts and elements of the organism continue to exist identically. To say, "this human being lives," necessarily involves the proposition, "this human being is," or, "this human being *exists*."

This does not exclude the possibility of a life of the soul (person) after death, nor does what we say exclude that human persons, if their primary identity resides in their soul, can live after their death. The death of a human person, which destroys the biophysical unity as an integral human being consisting of body and soul, does not exclude the continued existence of the ultimate personal self, which can, as we shall see in Chapter Three, be attributed to the soul.

"To live," then, refers to a specific mode of existing proper to living things. When "to live" is used in this sense, the statement, "A exists," is part of the meaning of "A lives." Understood in this manner, life appears to be situated at such a deep level of a being that the life of a being is its existence, and its existence is so inseparable from its life that life is in a sense the existence of the living being, as Aristotle and Aquinas say.

When taken in another sense of the term, life belongs to the essence of things. Therefore, the answer to the question whether something is "a living thing" or an inorganic and "dead" entity constitutes an answer to the question about what and how something is. In this sense, Bonaventure rightly says[73] that life is essential to the living organism ("*est essentiale animali*"). At the same time he says, indicating the strange conflation of essence and existence in life: "*Vivere est esse viventis et ei essentiale*" (to live is the being of the living thing and is essential to it).[74] Life encompasses both the essential and existential identity of a being. It belongs to it essentially for two reasons. In the first place, part of the *nature* of a being is to possess life. In the second place, the *reality* of its nature and of its life requires *real existence* so that really *to be* and *to live*, to exist, is essential to a living thing in that it would not really be living if it did not really exist. Heteronomous or purely intentional objects of a conscious subject can never possess actual life.

We can see the first of these connections of life to essence in games where someone has to guess what other people are thinking of. One of the first questions in the game will be: "Is it some living thing?" If the other is thinking of "bird" and answers "yes," that person understands life not as the concrete existence and *actual* life of any bird but as a property of the bird's essence which distinguishes birds from stones and other inanimate objects. The person can even refer to non-existing but essentially living things, as, for example, nymphs.

How can we solve this puzzle as to whether life signifies the essence or the existence of living things?[75] Perhaps in life essence and existence meet and merge in a unique manner. I think, however, that we come closer to the truth when we say that we can speak of life in two senses. Sometimes we mean its essence, while at other times we mean the existence proper only to living entities.

Yet when we attribute actual life to an entity, saying, "yes, this woman actually lives," we seem to indicate at the same time an essential trait and the actual existence of that woman. Life, as Aquinas notes, belongs both to the order of essence and of existence; it constitutes both a more perfect mode of *esse* and a determination of essence.[76]

G. The Situatedness of Life on the Level of Substance or Its Character of an Accident

Another purely philosophical question about the intelligible essence of life regards the problem whether life is just an accident, similar to color or extension, or belongs to the substance of an organism, or even is a substance itself.

By "accident," or "accidental," Aristotle means two quite different things, without distinguishing them clearly. An "accident" is any being that does not stand in itself in reality but inheres in another thing, as, for example, qualities, quantities, relations, acts, and all categories of being except substances. The opposite of an accident in this sense is substance. Substance then signifies that ultimate entity which is not in another thing but stands in itself in reality, the human being itself, the tree itself, etc. A second and quite different meaning of accidents (*ta symbebekota*) signifies non-essential properties. Its opposite is not substance but those properties of a thing which constitute the thing's essence or vocation. Life is not merely an accident of an organism in the second sense in which the organism's size or shape are accidental, in quite different degrees and ways, although a fundamental shape and form of an animal are essential to its species. For example, the basic form of the horse belongs to the horse's nature and is not accidental in the second sense of this term. "Accidental" in this use of the term, while it may imply that the "accidents" inhere in a substance and do not stand on their own feet in being, means that the "accident" has the character described by Aristotle's term *ta symbebekota*, as that which is not necessary and superadded to the essence of a thing. Life is surely not accidental in this sense. It characterizes the most elementary *what* and *how* something is, its substantial being and essence, and the activity and operation of an organism. Here again, Bonaventure points out this double aspect of life, when he says that life can refer to the essence but also to the actuality and operations of a being.[77] At the same time, life is not just some abstract entity or principle of being but coincides with the substantial principle of being of the individual organism. This shows that life belongs to the essence of the organism and is no mere accident in the sense of a nonessential property. In my *Essere e persona*,[78] I have tried to develop a metaphysics which recognizes accidents in the first sense which are in no way accidental in the second sense. I tried to show that Aristotle in his *Metaphysics* fails to make this crucial distinction and therefore was seduced into the erroneous opinion that metaphysics studies only substance and not accidents.

Turning into a dead corpse, the organism changes its essence and loses its substantial identity. The corpse is no longer this animal or this human being: these no longer exist. Mere parts and external elements of the organism continue to exist after death that are not identical with the living whole that we call organism. Thus, life is an act or inner actuality that co-constitutes what the medieval philosophers called the "substantial form," the essential and substantial identity of a substance:

> To live is a first act, which belongs to the genus of substance.[79]
>
> it is the actuality of substance[80]
>
> To live is the act(uality) of the living being.[81]

The organism lives in virtue of its essence and substance, not as to exist or to live necessarily, absolutely speaking, but living necessarily as long as it possesses existence (the *actus essendi*). Its being, as essentially ordained to life, is to live. We cannot retain the living being, while abstracting from its life, nor is life an entity separate from the being that lives. The living organism or the living soul is always what lives and to which we attribute life: life pertains to the *ens vivens*, to the *être vivant*.[82]

Nevertheless, the radical newness of life, of the *psyché*, the recognition of which we found to be the most important philosophical step in the discovery of the essence of life, shows that in addition to the living organism life itself is a real entity. The principle of life, which in a sense is life or merges with it, is, at least in human persons, a substantial entity, a soul. With Plato, we recognize that life is inseparable from soul in that no dead soul can exist. Even in plants and animals we find some soul as the principle of life, and, if we do not want to call the plant life or the principle of life in the animal a substance or a soul, we must call it at least a "substancoid" or a "psychoid," meaning that it is a reality which possesses some autonomous existence in itself. Therefore, life cannot be reduced to just a principle of being in which the essence and existence of an entity are only *in real entities* and not autonomous realities and are not beings in their own right. Instead, life as soul, and the real active principle in plants and animals that is life and bestows life, is a real entity itself, like a substance, but in animals and even more in plants fully "immersed" into matter, something "in a body and for a body," as Aristotle says. In human beings, on the contrary, as we shall see in Chapter Three, the living soul as the seat and principle of human life is itself a fully real, substantial, and living *ens*, and even a separable spiritual entity and substance in its own right, although it also is part of the whole human essence and substance, and therefore might be called "substantial form of the human being" or "incomplete substance" (*substantia incompleta*).

The *psyché* is, in different degrees, dependent on the type of soul in question, a substance in itself, that is, it stands in itself in reality and is not reducible to the existence of an organism. The *psyché* is not the organism's existence nor an essential substantial trait of the living substance, not even in plants and animals, and certainly not in the human person. Instead, the soul itself that possesses and bestows life, possesses being, and, as Plato saw, exists much more essentially than any other thing.

While we do not attribute fully autonomous substantial being to the life-principle of plants or to animal souls, because they are, as Aristotle puts it, something in and for a body, the *psyché* in all its forms still possesses an actuality and a being distinct from that of the body. The human soul, however, constituting the core of the human person, clearly and unambiguously possesses substantial character. The human soul is a simple substance that stands in itself in being and is not just a principle or actuality of something else or of the human "organism," as I shall show in Chapter Three.

Plato thinks that life is absolutely inseparable from a soul as long as it lives and that life belongs to the soul eternally and immortally and as necessarily as being odd necessarily belongs to the number 3. The comparison with the mathematical essential necessity obtaining between three-ness and odd-ness is found in Plato's *Phaedo*.[83] On this, Plato bases a key argument for the immortal nature of the soul, an argument which cannot satisfy me.[84]

Inasmuch as soul constitutes the essence and reality of life, life essentially belongs to the soul so that a "dead soul" would be a contradiction in terms, and inasmuch as the soul is the source and seat of life, life itself, understood as principle, seat, and source of life, can be regarded as soul and thus as substantial reality.

This is one of the reasons why I reject as false any philosophical answer to the question about the essence of life that sees the essence of life only in an accidental feature of a being. Life belongs to the substantial being of a living thing and subsists itself in a substantial soul or in a substancoid principle of life. This critical remark also applies to Helmuth Plessner. For this reason, Plessner's attempt to capture the essence of life chiefly through the "positionality" (*Positionalität*), an obscure term which refers to the open relationship of living beings to their limit and to the world beyond their limit, cannot convince me. This "positionality," which he defines in terms of a relationship of an organism to its limits, is of the order of qualities, properties, or accidents and thus cannot adequately capture the substantial reality of soul. However significant this feature of living things might be, it always remains at the level of a non-substantial, and in this sense "accidental," characteristic of living beings and hence can at best be an indispensable essential moment of living things but never coincide with their character as living beings.

At this point, we might ask other questions: *Is* the soul life, or does the soul just *possess* life, or does it bestow life on that which has a soul? The answer to this question will partly depend on the kind of life of which we are speaking. The life of a whole human being seems to be bestowed by the soul and in no way identical with it. If we speak of the life of the soul itself, however, we find it extremely difficult to consider life as distinct from soul. This is true both when life is understood in the essential sense and when it is understood in the existential sense. No dead soul can exist, and to consider life as something extraneous to the essence and existence of the soul is incomprehensible and unintelligible. Nevertheless, an irreducibility of soul to its life seems to tell us that the soul is not simply identical with life but "has" or "possesses" it. This is linked to its contingency. The soul neither exists nor lives with absolute necessity. Therefore, metaphysically speaking, the soul could have remained, as without existence, so without life.

H. Life and Value of Biological Life

The value of life, the non-neutrality of life, is quite a different essential mark of life the exploration of which is specifically reserved to philosophy. When we consider all the discussed essential marks of life, especially the different dimensions of entelechy, we arrive at an entirely new axiological insight into the fact that life possesses a positive importance that lifts it out of the sphere of the neutral. Grounded in its essence, life possesses a nobility that surpasses that of any dead being and of any being deprived of life.

This positive importance and nobility of life is not a "natural property" of the sort, say, of cellular structure or nutrition. It is in a precise sense a "non-natural property" that grows out of all the other characteristics of life.[85] It is in this sense also a "supervenient property" of life. Yet this value of life is a central property of life metaphysically speaking, because it refers to the *agathon*, to the goodness of life, which we can recognize, with Aristotle, as the final cause, as the *raison d'être* of life.

With Dietrich von Hildebrand, I add that this value of life is not only of the category of the "agreeable" or of the "subjectively satisfying," or even solely of the type of "objective good for someone" (for an animal or for a person). Instead, we encounter here an intrinsic value and superiority, a positive importance as an intrinsic and objective preciousness and nobility so that the addition "(*good*) *for* someone" contradicts the essence of the objective value if this formulation seeks to describe the essence of this value of life. This is not to deny that all things which possess intrinsic and objective value are also, and even therefore, able to become objective goods for persons.[86] With Bonaventure, Nicholas Malebranche, and Max Scheler, we can say that the living being possesses a higher value than the dead, and that this value of life possesses an ultimate and irreducible value-quality:

> The being of the living entity is more nobly and more truly being than the being of that which is lifeless.[87]

Scheler adds the important insight that any vitalistic relativism of values that declares *all* values relative to life could not attribute to *life itself* a value and yet necessarily presupposes life's absolute value. A life that would be neutral in itself could not give rise to any other values, while any attempt to explain the value of life itself as being relative to life would be circular.[88]

At this point of our investigation, we might ask what in this biologically living being is the bearer of the value of life. I suggest that we can identify the value of life as situated on four different levels within the living entity. At first, we can say that the actualizations of the essential properties of life in themselves, of nutrition, growth, regeneration, and of each of the elements involved therein, possess an ontological value and are not something neutral. Secondly, we find that – in the frozen plant, for example – even the potency to actualities proper to living things is the bearer of an ontological value of life. This value is absent in a stone which is bereft of all the potentialities proper to living things. Thirdly, we discover that life itself is irreducible to its operations and that life as fountain and source of the activities of living things is itself the bearer of value. Fourthly, we are led to a similar conclusion as it corresponds to a personalist metaphysics: the deepest value of the living plant or animal does not just reside in its ontological being alive and in having the essential properties of living things but in fulfilling the vocation of the living being. The most significant value is possessed by a plant or an animal when it is healthy and embodies qualitative values of beauty, of order, of meaning, and of integration with other beings. These properties alone – which are accidents in the first sense of the term as inhering in the organism – perfect the living thing and bestow on it its ultimate value. Imagine a monstrous animal, misformed, ferocious, that devours all human beings, has perverted instincts, threatens beings higher than itself, an animal that emits the most horrible stench, and has the appearance of a malformed dragon invented by a devil and emerging from a demonically malformed underworld. We would try to kill this animal, thinking that it had better die. Or imagine a plant that is ugly in all respects, is a terrible weed, a noxious, aggressive, and invasive plant that kills all life around it. Certainly we would prefer that this plant did not live or exist. Thus, we see that the deepest value of living things does not merely reside in their substantial being and life, but in those qualitative values which perfect them and bestow their innermost meaning on them. Even the ontological values of living beings *per se* receive fulfillment only when these living beings serve the realization of the higher values and when the ontological values themselves are perfected by them. The wonder of being alive manifests itself and is fully real only in and through these additional values which have to do with the beauty, grace, comely form, order, and meaning of living things. I will return to a metaphysics of accidents in Chapter Three when dealing with the life of persons.

4. Essentially Necessary (*A Priori*) Characteristics of Biological Life in Terms of Chaos Theory and Their Ambiguity

Whereas classical forms of materialism and materialist monistic identity theories attempted to show that life and mind were nothing essentially new with respect to closed and fully determined systems of material elements, governed by the laws of physics and chemistry, the life-sciences increasingly observed living organisms to be radically new systems of physical entities which are more complex and obey other laws than inanimate objects. Jay Roth expresses this well:

> If one considers even a single protein, for example, glycogen phosphorylase, this displays such an immense complexity that it boggles the mind. Considering the processes of protein synthesis, DNA replication and repair, and hundreds of equally complicated processes, one is left with a feeling best described as awe.
>
> I have carefully studied molecular, biological, and chemical ideas of the origin of life and read all the books and papers I could find. Never have I found any explanation that was satisfactory to me. The basic problem is with the original template (be it DNA or RNA) that would have been necessary to initiate the first living system that could then undergo biological evolution. Even reduced to the barest essentials, this template must have been very complex indeed. For this template and this template

> alone, it appears it is reasonable at present to suggest the possibility of a creator.
>
> I must be honest and point out that even though, as some have calculated the odds of such a template forming by chance are 1 in about 10^{300} or, possibly, a much larger number, it is always possible to win the lottery ... .[89]

Similar ideas are expressed by Henry Margenau:

> The British Astronomer Fred Hoyle is widely noted for the statement that believing the first cell originated by chance is like believing a tornado ripping through a junk yard full of airplane parts could produce a Boeing 747.[90]

A similar thought was expressed in 1921 by the discoverer of the biological notion of *Umwelt* (surroundings), Johannes von Uexcüll,[91] with respect to the immense improbability that an amoebae could come to exist by chance and had to find a surrounding in which to live and then propagate itself regularly. He compares this with the idea that by accident a car be formed out of different parts of metal, a key falls – by accident – into the key-hole, gas flows – by accident – in the tank, the key turns by accident, by accident a street appears on which the car can drive, etc. And when this car crashes and breaks, from its parts by accident it is restored or else little cars emerge from the pieces of the preceding one. This would go on all the time and quite regularly, millions of times, and not just one time per 10^{300} – all by chance. Uexcüll adds that to assume this origin of cars would be an incomparably more probable assumption than a transition from lifeless matter to the simplest organism, which is far more complicated than any car, let alone the assumption of the production, by chance, of the entire cosmos of organisms on earth. He also makes the excellent remark that if the most intelligent scientists, studying all laws of nature and creating artificially the conditions under which they believe life to emerge from lifeless materials, were ever to succeed in their efforts, they would not prove that chance can produce life, but only that the highest terrestrial intelligence, after years of study, was able to produce one simple form of life.

Following the lead of Erwin Schrödinger, scientists observed that organic substances are partly governed by principles that are antithetically opposed to those of inorganic matter.[92]

Schrödinger's book *What Is Life?*, especially the Epilogue, is profoundly confused philosophically speaking and advocates a strange thesis of an experienced all-identity of a pantheistically conceived single "Consciousness." But it introduces important categories which show the newness of life as manifesting itself through laws and activities contrary to those which govern inanimate matter, as, for example, "negative entropy" (called *negentropy* by

Bertalanffy).[93] By having noted these phenomena consciously, Schrödinger made a significant contribution toward a critique of materialism, although his book later seeks to explain these phenomena in terms of quantum physical laws. Whereas material things, for example, underlie the thermodynamic laws of the inanimate cosmos and obey principles of entropy which involve a growing transition to lower forms of energy and less ordered material wholes, the living organisms develop in accordance with principles of "negative entropy" which here indicates a positive phenomenon of living organisms developing toward more ordered and organized material and energetic systems. Schrödinger says that the organism "drinks order from its surroundings" and nourishing substances and resists the tendency to reach a static state of thermodynamic equilibrium (which Schrödinger compares to death).[94]

Unlike many other laws in physics, the increase of entropy appears to explain or to presuppose the directed flow of time.

> The future and the past seem physically to be on a completely equal footing, Newton's laws, Hamilton's equations, Einstein's general relativity, Dirac's equation, the Schrödinger equation – all remain effectively unaltered if we reverse the direction of time. (Replace the coordinate *t*, which represents time, by *-t*.)[95]

Also Max Planck[96] and Ilya Prigogine[97] explain the connection of the second law of thermodynamics and the flow of time, the "arrow of time," as a most fundamental physical fact.

Entropy was also defined as "the measure of the degree of disorder in a substance or in a system." And the laws of entropy involve a directedness of a physical system to lower and lower forms of energy and to growing disorder. In 1854, Rudolf Clausius had formulated the Second Law of Thermodynamics in the following form: "The entropy of an isolated system never diminishes." Ludwig Boltzmann later formulated it as, "Any closed system tends toward an equilibrium state of maximum probability, which is associated with equalization of temperature, pressure, and so forth."

Life resists these laws of lifeless matter. Expanding on Schrödinger's terminology, we could say that life shows a transition to "order from order,"[98] inasmuch as living organisms possess in themselves an order which they pass on through propagation, and which they do not receive from without, in the manner in which inorganic matter is formed by an artisan or an architect into a given shape. Inorganic matter produces order only from disorder, and this order is produced from without by some external cause as, for example, a beaver, an ant, or a human artisan or architect.[99] Otherwise, the thermodynamic laws lead to a "negative order"[100] of a thermodynamic equilibrium that tends toward extinguishing the differences of temperature, structure, etc. – elements that belong to order in the physical world. Schrödinger links, somewhat confusingly, the irreversibility of physical entropic developments to this sense of "order" which he calls elsewhere disorder. Thus life expresses itself through an entirely new "negative entropy," a tendency from disorder to order, from lesser levels of orders to higher ones. A strange phenomenon in the physical universe, however, which resembles life in some respects is the crystal and its growth into a highly ordered form.

Therefore, a material universe governed by the laws of thermodynamics and entropy cannot explain life. Ulrich J. Becker states this well:

> It [the origin of life] happened $3x10^9$ years ago. Luria and Ziegler argue on plausibilistic levels to overcome the minute probability of an accidental start as scientifically rigorous thermodynamics predicts. Even if new "chaos-to-order" models enhance the probability by many orders of magnitude to form the first reproducing entity, the question of the origin is not answered without addressing who arranged for these laws to cooperate so well.[101]

While the principle of "order from order" indicates well phenomena such as propagation of living organisms, as opposed to the ways in which higher order is produced in inanimate matter from relative chaos and from without, we could also use the opposite terminology. We could say that, by the processes of assimilation and the nutritive system, the living organism creates higher order from relatively disordered materials and foods (order from disorder), whereas the inorganic physical systems undergo a movement from higher order organization to growing disorder or to more primitive levels of organization and energy (chaos from order).

Although Schrödinger's book is a great witness to the inexplicability of life in terms of physics and a testimony to the newness of life, Schrödinger himself attempts to give a new reductionistic explanation of the living cell and the living organism. While he admits that classical mechanistic theories fail in their reductionistic explanations of life in terms of physics and chemistry, he proposes an ambiguous quantum-mechanical and purely physical explanation of life. The ambiguity of his position on biological life allows proponents of reductionist explanations of life as well as defenders of the radical newness of biological life versus non-living substances to refer to Schrödinger as their inspiration. Considering his many expressions of awe and profound wonder at the newness of life from the standpoint of physics, his thought inspires those of us who insist on the newness of life and who stress the irreducibility of life to any physical system. In proposing a quantum-mechanical theory of life, however, Schrödinger develops a theory of life which seeks to explain the "order" of organisms in the last analysis through a principle of a physicalistic transition from apparent chaos to order.

This concept finds ample nourishment in the recent advances of chaos-theory, which is not only applicable to physical and biological theories but even to the theories of the laws which govern the order of prime numbers,[102] and in the new method discovered by Chaitin and others to analyze chaotic orbits mathematically.[103] By the notion of non-chaotic physical systems, I mean physical systems that obey well-explored laws, those of classical physics possibly including the statistical laws of quantum-mechanics. By the term "chaotic physical systems," I refer to physical systems which appear to be chaotic and to follow hitherto unexamined laws or disordered patterns but which can be proven to obey some laws according to which certain effects are produced with higher frequency than would follow from the general laws of probability *per se*. To this class belong all those phenomena the laws of which we do not understand, as, for example, the sudden changes of weather or the changes of which contemporary scientists assume occurred during the alleged Big Bang, or other material events and results which occur under unexplored combinations of factors and which could have given rise to nucleic acids and other molecules that compose living organisms. A modern chaos-theoretical explanation of life is proposed, for example, by Ilya Prigogine. (Ilya Prigogine, who received he Nobel Prize of Chemistry in 1977 for his discoveries in the field of non-equilibrium thermodynamics, and other scientists do not believe in the Big Bang theory.) He writes:

> I do not believe in life as a unique phenomenon. I believe life is a cosmic phenomenon, which appears where the right conditions (distance from equilibrium, non-linear processes, chemical composition, and so on) are satisfied. The main difficulty with the classical view of its origin was the high "improbability" of the complex organization which we find in living beings. With the discovery of complex structures arising in non-equilibrium linear systems, this objection can be discarded. In a hydrodynamic process such as Benard instability, we see complex phenomena which at equilibrium would be quite improbable, too. But the non-equilibrium provides the necessary environment for these self-organizing processes and permits the realization of processes whose probability at equilibrium would be nil ... . A recent book gives ... a balanced view on the role of chaos and bifurcations in living systems.[104]

This opinion could be further explained in the following way: Given that what the term "chaotic physical systems" allows for unexpected variations of the laws of chemistry and physics, or for unpredictable applications of them in view of our ignorance about the exact initial states and factors preceding a given event (the German word *Rahmenbedingungen* might best describe what I mean here), we cannot speak of the extent and limits of chaotic physical events with any authority of natural science that has not yet finished exploring the possibilities of these chaotic physical systems.

On the other hand, one has to admit that also the contrary assumption is not demonstrable. The absence of any empirical proof of chaotic events giving rise to life is also expressed by a physicist who believes in a materialist explanation of the origin of life:

> To assume some higher organizing principle outside and above these physical and chemical laws is unnecessary in my view. But that's my opinion. Nobody has demonstrated that life, even a simple bacterium, can evolve form a broth of molecules.[105]

Scientists qua scientists, attempting to explain the emergence of life from matter through chaos theory, find the sphere of the unexpected to which chaos theory refers such that they cannot impose on it precise "cans" and "cannots." We are still far from having explored the immense wealth of contingent facts concerning matter and life which are open to empirical testing and research, supported by hypothetical theories which appear to defy traditional logic, theories like the uncertainty relation of Werner Heisenberg, Bell's theorem, or various principles of physical chaos-theory.[106] Therefore, the defenders of a materialist reductionist explanation of life argue, life can very well be explained through the laws of the physical universe.

My position, however, is that inasmuch as the necessary essential features of matter and life, as well as their essential differences, are concerned, philosophical knowledge can reach an understanding of both life and matter, and thus determine limits of what any future development of chaos-theory could explain.[107] A philosophical knowledge of the limits of what chance and laws of chaos can explain is enough to demonstrate the irreducibility of life to chaotic and non-chaotic physical systems.

Quite apart from this, the theory of chaos is, philosophically speaking, ambiguous, and often the term is introduced more as expression of an intellectual fad than as a clear notion.

A. Three Meanings of Chaos

Chaos was introduced into the modern discussion by James Clerk Maxwell, who was aware that the evolution of a strictly deterministic physical system could be essentially unpredictable. The later states of the system could depend so sensitively on its initial states that an infinitesimal error in the initial conditions might result in a large error in later states.[108] Chaos theory is much older, however, and goes back to Greek philosophy, as Enrico Berti's contribution to the volume *Cosmos*[109] shows. Today, the term "chaos" is used in many senses.

(1) The terms "chaos" or "chaotic events" mean at times a macrophysical application of microphysical concepts from quantum-physics (so-called indeterministic chaos which Schrödinger introduces to explain the occurrence of life). Then "chaotic events" would be undetermined and uncaused, and therefore unpredictable, events. As Heisenberg's book, *Philosophy and Physics*, demonstrates, he was quite interested in philosophy and had a good philosophical education which allowed him to make many fascinating applications of classical philosophical distinctions and questions to modern physics. Nevertheless, many of his philosophical ideas are open to serious criticism. Specifically, Heisenberg's philosophical interpretation of "chaos" and quantum physics – as demonstrating events which are in themselves undetermined or uncaused – contains philosophical confusions between various epistemological and ontological issues. I will return to this point.

(2) Another concept of "deterministic" chaos is based on the notion, introduced in the last century by James Clerk Maxwell, of unpredictable complex events[110] that can be calculated only in terms of non-linear equations or where the exact conditions found in the original starting point of a given process are not known. We may say with Morton, "The world is full of systems which are in principle unpredictable." Unpredictable complex events are explored in recent attempts by the Oxford Forecasting Services Company to use chaos-theory in predicting the development of currency-exchange-rates and other economic factors. If the events were known exactly, the calculation, in cases of "deterministic chaos," where all applicable general laws of physics and chemistry are known, could achieve exact results. As long as the starting conditions are insufficiently known, chaotic processes and their chaotic results are not predictable with precision and have to be referred to with non-linear equations and principles of chaos-theory.

(3) A third meaning of chaos is the following: facts or processes, which science considered for a long time as occurring just by chance, are governed by some laws which cannot be explained until now where science can prove that determined processes or facts occur more frequently than expected just by the laws of probability:

> In chaotic systems uncertainty and approximation are rapidly amplified. This precludes not only long-term prediction of their behaviour, but also the closed-form solution of their equations of motion.[111]

See also the following text by James P. Crutchfield:

> The error in this prediction can be as large as the attractor itself. The refinement of a "theory" for a single chaotic orbit cannot be improved beyond that irreducible and large error. One response is to use probabilistic descriptions of the apparent random behaviour. This ignores the tremendous structure in deterministic behaviour, such as the short-term predict-

ability and the shape of the chaotic attractor. Qualitative dynamics is a geometric approach intermediate between exact solution and probabilistic methods.[112]

Thus, even where the alleged firm order of the world of physical laws is broken into by new anti-thermodynamic laws of life which appear to be inexplicable in terms of physics, it appears possible to introduce notions as, for example, the Big Bang, explosions, mutations, and quantum-mechanical factors which give rise to new orders including organisms. These new and higher orders occur according to higher probabilities than those which would correspond to the laws of probability and according to mathematical laws involved in the transition from chaos to order. A reductionistic explanation of the emergence of life from physical systems along the lines of this third meaning of chaos is also suggested by Schrödinger. He relativizes the physicists' principle of "disorder [chaos] from order" and the biological principle of "order from order,"[113] implying that also clocks show signs of "order from order."[114] Yet, claims Schrödinger, just as a clock is more than a mechanical system because it needs a spring and, to function, has to be rewound, so the living organism is not an autonomous mechanical system but the finest masterwork of a divine quantum mechanics.[115] Thus, life appears again to be reducible to the product of fine mechanisms of nature that go beyond any normal origin of order and which lead to entities that surpass in artfulness all clocks and other human artifices.

I will reflect on this view, though not from the standpoint of the scientist, who can describe life excellently in terms of its empirical properties and of the empirical laws that govern it, but who cannot grasp, with methods of natural science, the essence of this unique phenomenon of life. Nor will I approach life from the point of view of the mathematical chaos-researcher, but from that of the philosopher who seeks those necessary and highly intelligible aspects of life that are accessible to rational philosophical insights and arguments.[116]

B. Four Meanings of Big Bang

Before I investigate the issue of the reducibility or non-reducibility of life in greater depth, I will reflect critically on the idea of the Big Bang, which demonstrates, as few other modern conceptions in the context of which chaos-theory is used, how philosophically involved yet how ambiguous and philosophically unclear the notions of chaos and of chaotic physical events are. In some of its forms, for example, in Andrej D. Linde's cosmology of "chaotic inflation," chaos-theory is used against the Big Bang theory.[117]

Some notions of chaos, or Jacques Monod's notions of chance and necessity, go far beyond the idea of complex and unpredictable causality or of events that must be described with non-linear equations. Reflection on the idea of the Big Bang also shows that such distinctions as between "deterministic chaos" (in macrophysics) and "indeterministic chaos" (in quantum physics) are philosophically insufficient and confused. Besides possessing a more precise scientific meaning, the term "Big Bang" in some of its more philosophically involved usages is a prime example of a reductionist explanation of the world and of the origin of life. The term "Big Bang" has the following quite different meanings:

(1) We find a philosophically and metaphysically undetermined notion of the Big Bang as an event that marks the beginning of our cosmos and took place about 150 billion years ago.

> The fact that physicists are able to situate the origin of the universe in time at fifteen thousand million years ago is ... a consequence of two events ... first, the discovery by Edwin Powell Hubble ... of the recession of the galaxies, which gave rise to the notion of an evolving universe; and, second, the famous measurement of the fossile radiation of 2.7°K (about -270°C), which gave this evolution an origin in time, that is to say gave the universe a definite age.[118]

In this sense, to speak of the Big Bang says only that our cosmos, especially the motion of the astronomical bodies and systems away from an imaginary center, has had a beginning at an approximately calculable time of 150 billion years ago. Essential for this first meaning of Big Bang is that of what nature this event was remains open. It could, so runs the interpretation of some theistic scientists, even be the moment of the creation of the world from nothing.

(2) Another notion of Big Bang refers to a far more specific event in the physical universe, namely, a massive explosion described in detail by some physicists (in terms of the temperatures preceding the time when it took place, etc.), which marks the beginning phase of the cosmos. Whether this state is an absolute beginning of the universe or only the initial event of a new "cosmic age" is left open. This notion of the Big Bang neither denies nor asserts that this event itself and its ensuing consequences require a final cause as explanation of the cosmic order that emerges from it. The metaphysical question remains equally open whether the static and dynamic beginning state of the world (and the Big Bang) required a personal Creator and whether the world stands in need of many further creative interventions of the supreme Being; or whether this beginning state is to be conceived in atheistic terms according to which the physical event called "Big Bang" is the absolute cause of the universe: a quasi-divine and creative Big Bang. In contradistinction to the first meaning of a sudden physical or metaphysical event 150 billion years ago which led to the emergence of the universe, this second meaning of Big Bang

refers to a physical event of a nature describable in terms of physics. Scientifically speaking, this meaning is much more specific than the first one. Philosophically speaking, however, it constitutes an equally indeterminate concept inasmuch as it leaves open all the questions concerning the ultimate final and efficient causes of the cosmos.

(3) A notion of the Big Bang in the spirit of Pierre Teilhard de Chardin is necessarily connected with an evolutionism that assumes a continuous causal chain and development such that all later developments and forms of life developed "out of this event" and were caused by it. This monistic evolutionary notion of the Big Bang can be theistic (assuming that the Big Bang and the anthropic principle necessary to explain the emergence of life and human life had to be planned and initiated by a transcendent intelligent God) or atheistic-materialistic-monistic (alleging that this event alone constitutes a sufficient cause of the universe). But in both cases the third conception of this event attributes to the Big Bang and to the first material elements and events in the universe leading to it and following upon it all the evolutionary germs which then give rise – in an immanent development – to the coming-to-be of the whole universe. The world can, in keeping with this conception of Big Bang, also be conceived as a huge entelechy and organism, along the lines of Schrödinger. A linear evolutionary development, however many qualitative leaps of chaotic nature it involves, leads, according to this third and definitely philosophical interpretation, from the physical event of the Big Bang to the end of human history and of the cosmos. This theory of the Big Bang is no mere hypothesis of natural science but a philosophical and even metaphysical theory.

(4) An even more pronouncedly metaphysical notion of the Big Bang is that of a purely physical-chemical event which *per se* and without any transcendent intelligent or divine causality produced the whole universe by some chaotic and non-chaotic laws and events. Thus understood, the Big Bang constitutes the beginning of a materialistically, atheistically, and immanentistically conceived universe and evolution. This fourth understanding of the Big Bang is neo-darwinistic and monistic and seeks to make quantum-mechanical indeterminacy and deterministic chaotic laws of chance and necessity the "divinity" responsible for the origin of the world.[119]

We see how many meanings the concepts of the Big Bang and of chaos can contain and how confusing they turn out to be. I am reminded here of Benedetto Croce's view that natural science does not use authentic concepts but words without definite meanings, something like non-concepts which perform functions in scientific systems but remain conceptually undetermined.

What should we think about the four meanings of "Big Bang" that I have described?

(1) The first sense of Big Bang corresponds to many facts of science and is a reasonable assumption fully compatible with metaphysics and with present astronomical and cosmological knowledge. It is well-nigh universally accepted today but could be opposed by those philosophers, including most philosophers in antiquity and modern Parmenidean thinkers like Emanuele Severino, who deny any beginning of a universe which they regard as eternal or as static. It could also be rejected by those who hold the opinion that the cosmos moves in cosmic cycles subjected to some firm unexplored law of eternal recurrence. Friedrich Nietzsche defended this theory, although he might have understood the teaching of eternal recurrence more as an expression of a nihilistic will to power – which culminates in the will that the value-less absurd cosmos lasts or returns eternally – than as an objective metaphysical thesis.[120] Finally, this view of the Big Bang could be criticized by those who interpret and believe in a literal sense the Biblical account of creation (in a six-day sequence). Others hold religious views which make them doubt the absolute validity of the modern systems of science to determine the boundaries of the temporal beginnings of the universe by their methods which are not free of untested philosophical assumptions implied in all inductive methods. The scientific methods mentioned above, on which scientists rely when they estimate the age of the universe, could be drawn into doubt by philosophers who criticize inductive knowledge in part or in principle, as Sir Karl Popper does.

(2) The second meaning of Big Bang constitutes a scientific hypothesis – or myth – which is impossible today to demonstrate conclusively but which can be introduced as a reasonable working hypothesis for cosmology and cosmogony. It was accepted widely by scientists over recent decades. But it is quite controversial. Some leading scientists criticize it sharply and hold it to be an unsuccessful hypothesis for various alleged or real scientific deficiencies. Among its detractors are Hannes Alfvén and Fred Hoyle. They think the Big Bang theory in the second sense has not been successful and does not account for elements heavier than helium.[121] These scientists admit a temporal origin of the cosmos (and thus a Big Bang in the first sense) but reject the assumption of a Big Bang in the second sense at the origin of the universe. Instead, they introduce other cosmological hypotheses about the origin of the world.

A more philosophical criticism of the Big Bang theory in its second sense would emphasize that the purposeful aspects of the universe cannot be explained by a concept of a Big Bang which seeks to identify only the efficient cause (and here only the physical part thereof) which produced the cosmos. Instead, any proper cosmological explanation has to take into account the obvious teleological aspects of the universe. The so-called "anthropic principle" which shows how many astonishingly delicate conditions in the universe had to be fulfilled in order to render human life possible on earth, emphasizes this teleological aspect in modern cosmological reflection. Inasmuch as, physically speaking, only incredibly improbable combinations of material conditions in the universe as habitat of life make possible any terrestrial form of life, and not only human life, this principle could also be called a teleological "biotic principle" which governs the rise of the universe. This teleological cosmological principle, like the rise of any other complex and intelligible order in the cosmos, demands in addition to meaning and purpose an intelligent efficient cause behind any Big Bang. Plato and Aristotle saw this clearly.[122] I will return to this point when discussing critically the fourth meaning of Big Bang.

(3) The third meaning of the Big Bang can never be demonstrated by science and is a philosophical theory of evolution. It contains monistic and evolutionary conceptions of the structure of the universe which fail to recognize any of the significant essential and unbridgeable differences between various beings on earth, as I will substantiate them in my arguments for the irreducibility of biological life and for the reality of the human soul.[123] If the arguments against the reducibility of *bios* to physical systems and those for the existence of the soul presented in the third chapter of this book hold, then the third meaning of the Big Bang theory is false. It contains the impossible assumption that entirely different and irreducible phenomena and realities (life and lifeless things; matter and mind) could "develop into each other" and explain each other in terms of an "evolution." Evolution is only possible where no radical necessary and essential differences exist between different species, differences which cannot in principle evolve into each other. Only where accidental (contingent) differences occur which do not touch the principal essence and substantial nature of beings, is evolution possible through series of genetic mutations, similar to the amazing possibilities of metamorphoses which we witness in nature.[124] But lifeless things can never, in an immanent development, evolve into living things, and even less can matter evolve into mind.

(4) The fourth meaning of Big Bang rests upon still heavier metaphysical assumptions which imply a philosophically false materialist and atheist explanation of the coming to be of the world which is entirely unfounded by scientific facts and is purely philosophical in nature. Drees shows the metaphysical and religious neutrality of the Big Bang theory and the fact that some interpreted in the first sense, others in materialist and atheist senses.[125] As philosophical cosmology, however, it falls behind the level of cosmology of the Presocratics, a regress in cosmological sophistication hardly understandable given that the astonishing inner meaning and order of protein-molecules, of life and of the genetic code, as well as of countless teleological aspects of the development of the universe, as those contained in the ideas of the biotic and anthropic principles, are much better known today than ever before. I introduce this terminology of biotic and anthropic principles for the above-mentioned reason that not only human life but life in general requires a teleological explanation. From Xenophanes and Thales of Miletus, and from

Anaxagoras on, philosophers have understood that the teleological aspects of the universe require an intelligent author of the cosmos. As mentioned, Plato developed a highly sophisticated metaphysical cosmology in this direction. The purpose of my present investigation forbids a detailed analysis here of the ultimate origin of the universe. I tried to demonstrate the untenability of an atheistic reductionism elsewhere.[126] May it suffice to insist on the untenability of all those meanings and theories of chaos-theory and of Big Bang which involve a reductionism that does not do justice to the irreducible essence of life. This irreducible essence of life forbids any explanation purely in terms of events that take place in inorganic matter, as I have argued before.

5. Two Irreducibilities of Organic Life to Material Systems Governed by Chaotic and Non-Chaotic Laws: Irreducibility in Essence and in Fact

In excluding reductionism, a philosophy that is conscious of its fundamental method, which I call realist phenomenology,[127] begins with a simple intuition into the irreducible essence of life, the philosophically given marks of which were expounded above. Considering these marks, particularly that of life originating in *psyché*, we see that the essence of life is irreducible to physical systems of any sort. Therefore, if a reductionistic explanation of organisms in terms of chaotic or non-chaotic physical systems was successful in accounting for the phenomena we observe in organisms, then all this theory could possibly prove is that what appeared to be living substances are nothing but machines and do not live at all. Scheler points out that any reductionism with respect to life presupposes an intuition into the essence of life, which the defender of this type of reductionism denies.

> In those cases in which we deceive ourselves – for example, by taking something to be alive when it is not – the intuited *essence* of "life" must be given in the whole of the constituent elements of the deception.[128]

As to reductionistic explanations of life, it would not follow automatically that even if life on level (1), as explained above, that is, in single cells, could be defined by physical events, life on the further levels, even on level (2), as life of the organism as a whole, could be thus reduced. The cells in a cell-culture "live" only analogously when compared to the life of an organism as a whole, a plant, an animal, a human being. The whole of the organism is more than the sum of its parts, and so is the life of the whole more than the sum-total of living cells.

In unicellular organisms, the distinction between these two senses of life collapses into one. Nevertheless, conceptually and essentially, even here the life of the organism qua organism is not simply identical with the life of this cell. For example, it would be conceivable that a unicellular organism, a kind of monster in the unicellular world of organisms, could grow a second cell combined to the first, and still remain one and the same organism. The living cell-cultures of an animal or human body must be distinguished from the life of that animal or human being, given that single cells of our bodies die daily and that the respective organism may long be dead when organs and other cell-cultures are still alive.

Understanding biological life as the life of a living cell and as the life of an organism as a whole, a distinction which applies to all multicellular organisms and which plays a significant role today in the definition of brain death,[129] we may say the following. Even granted that so-called living organisms were mere physical systems governed by chaotic and non-chaotic physical laws, this would not explain life as nothing but physical systems. Instead, it would amount to the following explanation: so-called organisms simply do not live at all. In other words, this explanation would amount to saying: what you call life, is not really life; it is something else, namely, a complicated machine or a physical system. If the organisms were machines, they would not live and thus not be real organisms. They would be nothing but machines. I will return to the difference between computer functions and thinking in Chapter Five.

A philosophical understanding of the essential irreducibility of life to chaotic and non-chaotic physical systems is required for the insight that a machine or any purely physical system, however complicated it may be, would not live even if it accounted for all the phenomena we observe in living entities. Even if the laws of quantum-mechanics and their statistical character applied to macrophysical objects, and even if a macro-physical system were designed according to the most unexpected and manifold principles involving chance and necessity, and if it contained countless indeterminacies defying our understanding of logic, this physical system would still not live. A purely philosophical method can show that the essence of life can never be explained physicalistically. This method involves two steps that show the irreducibility of life in essence and in fact to physical systems.

(1) A simple rational intuition (of the sort Aristotle, Franz Brentano, or Adolf Reinach explained so well as origin of all rational knowledge) into the essence of life and the accompanying intuitions into the described marks of living organisms reveal these to be distinct from physical systems of any chaotic or non-chaotic kind. In this intuition, we rely on the notion of an intuitively given essence of life which allows us to say that any conceivable reduction of life to physical inorganic systems of chaotic and non-chaotic properties would never explain life but only show that what appears to live does not live at all. Life, whose real existence is given indubitably and from within in our

own conscious and living being, in the *cogito*, would remain distinct from any physical system.[130]

(2) A second and less simple philosophical problem to solve is that of the irreducibility of life *in fact*: are the biological organisms which we believe to live really alive? It is equally significant to show philosophically that the phenomena which we observe in real or apparent organic life cannot find a sufficient explanation in mechanical or chaotic events in the material universe, to show that organisms indeed are living and not machines. This is, in the last analysis, equally a philosophical question, although science alone can explore the empirical side of this question. Because scientists investigate the empirical phenomena of life, it is understandable that they believe they will have proven the reducibility of organic life to material systems should they ever succeed in their effort to produce substances that manifest the marks of life (and not only highly complex proteins) from inorganic matter.

Thus, regarding this interdisciplinary question, science and philosophy meet, and each possesses some authority to claim whatever it can justify rationally by its respective methods. Living organisms have never been produced artificially. Viruses, which lie in a nebulous sphere between life and inorganic matter, as far as our knowledge is concerned, have not even been produced out of inorganic matter, so that many distinguished scientists insist that viruses are living organisms, while others deny life to them. But apart from the fact that scientists have not succeeded in producing life from inorganic matter, empirical science can only investigate those phenomena that lie "before" the solution of this question. For this reason, even if a scientist could prove that a living organism comes to be out of some broth of molecules, she or he could not presume to have answered the question of the reducibility of life to inorganic matter itself because life qua life escapes the scientist's methods of observation and cognition. Even if we could produce a living organism by combinations of inanimate chemical substances, we would still not have demonstrated that no entelechial principle of life is required to explain the coming to be of an organism, just as the fact that *in vitro* fertilization or natural conception give rise to a human person does not prove that mere biological causes explain sufficiently the coming to be of a new human person, an assumption that I shall refute philosophically in Chapter Three. Natural science cannot answer the question whether the biological phenomena are sufficiently explainable in terms of physical systems, because the principle of life is essentially invisible and empirically unobservable. Thus, not only the question, "What is life?", but also the quite different question, "Can the phenomena of life be accounted for in terms of mere physical systems?", are philosophical questions toward the clarification of which natural science can only conduct preliminary investigations and make preliminary contributions.

I argue that only philosophy can do justice to the ultimate essence of life as well as of matter, recognizing the ultimate irreducibility of one to the other. I see this irreducibility most clearly and indubitably with respect to "mental life" or personal life to which the next chapter is dedicated, but a high degree of philosophical certainty also allows us to reject any explanation of biological phenomena in terms of chaotic or non-chaotic laws of the physical universe. I hold that also the biological life in plants, animals, and in human beings, to which Chapter Two is devoted and the essential marks of which were unfolded above, is given as irreducible to material systems of any kind and resists any physicalistic explanation. We can say, with the authority of the philosopher, some things about what follows from the observed marks of living things, and about what is rendered impossible by the highly intelligible and irreducible necessary essences of life and of matter. The explanation of living beings and of life in the light of their deepest *a priori* structure and essence (not regarding their empirical contingent sides) is ultimately an object of philosophical knowledge alone. This refers only to the necessary and supremely intelligible dimensions of the essence of life, not to the contingent and morphic aspects of life which are accessible only to empirical science. By *a priori*, I mean here objective essential necessities, not subjective forms of perception and thought.[131]

6. How Do We Know Biological Life?

I should summarize and develop a bit further the epistemological results of the preceding analysis into the modes of gaining knowledge concerning life. In the observation of biological life, the senses play a key role, but more important is our understanding which is guided by knowledge of the universal essence of life. The method by means of which we understand the essence of life as an absolutely irreducible kind of dynamic and self-engendering structure is a philosophical understanding (intuition, insight) by which we grasp not only, say, this concrete dog as living, but also the essence of life and of its essential marks. Only by means of this method, which is implicitly present in scientific investigations and even guides the scientist when understanding and interpreting what she or he observes, not by sense-observation and inductive methods of natural science, can we understand the living organism to be an entity which builds itself up and regenerates and engenders itself in nutrition, in regeneration and growth, as well as in propagation. Only by means of this method, we understand the entelechial structure of the organism in the three senses expounded above. Any biologist who understands this, is not just observing with the senses but using intellectual and even philosophical understanding. To apply a word of Kant: without this understanding the sense-perception of the external manifestations of life and induction would be blind.

This very same understanding which allows us to grasp the unified self-engendering structure of *bios* and of biological life, also permits us to understand that this life does not exhaust itself in the described essential functions in which it only manifests itself. This life underlies these functions as their principle, active or passive, in a potential or actual state, and this principle is an entelechy or *psyché*. We understand that cryo-conserved organisms or live seeds, in which none of the described functions of self-engendering, growth, nourishment, regeneration, or propagation are noted, still preserve life as the only principle from which, after their being thawed out or under other physical conditions, the essential manifestations of life can again spring. Thus, we understand that the potentiality to perform functions like growth or regeneration already involves life, and that life, also for this reason, lies deeper than the described essential notes of life. Life does not coincide with these functions but is their intelligible cause and root. Life accounts for these features rather than the features constituting life or giving life to life.

All the things I said about the givenness of biological life are accessible to us by means of two methods. One method is external observation and perception of entelechial self-movement, nutrition, etc. or a – still relatively external – "inner" bodily experience of our heartbeat, breathing, etc., coupled with inductive methods of science. Entelechial self-movement, *eigengesetzliche Selbstbewegung*, is distinguished well by Conrad-Martius from the self-movement of atoms or heavenly bodies.[132]

On the other hand, we use a philosophical intuition into the intelligible and necessary essence of life, and arguments based on these philosophical insights.

The first of these methods and ways of noting life is based on sense-perception, guided by inductive and intuitive ways of understanding. It involves, from its inception, cognitions that go beyond the sensibly and immediately given, but is still an empirical method studying the contingent factual sides of life. The second of these methods is a rational philosophical understanding that involves intuitions into highly intelligible and necessary facts and arguments based on them.

The experiential datum from which these methods proceed, biological life, in its existence and actual structure, is observed from without and never quite directly accessible except in its abstract essence as is accessible to philosophical insight. But a second mode of experiential givenness of life is a far more direct and immediate givenness of life than the experience of *bios*-life. To this entirely new experiential access to life we now turn.

Three

THE IRREDUCIBILITY OF MENTAL LIFE AND OF ITS SUBJECT (SOUL) TO ORDERED AND CHAOTIC PHYSICAL SYSTEMS

... because he does not actually understand ..., he does not live perfectly, but possesses only half of life.

Thomas Aquinas, *Sententia libri Ethicorum*, 9, 1.3.19 - 21

1. The Immediate and Indubitable Givenness of Conscious Life

When our inquiry starts with the second type of experience of life, namely, with the immediate inner experience of our own conscious experience, and proceeds to a philosophical discovery of the irreducible character of life, we are epistemologically speaking in a far better position from which to reject any reductionistic interpretation of life than when we are dealing with plant or animal life. Consider that René Descartes could suggest as a rational, albeit most implausible, hypothesis an interpretation of animals as *automata.* Why? Because their life (and thus their being more than divinely designed marionettes drawn by invisible strings of nature) is not immediately and indubitably accessible to our knowledge. Therefore, it is conceivable, however contrived this theory may be, that the animal life amounts to nothing but to a set of operations of a machine, or to characteristics produced by inanimate matter, by magic evolution, or by an artful mechanical device of nature designed by God.

But when it comes to conscious life, we possess a uniquely intimate acquaintance with the stream and actuality of our conscious life. This life is life in a higher and more proper sense of the term than biological life.

This superior mode of life of persons brings to mind a historical fact worth noting. While Aristotle gives ample room to the exploration of animal and plant life, Plato almost exclusively speaks of life in the context of human life, conscious life, moral life, and the life of the Demiurge, as if this personal life, when coupled with justice and knowledge, were the only life worthy of this name.

Compared to conscious life, which is lived and experienced from within, the vegetative life of plants can hardly be called life at all. This manifests itself even in the fact, regrettable though it is from other points of view, that we speak today of "brain death" when the central organ of biological life and of conscious life is irreversibly dysfunctional.[1] The truth at stake is that if human life were reduced forever to a vegetative life, entirely and eternally lacking the conscious life of the mind, even in forms hidden to our experience, it would cease to merit the title of personal life. A more metaphysical investigation would show that the life of the personal subject is deeper than consciousness which has the character of an actualization of this life. Therefore, the life of an irreversibly unconscious human being is still human life.

Apart from embodying life in a much higher sense, the conscious life of the human person can be known and is experienced in a completely different and far more perfect way than vegetative life. We can gain apodictic certainty about its existence and scientific-philosophic evidence about its essence and about the irreducibility of the mind's life to chaotic or non-chaotic physical systems.

This second mode of knowing life does not combine empirical observations of the signs of life with philosophical intuitions into its essence but is based on an immediate inner experience of life as *zoee* and involves the intuition that life is an absolutely necessary condition of the being of the person:

> A nature which lacks life also lacks the excellence of the personal nature.[2]
>
> To live is of the very substance of the soul.[3]

This explains why my being and my life are given with the same inseparable indubitable evidence. In this sense, Augustine has spoken of the indubitable evidence of the skeptic that the skeptic *is* and that he *lives*:

> On the other hand, who would doubt that he lives, remembers, understands, wills, thinks, knows, and judges? For even if he doubts, he lives … .[4]

This life is inseparably given with our existence. In the *cogito*, our being is given with its life. The *sum* (I am) of the *cogito* (I think) is inseparable from the life of the *ego cogitans* (thinking I). The being of and in a living Self is indubitably given in the *cogito.* Life as attribute of the irreducible essence found in the operations and in the being of the ego-subject of conscious acts is accessible to us entirely from within, in an experience much more intimate than introspection or inner perception, namely, in a differentiated experience of consciousness and of conscious life.[5]

Speaking of an equal degree of evidence and certainty found in the cognition of the *sum* and of the *life* of the ego, I do not wish to assert an absolute identity of being, life, and consciousness of the subject. Instead, the relationships between being, living, and consciousness to the subject of the *ego cogitans* are given to us in their difference. Only here do we encounter directly in experience the subject and principle of life itself. We have found that the deepest philosophical mark of life is its root in a *psyché* or in an entelechial principle of life, as we find it in plants as the principle of explanation for the phenomena of life found in vegetative life. We have also seen that the principle of soul in plants and animals is only experienced and given in an indirect way. This applies to the experience of the personal mind of other human beings. But in the *cogito*, we have a privileged access to conscious life itself and to its subject, to the *ego* which turns out to be the very soul itself that underlies all conscious operations and activities. In order to see better that here alone do we have an immediate cognitive access to the *psyché*, which we recognized with Aristotle as the ontological subject and source of life, let us now turn to the arguments for the existence of the soul.

2. Four Arguments for Mental Life Inhering in a Spiritual Substance (Soul)

The following analysis is based on philosophical proofs for the substantiality of the human soul that were expounded elsewhere,[6] and of which four will be summarized.

1. The first argument takes its starting point in the Aristotelian discovery of a fundamental distinction within real being: between (1) "accidents," that is, between those acts, activities, qualities, attributes, etc. which inhere in something else and cannot stand in being in their own right, and (2) their ultimate ground in those beings that exist in themselves (*in se*). The ultimate subject and ground of being, that stands in itself, is what Aristotle calls *hypokeimenon*, *ousia*, *hypostasis*, or substance.[7] Only these beings which stand in being on their own right can lend ontological support to the first group of categories of being, that is, all the accidents and dependent principles of being. Among these we cannot count real existence. It is an actuality that neither stands in itself nor can be said to be an accident of substances. For it is that actuality which makes the substance be, the most intimate actuality which posits in being that which exists, including substances.[8] On the basis of this distinction, we can understand that any conscious thinking, knowing, feeling, or willing, and thus any conscious life, does not exist as a thing as such, or better, as an entity which stands in itself. It is not a subject but an activity (accident) which requires a substance. Thinking or willing are "in another entity" and require a subject which is not like these activities, an attribute of another thing, but stands in itself. This is what Aristotle means by substance. "Substance" in this sense has nothing to do with a thing (*res*) as opposed to a person but indicates only the irreducible trait of "standing on its own feet in being," as opposed to inhering in another entity. Thought and any conscious life require a substance-

subject, someone *who* thinks, wills, etc. The character of substance in general and of the soul as a simple and indivisible substance has been explored recently by Roderick M. Chisholm.[9] There are some points of fundamental difference between Chisholm's and my own views concerning the spirituality (or possible materiality) of the simple self.[10]

Scheler, unfortunately, thinks that he can save the category of person only by denying its substantial being and standing in itself. So he says in his *Position of Man in the Cosmos:*

> The center of the spirit, the "person," is therefore neither an objective nor a thing-like [which Scheler understands as "substantial"] being but only an ordered whole of acts which lives itself.[11]

But this I or self, this person who wills or thinks, is clearly given in our experience as one single and indivisible subject.

Gottfried Wilhelm Leibniz insists on the utter and evident impossibility that a composite entity could think.[12] The non-spatiality and the indivisible unity of the subject of thought excludes that it be matter which possesses necessarily parts outside parts. In contemporary thought, this point was well explored phenomenologically by Roderick M. Chisholm, who, like Kant and Leibniz, does not distinguish clearly enough the simplicity of the mathematical point from the soul.[13] Aristotle stressed the non-spatial and absolutely indivisible unity of the soul, distinguishing it sharply from the simplicity of the mathematical point:

> Hence mind cannot have that kind of unity either; ... How, indeed, if it were a spatial magnitude, could mind possibly think? Will it think with any one indifferently of its parts? In this case, the "part" must be understood either in the sense of a spatial magnitude or in the sense of a point ... .[14]

Material objects can carry many properties, as, for example, color and beauty. A material object can store the physical substratum of information, for example, a letter, a piece of paper, or – in a far more complicated manner – a computer disk. But can a composite thing, as our brain, think? We understand that this is impossible. We arrive at the following insight: the mind as subject of our thought-life is an absolutely indivisible, simple subject that cannot be observed by the senses. To say that my ego is divided into two is absurd. Even the phenomenon of schizophrenia presupposes the undivided and indivisible unity of the ego of the schizophrenic person. Because of the evidence of the unity of the subject of consciousness, some thinkers have argued that the earliest phases of embryonic life cannot involve personal life, since twinning is still possible. Even if they err in this assumption, they recognize the non-duplicability and non-divisibility of the individual person which manifests itself most clearly in self-consciousness, as Sir John Eccles has repeatedly noted. Now the brain and any other bodily organ possesses billions of non-identical cells and parts, into which – as Leibniz remarks in the *Monadology*, no. 17 – we could enter, if they were enlarged, and which we could observe through the senses. But we understand the non-sensible nature, the simplicity, and the necessary indivisibility of the I-subject of mental life and thought. Thus, neither the mind nor its life can be reduced to physical systems.

2. Another argument for the reality of the mind and the irreducibility of its life to chaotic or non-chaotic physical systems is based on two evident premises. (1) It is based on Aristotle's intuition that the subject (substance), as what supports in being every attribute inherent in it, constitutes the primary reality of a thing. This subject surpasses in "actuality of being" (in reality, properly speaking) what just exists in dependence on it. Substance is the supporting ground of being for everything in it. The subject (substance) is the most real part of an entity. (2) While small physical causes suffice to kill human beings, human beings are still nobler and possess an incomparably superior reality than the whole universe of bodies. By knowing and in virtue of our free acts and moral conscience, human beings surpass in reality the entire cosmos of physical substances, including the perennial mummified existence of our body. Conscious and rational life possesses an actuality and contains a self-possession of being compared to which the universe of material substances is like nothing. For the conscious life of the I to be reduced to the being of a material substance would be equivalent to its annihilation.

From these two premises follows that the incomparably higher life of the spirit, which is more properly real and of greater dignity than all material substances of the universe, cannot possibly be a mere function or accident of one of them, the brain. If the substance is the most real entity in the world, that which is primary being, as Aristotle holds, then the conscious self whose reality and life surpasses that of all material bodies put together (which are "nothings" compared with it), cannot coincide with the material substance of the brain and even less with some accidents or epiphenomena of it.

3. A third argument in favor of the reality and substantiality of the mind, and in favor of the irreducibility of the mind's life to physical systems, is based on the specific essence of certain acts. Knowledge, for example, in order to be knowledge, must depend in its content on the nature of that of which it is knowledge. As subjects of knowledge, we mentally grasp the nature or existence of what we know. In certain knowledge, such as that you yourself exist, you as knower can be equally certain of the object of knowledge and of your own receptive mental grasping. You know, for example, that you truly exist and are a subject and that you know this. Knowledge exists only to the extent that someone grasps *that* or *how* something is, because it is and is in a certain way. Cognition possesses an intentional relationship to its object and is char-

acterized by a receptive transcendence of the subject in the cognitive contact with the object of cognition. Knowledge must not only be formed objectively by the nature of the object, as a piece of wax can be objectively formed by a mold, but it must mentally reach this object, cognitively touch it so that it discovers *that* and *how* something is. Cognition would therefore be impossible if knowledge were just dependent in its content on brain-functions which are subject to causal laws and are entirely determined by external material causes which have no intrinsic relation to the true nature of the objects of knowledge. Just as it is impossible that a computer, whose output is entirely dependent on physical events, could know or check its own program in any real and ultimate way, so we human beings could never know anything if our knowledge were causally dependent on material processes and their causal connections, and if we did not have a mind distinct from matter and its causal effects. But human beings know with certainty some things. Therefore, they have a mind. Any assertion, including that of radical skepticism, is absolutely impossible without cognitions, as, for example, that I exist, that I doubt, that I am aware of objects, that I pose a question, that the two contradictory states of affairs which I consider in doubt cannot both be. These and countless other such things not only *can* be known but they *are* known by all of us. We claim and possess this knowledge inevitably in any assertion or thought. Hence, any assertion of the identity of knowledge or of the cognitive life of the mind with brain-processes, or of its causal dependence on the brain, is self-contradictory. This does not exclude the manifold dependence of the mind on the brain and on the brain's activity as the *empirical condition* of mental activity. But we must distinguish *cause* from *condition*, as well as empirical and absolutely necessary conditions. Cognitive acts can never have their efficient cause, nor their *absolutely necessary* conditions in the brain, but only their empirical conditions.

The untenability of any reduction of consciousness to an epiphenomenon of brain events or to these events themselves (in the mind/brain identity theory) could also be shown regarding freedom and promising. Jonas[15] has demonstrated the absurdity of the mutual promise of Hermann Ludwig Ferdinand von Helmholtz and his friends to promote materialism. They pledged to promote a theory of the power of matter over mind, but they presupposed, in the very assumption that their promise could and would be kept, an original power of the mind over matter and its independence from chemo-electrical processes in the brain. A promise or any other free act is necessarily impossible, nay absurd, if this act is identical with, or determined by, material or organic processes, or if it is a causal product of evolutionary developments. Every person presupposes some free acts, as, for example, searching for truth, asserting, or promising, even when she or he resolves to investigate or to defend materialism. Hence, materialists who give promises contradict their own theory in every moment in which they – inevitably – presuppose their freedom. We are dealing not with an inevitable subjective presupposition *à la* Kant but with an evident datum of the essence of freedom and of its real existence in us. When we act in a way which implies the free initiating of acts which do not proceed from another cause but from the self itself, these acts would not exist if we had not willed them to be. They involve the fact that we are master over their being or non-being. This datum of freedom refutes materialism, according to which free acts could not exist. Philosophies which recognize the existence of a soul can embrace determinism, but materialistic philosophies must inevitably do so. Thus, the life of free acts and of their subject is irreducible to the brain and to any conceivable material system, whether it is dominated by well-explored or by chaotic rules. This is overlooked by James P. Crutchfield, when he links freedom to chaotic events in the brain as if freedom could be reduced to them or explained by them.[16]

Cognition and free actions contradict their being an epiphenomenon of, let alone their being identical with, the brain or its functions. This becomes evident when we consider the cognitive transcendence in which the being or essence of something discloses itself to our mind as it is in itself. It is also evident when we consider the transcendence of our freedom (in the morally good act and in love) which is capable of responding to a good for its own sake, to give it the proper value-response, and to transcend all immanent unfoldings and self-actualizations of our own life. This feature of transcendence is absolutely essential for any understanding of the person who can be better characterized as a trans-telechy than as an en-telechy. In the next chapter, I will examine the beautiful "definition" of the essence of the human person given by Max Scheler in terms of transcendence and self-transcendence:

> The core of his [man's, the human person's] nature – apart from all special organization – is in fact this movement, this spiritual act of transcending himself![17]

Thus, to explain cognitive and free acts and their capability for transcendence in the cognition of what and how things are, and to explain the transcendence of the human person in the free stances taken by persons toward them, in terms of a psycho-physical identity or radical causal dependence, involves a necessary contradiction to the nature of these acts. This position leads anybody who asserts it into a self-referential contradiction. Nevertheless, attempts at a reductionistic explanation are undertaken by the "bio-psycho-social model" of the human mind popular with many scientists.

4. The most striking argument for the irreducibility of the mind and of the mind's life to material systems is taken from a reflection on the immediately experienced "I" which "accompanies" all our experiences and which is the self-conscious subject of any mental life. In this "I," we encounter a subject which we do not have to *infer* as the cause of our acts but which we expe-

rience immediately as subject and which we understand to stand in itself and to act. This subject of consciousness, which we encounter immediately in our experience along with our acts, has a set of predicates that differ from those of any conscious experience *per se*. Not our experiences are conscious of each other, but we as subjects consciously live them. They cannot reflect upon themselves and know themselves, but we as subjects can reflect on them and on ourselves.

To overcome the reductionism that is inherent in many forms of structuralism, we need to overcome the attempt to reduce life to non-living entities and functions and the reduction of consciousness to life. Consciousness and conscious life are essentially distinct from biological life. Consciousness belongs to the essence of the actualization of this higher and specifically personal mode of life. Life is *given in* the consciously awakened life. But the life of the soul thus given must not be reduced to consciousness, as many idealists and transcendental phenomenologists seek to do. On the contrary, the life of the person given in consciousness reveals itself to be more than consciousness and as something which can be preserved, though not properly actualized, without consciousness. The unconscious states of sleep or loss of consciousness and the experience of regaining consciousness prove this irreducibility of the life and existence of the conscious subject to consciousness or to its consciously lived and awakened state.

Nevertheless, in its awakened and conscious state, life exists in an incomparably higher form than when it is deprived of consciousness.

When I consider carefully the self-given subject of consciousness, I discover that this "I" shows itself to differ from any mere function of another thing or of a brain and is immediately given as substantial subject. I also discover that the human mind possesses each trait of substance in an incomparably superior way to the weak and analogous manner in which material entities can be substances. This can be seen from the following considerations. The mind is the ultimate subject of acts, as thing-substances are of accidents, but the mind is also a consciously living subject. For this reason, we reserve today the term "subject," which originally designated all substances, for persons only. The subject is not an "it," but a "he" or "she." The person's acts do not merely "inhere" in a mind-substance but are performed and lived by the mind-subject. As one single, non-composite self and as conscious of herself or himself, the person stands in herself or in himself and is "this single substance-subject" in a way quite incapable of being matched by the material world where accidents inhere in various parts and appearances of bodies and not in one single material subject. In sharp contradistinction to this material world, my identity as one simple (non-composite) "I" – the subject of myriads of experiences – is given to me. An investigation into memory, retention, and "superactual consciousness" in Hildebrand's sense might help elucidate the lasting identity of the subject of consciousness.[18] The character of the self as indivisible substantial subject involves its difference from the brain and from any totality that consists of non-identical distinct parts. Material things are not indivisible, nor do they possess an inner unity of substance comparable to that of the mind. The subject of personal life possesses other traits of substance (identified by Aristotle) more properly speaking than any material substance could possess them: lasting identity throughout many states and accidental changes, reality in the proper sense of this term, and individual thisness. Material things lack individual thisness in the sense of the absolutely indivisible, irreplaceable, and incommunicable identity of the sort that is found in the personal self that can think, act freely, and love. While material things or paintings by Rembrandt also possess these traits in some way, each material substance and each part thereof can be replaced by another one, without this making a big difference, whereas persons cannot be replaced or substituted by others. Even masterful paintings could conceivably be replaced by a perfect copy. Moreover, in material things the different traits of substantiality are somewhat separate from each other. For example, their individual thisness and distinctness stems from an external form which does not coincide with their self-standing substantiality. Again, what is lasting in them is not the material substrate of body cells which are entirely renewed every seven years. In contrast to this, in the subject of the conscious life that is immediately experienced by us from within, the various traits of substantiality are united. The same subject lasts, is substance, is an individual self.

These considerations make evident that the mind cannot be a supervenient attribute or epiphenomenon of brains. The "rational substance" of the self-experiencing mind possesses traits which make it necessarily different from the brain with its billions of replaceable cells. The mind is different from each one of these cells with its countless non-identical parts and with its poor embodiment of the general traits of substance. We see again the impossibility of considering this second type of experience of life and the conscious life itself, as an emergent property of complex material systems of any kind and of their immanent internal laws. The magic words of "emergence" or "laws of chaos" cannot help, because chaos never can bridge intelligible essential differences, and the laws of chaos can never explain what is intrinsically impossible: that the operations of the mind which reveals itself as a substantial entity distinct from matter could be produced by unexplored laws of matter.

3. Life and Death: The Unity of Biological and Mental Life in the Human Being

If we distinguish carefully this distinctness of mind and body, indubitably demonstrated through the arguments sketched above, from any separation, also keeping apart entirely different senses of "dualism," we shall find that the unity of human beings as consisting of body and soul is not threatened or rendered impossible by the mind. Quite the contrary, the difference of the mind from the body constitutes the only conceivable basis for doing justice to the unity of the human being and of human life, in whom body and soul are joined to form a much more unified being than two sorts of matter, or a material thing and its accidents, could ever constitute. Only a mind distinct from the body can become "form" and animating spiritual principle of the body, in sense-perception, in action, in speech, or in love.

The unquestioned manifold dependence of the mind on the body, especially on the brain, is by no means incompatible with the superior actuality, life, and reality of the mind. Neither the psychophysical dependence on the body nor the manifold dependence of bodily motion and action, speech, and expression on the life of the soul are incompatible with the unity of the human being. Just as the union of two persons who love each other requires the duality of persons, and as the unity of the word requires the radical distinctness of its meaning from its audible *Gestalt*, so the unity of the human being requires the duality of body and mind.

Another significant discovery concerning substances will help us, finally, to understand why the subject and the life of consciousness intrinsic to it cannot be reduced to the brain or to any other complex material system. The following distinction will clarify the unity of organic and mental life in the human being and the need to assume the presence of the human soul in the human body throughout the duration of organic human life. Every occurrence of accidents in a substance presupposes some real potentiality in that same subject. For example, acts of understanding cannot arise from nowhere but presuppose a faculty of intellect. The being of potentialities, faculties, and potencies differs greatly in nature according to the kind of subject and of activation of which we are speaking. The "passive potency" of a destructible piece of wood that can take on billions of forms differs from the inherent, active, and essential potentialities of the person. Some of these potencies and faculties are inseparable from the substantial being of the mind. They are not inborn capabilities of immanent activation but "transcendent potencies": They open the cognitive, volitional, and affective powers of the person to the world, to all beings.[19]

In view of the philosophically evident distinction of body and mind, we recognize that the individual human personal life on earth objectively begins when the spiritual human soul is present in the human body, that it continues as long as the mind is united with the body, and that our bodily mundane life objectively ends at the moment when the human mind definitively leaves the body which becomes a soul-less material thing. Death is the ultimate and terrifying demonstration of the irreducibility of human life to physical systems.

But the question remains as to how exactly in the human being the biological life, treated in Chapter Two, and the mental personal life of the human being are related to each other. Some distinction must exist between biological and personal human life, especially in view of the divisibility and lack of strict individuality of biological life-processes and genetic codes versus the absolute indivisibility of the mind. Admitting this difference does not force us to admit the separability of the human soul from our vegetative and sensitive life. The close union between personal human life and the biological life of the human organism as a whole is obvious. As long as the biological life of the human being as a whole is present, then, in virtue of the unity of body and soul and in virtue of the profound formation of the human body by the human spirit, we have the best reason to assume the presence of the personal human mind.

This does not sufficiently solve the problem of how "biological human life" is related to personal human life. We must consider human biological life as the life of the human organism as a whole, not just as the life-processes in a single isolated organ. Thus, if we can keep "alive" some cells in a cell-culture, these certainly do not possess the biological life of the human organism as a whole. They do not possess human life in the sense of the life of a human person. Organs and cells can outlive their master. Thus, the death of the "human organism as a whole" cannot be identified with the death of the "whole human organism," including all its organs and cells.

A radical materialism and a new form of Cartesianism postulate the separability of biological human life from human personhood. These philosophical anthropologies, whether they are forms of monist materialism, of neutral monism, or of neo-Cartesian dualism, throw into question the unity of life in the human being. They lead to a new form of dualism between human organisms and human persons. According to this view, the embryonic life before brain-birth (or some other prenatal or post-natal event) is only biological human life but not personal human life. Again, the philosophy and medical-legal theory of brain-death separates the biological life of organisms of the species *homo sapiens* from its personal human life. If the mind coincides with, or totally depends in its existence on, higher brain functions, then the mind cannot precede or survive irreversible dysfunction of the brain.[20] Otherwise, the mind is nothing but these functions themselves, albeit experienced in different categories, or it is a set of effects or epiphenomena of brain processes. Thus, a materialist and monistic ontology of the mind logically leads to a radical dualism between biological human life and human personhood in that, according to this theory, many live "human beings" are not "human persons," and all those whose brain does not function cannot have a mind or be persons. This reductionism reduces biological human life to one set of physical functions and human mental life to another set of physical properties.

Late ensoulment-theories exist along with theories about the premature leaving of souls from human bodies which are then conceived only as remaining human animals or vegetables. These theories also allege the separability of human minds and human bodies. Against this, I have insisted elsewhere on the absolute inseparability of biological human life of the human organism as a whole and of the life of the human mind or soul in union with the live body.[21]

Any claim of a real divorce of human biological life and human mental life on earth and any failure to recognize the striking though composite unity of the human being as a whole, constitutes an inadequate dualism that does not do justice to the unity of human life in which the mental *zoee* and the biophysical life of the human being must not be divorced.

4. The Death of the Human Being – Radical End of Human Life? On Death and Immortality as Subject of a New Book

Without going beyond the topic of a work on the question, "What is life?", I cannot treat the big question of what death is. Death is the opposite of life. Death makes life more intelligible by standing in contrast to it. Death is the point toward which life always tends as the end of life. Does death constitute, then, the culminating point of life, the utmost possibility of being for a living thing, as Heidegger formulates in *Sein und Zeit*? Or is it the radical destruction and annihilation of life?

Heidegger mystifies death qua death (and not qua beginning of a new life). He thereby conceives of the human being not only, as Gabriel Marcel notes, as of a being toward death (as *être vers la mort*) but also as a being destined for death (as *être pour la mort*). But in many atheistic philosophies, the death of the human being is conceived as radical annihilation of consciousness and personhood, as that great nothingness which Hamlet ponders in posing the question in the face of death: "To be or not to be ... ."

Another question of the highest significance poses itself, a question crucial for the meaning and essence of life, especially of human life: Is human life, as the life of the human soul, mortal, and will it end forever in death? Or is it destined to a transcendent and immortal life, as many philosophers from Plato to Marcel taught, and as I have argued elsewhere? But these questions would lead us to another book on the topic, Death and Immortality.[22]

Four

VALUE AND DIGNITY OF HUMAN LIFE

1. The Value of Human Life and the Fourfold Root of Its Dignity

Our investigation into the evident givenness and nature of our mental life and its ontological ground in a substantial soul would remain incomplete, were we not to address the question of the ultimate *raison d'être* and value of human life. We have seen in Chapter Two that one of the crucial questions of philosophy touches the problem of the value of biological life. This is even more true of human life. Is this life just a neutral fact that can be disposed of according to the whims and wishes of individuals or political powers? Is the destruction of millions of human lives in Auschwitz or in the Gulag Archipelago just a neutral fact? If so, then a philosophy of the essence of this life would be of little existential impact and interest. Or is this human life, in virtue of its essence, endowed with a high value and preciousness, in a word, with a dignity that constitutes a decisive standard for political and private actions? In this case, the investigation into the essence of human life should culminate in an investigation into its axiological dimension, into its dignity.

The questions relative to the dignity of the life of personal beings, a life which we experience with indubitable evidence in ourselves, and even the questions pertinent to the value of all living beings, were present all along in our preceding investigations. From their inception, we have investigated life not as a neutral fact but as an astonishing and irreducible datum of high value. Now we have to address thematically the value questions which aim at the core of life and its meaning.

These questions are decisive for philosophy of the human being and ethics, as well as for any legal philosophy which recognizes a "just" and an "unjust," a "right" and a "wrong," not by any decree of positive legislation, but which precedes and grounds any rational positive law.

Thus, any philosophy which seeks to answer the questions, "What is life?", and "What is human life?", remains incomplete as long as it does not address the deepest problem about the essence of human life: "Does it possess value?" And if life does possess value, then, "What is the root of its dignity and value?"

2. The Question About the Value of Human Life against the Background of Today's Intellectual and Political Landscape

Against the vehement protestations of many human-rights groups and influential associations of the physically and mentally handicapped, Peter Singer's book, *Should the Baby Live?*, was recently published in Germany.[1] In it, Singer repeats his radical views according to which higher developed and healthy animals, as, for example, pigs, dolphins, or dogs, deserve more legal protection than those human beings, who, for one reason or another, are unable to exercise fully their specifically human abilities of thinking, speaking, etc. Singer considers the belief that each living being of the species *homo sapiens* is endowed with an incomparable dignity an expression of a new sort of pride to which Singer gives a jaw-breaker of a name derived from Latin words: "speciecism."

Singer's explicit program of "unsanctifying human life" launches, in quite radical form, a movement which is spreading more and more and which denies the essential dignity of the human person and of human life, implying that human life deserves legal protection only at a specified level of consciousness and "quality" of life.

This movement away from what might be called the human person's *Sonderstellung* (radically distinct position) in the universe does not restrict itself to the field of academic discussions and ideologies. Hitler's Third Reich and countless other political powers which deny that every human being possesses equally human rights constitute a major political attack in our century on the intrinsic dignity of each human being and of each human life. We cannot blame all violations of basic human rights on Nazi Germany or on the Nazi mentality. As many people were murdered in Stalin's Gulag Archipelago as in Hitler's concentration camps, or even more. Today, after the discovery of universal human rights and after the repeated public expression of universal consent on human rights and the inviolability of human persons in Western and global declarations of human rights, we are faced with the atrocious realities in Bosnia-Herzegovina and in many other spots in the world in the face of which every honest person of even the lowest moral sensibilities is shocked upon witnessing the most cruel neglect of any imaginable natural law and human right. In addition, in the "civilized" rest of the free Western world, millions of unborn babies and a considerable number of old and "socially useless" human beings die every year because of the same philosophical idea which Singer openly proposes that a minority, or even a huge number, of members of the human species are not human persons endowed with equal dignity and equal human rights.

Singer and others fail to recognize the existence and the four different sources of human dignity and of human rights to be discussed below, especially the first one. A book as Singer's and the development it signals away from human dignity becomes less and less confined to the level of dry theory. This new spirit of a negation of the intrinsic dignity and value of human life permeates more and more the camp of humanity's practical approach to human life in genetic experiments and abortion.

The official representative of China openly proclaimed the relativity of human rights in 1993 in Vienna at the universally observed World Convention on Human Rights. Anti-human rights *theories* and academic conceptions of a historical and cultural relativity of human rights, as well as the horrendous *practices* of the Nazi holocaust and present genocides, force us to think anew and more deeply about the foundations of the dignity of human persons, of their life, and of their inalienable human rights.

Against this background, we must seek a theoretical understanding of the unique value of human life. Let us begin by asking what the "dignity" of human life means and then proceed to discuss its fourfold root.

3. What Is "Dignity"?

A. What Is Value?

By "dignity," we mean a special kind of value of persons. Therefore, in order to discuss dignity in a meaningful way, we have to introduce first the notion of value the usage of which in ordinary language is by no means clear. Even though "value" or "the good" is an irreducible and ultimate datum which justifies the statement of George Edward Moore quoted before that "good is good" and not any other thing, this does not prevent us from being able to grasp more clearly what "value" means and to distinguish fundamentally different phenomena which are designated by this term. In the first place, "value" (as distinct from disvalue), and "good" (as distinct from "evil" or from the "bad"), indicates positive importance. The term "importance" designates that quality or characteristic of a thing that makes it not neutral and, lifting it out of neutrality, provides the ground for meaningful motivation.

Within the "positively important," we can still distinguish entirely different types. The distinction between them is the condition of understanding the dignity of human life and the foundation of moral imperatives. Some things may be lifted out of the neutral only subjectively: they please or displease us, they are agreeable or disagreeable for us, and this may change from person to person. One person likes cigars, another detests them; one finds chocolates wonderful, another extremely disagreeable. But this changeable quality that makes the pleasant and unpleasant different for different people is not the decisive point here. Instead, the crucial point is this: the type of importance we have in mind by the "disagreeable" or the "subjectively satisfying" is essentially dependent on our pleasure and displeasure, it is a subjective sense of the good which lives from the fact that it is pleasant or unpleasant *for a person.* But when we speak of the dignity of the person or the justice of a judge, we do not mean only a positive importance which depends on our pleasure. We mean an importance which characterizes the human being or justice in themselves and endows them with an inherent, intrinsic preciousness which makes them "good in themselves," and the worthy object of admiration or other value responses in which we acknowledge the intrinsic positive importance and preciousness of these things. We would not say that justice is good for me or for you, but simply that it is good.

What is only subjectively positively important invites or seduces us but lets us remain in our arbitrariness. We can eat a Swiss chocolate or refuse to do so without obligation arising from its pleasantness. As long as *only* the objects of subjective satisfaction or dissatisfaction are designated as "good" or "bad," we do not find a call addressed to our freedom. Instead, when what is at stake is "value" in the sense of what is good in itself, the justice of a judge, or the beauty of a work of art, then these intrinsic goods demand an adequate response. They do not leave us in our arbitrariness but impose a call to respect them, to respond to them, to show interest in them. Thus, they bind yet awaken our freedom.

When we turn to what is only subjectively pleasing, we subordinate the pleasant object to ourselves, we use it for our satisfaction, and we consume it. But when we encounter something which is lifted out of the neutral by an objective in-dwelling positive importance, by an intrinsic value, we adapt to the object, we give ourselves to what we recognize as intrinsically good.

Further, while the agreeable and the disagreeable have many degrees of intensity and many qualities of pleasantness or unpleasantness, this category of importance of the subjectively satisfying does not stand in a hierarchical relation and order of higher and lower good. As soon as we introduce these terms, we have objective importance in mind and we presuppose the intrinsic positive importance which I call "value." We can, with the brilliant ancient hedonist Aristippus, distinguish many things within the merely subjectively satisfying: what is more or less intensely pleasurable, pleasures which can be attained without displeasure, pleasures that can be enjoyed more easily versus those which can be obtained less easily, pleasures which last longer or shorter, pleasures which have unpleasant consequences, and those which do not, etc. But as soon as we say that the value of the human person is higher than that of a pig, we introduce an entirely different sort of gradation which presupposes the objective and intrinsic value.

Finally, the merely subjectively satisfying, while providing pleasure of various intensity, never bestows authentic happiness upon us. For happiness in the true sense presupposes an encounter with a thing of intrinsic value, the positive importance of which raises that thing out of neutrality by characterizing that thing "in itself and not just for us," by an objective value.

Distinct both from "value" as intrinsic positive importance of a thing and as the merely subjectively satisfying is a third category of the good, the *objective good for someone.* This type of positive importance is necessarily *for someone*, addresses itself *to* some person for *whom it is* good. But far from being a merely subjectively pleasant thing, it lies in the true interest of the person, constitutes an objective gift for him or her, and is thus objectively good for that person. However, this is relational and not intrinsic good. Therefore, the very same thing, the objective value of which is intrinsic, as, for example, the heroic and deep love of a woman, may be a great gift and objective good for the man whom she loves and at the same time a great objective evil for another man who is in love with her and from whom she turns away by loving the other. Here we find higher and lower goods for persons. I cannot develop in this context a detailed theory of value and of the good. The preceding short introduction to what I consider the best philosophy of value presented in our century must suffice for the moment. This philosophy of value was developed extensively elsewhere.[2]

When we speak of the dignity of human life, we mean an objective and intrinsic value. We speak of a value and intrinsic goodness greater than, and different from, a modest aesthetic value of an ornament or the intellectual value of a chess player like Wilhelm Steinitz, which do not directly impose *moral* imperatives on us. Instead, when we speak of human dignity, we speak of a *morally relevant value*, one which evidently imposes on us a moral call and an obligation to respect it. While Immanuel Kant does not generally recognize an intrinsic and morally relevant good as the ultimate source of moral imperatives, in one passage he does so explicitly:

> All these relative ends, therefore, are grounds for hypothetical imperatives only.
>
> But suppose that there were something the existence of which in itself had absolute worth, something which, as an end in itself, could be a ground of definite laws. In it and only in it could lie the ground of a possible categorical imperative, i.e., of a practical law.
>
> Now, I say, man and, in general, every rational being exists as an end in himself and not merely as a means to be arbitrarily used by this or that will. In all his actions, whether they are directed to himself or to other rational beings, he must always be regarded at the same time as an end. All objects of inclinations have only conditional worth, for if the inclinations and the needs founded on them did not exist, their object

> would be without worth ... on the other hand, rational beings are designated "persons" because their nature indicates that they are ends in themselves, i.e., things which may not be used merely as means. Such a being is thus an object of respect and, so far, restricts all [arbitrary] choice ... without them, nothing of absolute worth could be found, and if all worth is conditional and thus contingent, no supreme practical principle for reason could be found anywhere.[3]

B. Dignity as a Unique Excellence of Value

The term "dignity" goes beyond the terms "worth" or "value," even when interpreted as intrinsic value. It designates a unique value which endows each person with an intrinsic and objective preciousness, though this can also be said of animals and of all living beings as well as of dead material things, but which raises the person to an incommensurably higher level of value, to an axiological level incomparable with any other value which does not merit the lofty title of "dignity." As life, and human life, this value called "dignity" is an ultimate and irreducible phenomenon which cannot be defined properly speaking but can only be unfolded and brought to evidence.

C. On the Inalienability of Dignity: Dignity Is Inseparable from Personhood, and Personhood Inseparable from Dignity

Dignity then signifies an excellence of value which is so closely linked to the nature of a person that it cannot be understood independently of grasping the essence of the person in whose nature it is rooted, which I have discussed briefly in expounding the arguments for the existence of a soul. Whence, the definition of the person, through Alexander of Hales, in terms of this dignity: "The person is a substance which is distinguished through a property related to dignity."[4] The essence and real existence of persons give rise to an ontological dignity, of which we understand that it belongs inalienably to a being endowed with understanding, freedom, moral conscience, positive or negative religious acts, an absolutely irreplaceable and indivisible self (in contradistinction to the *Verzweigbarkeit* of plant life), in a word, to a *person*.

D. The "Inviolability" of Dignity: Dignity as Object of Moral and Legal Respect and of an "*Intrinsece Malum*"

"Dignity" means an excellence of value *per se* and bears an intrinsic relationship to being the object of morality and of moral imperatives. It signifies a high and noble value as, for example, that of the contemplative life which many persons are allowed to spurn, turning without any guilt on their part to the practical life, or a sublime value as we find it in art which fails to bind our moral conscience. Dignity also signifies a preciousness of the person which is so essential for personhood and so imposing that it issues moral imperatives to respect it. Even more: dignity imposes a strict obligation to respect a being endowed with it both legally and morally in an essentially higher and more absolute manner than those beings which also possess morally relevant value but lack this dignity, as, most notably, animals.

When, therefore, in 1993 a Swiss animal rights group repeatedly distributed in Liechtenstein material against the "Pig KZ" of the Prince of Liechtenstein in Austria, the equalization implicit in these flyers of the undoubted value of pigs and of the dignity of the persons who were murdered in Auschwitz and other concentration camps is ludicrous. Cruelty to animals is morally evil, but it cannot be compared to the violation of persons endowed with this lofty and morally imposing value: dignity. Dignity is then an especially clear case of a morally relevant value the violation of which constitutes not merely an immoral act but a special moral outrage.

"Dignity" signifies a morally relevant value that is able to ground an *intrinsece malum.* Actions which are essentially and seriously (gravely) directed against this dignity are also essentially directed against morality, that is, they are essentially and intrinsically evil and cannot become good and permissible under any circumstances or when they are performed for good purposes. Dignity indicates a "sacrosanctness" of the person which makes the person's value inviolable for any reason whatsoever. Kant says that dignity is a value which must not be *verrechnet* (calculated), that is, which has an absolute character in that it does not permit violation for any pragmatic reasons, even for a quantitatively higher good. Kant continues that the dignity of the person excels over anything that has a price; it is the irreplaceable value of a being which can never be negotiated (*das "über allen Preis erhaben ist, mithin kein Äquivalent verstattet.*")[5]

Therefore, respect (*Achtung*) is owed to every human being absolutely and in a way which does not allow us ever to use a human person just as a means.[6] The dignity of the person absolutely forbids, for example, to rape a woman, even if this action can save ten other women from a similar fate, because an attack against freedom and sexual integrity is in itself an attack against the inviolable human dignity and is therefore essentially and intrinsically wrong. This inviolability which is inseparable from the dignity of the person belongs both to the person and to the rights which issue from the person. Any form of purely teleological and consequentialist foundation of moral norms fails to recognize this aspect of dignity and must therefore be rejected.[7]

Inviolable dignity cannot have the sense that it, and the subject which possesses it, *cannot* be violated, but it has the sense that a person endowed with dignity *ought never to be* violated with respect to what constitutes this dignity.

The peculiar moral absoluteness and inviolability of the dignity of human life and of the human person was always seen to be a consequence of, and a reason for, any finite person's being in a special way similar to "that greater than which nothing can be conceived," to the *id quo maius nihil cogitari possit.*[8] For the highest and supreme dignity belongs to that being which is of pure infinite perfection, to God as the only absolutely perfect being greater than which nothing can be conceived. The infinite perfection of God can be treated purely in metaphysics[9] or, as in Rudolf Otto or Max Scheler, in philosophy of religion. Otto analyzes moments as, for example, the "*tremendum*," the "*sanctum*," the "*augustum*," the unique *majesty* and other numinous values which exclusively pertain to God but archetypally and most perfectly constitute personal dignity. He investigates also the strict intentional correlation between these moments of the Holy and the corresponding moments of the religious act. Scheler expands Otto's analysis and adds many critical comments, separating Otto's notion of the *A priori* in philosophy of religion from Otto's Kantian subjectivism. Scheler shows the full objectivity and intrinsic necessity of the divine attributes.[10]

4. The Four Roots and Sources of Human Dignity

A. What the Human Being Is as Person, not just What He or She accidentally Has: the Essence, Being, and Substance of the Person as Source of Human Dignity

Those who, like Peter Singer, seek to restrict human dignity to the sane and healthy and intelligent members of the human species deny that the very existence and substantial nature of the human person are the source of human dignity. The same is true of those who deny full dignity worthy of respect to children, as if only adults possessed dignity, an opinion which the great Janusz Korczak opposed both as author and through his actions in real life, up to his freely chosen death with a group of children in the concentration camp.[11] Authors who deny the dignity of the person to each and every human being and restrict it to exemplars of humankind seek to assign human dignity to our accidental features and remove it from our essence. We can see that the being of the person, and thereby also the dignity of a person qua person, reside not only on the level of acts and accidents but on the level of the person's essence and substantial nature, and hence is given with the person's very existence and life.

This becomes immediately evident when we consider that to be a person is always to be – in Aristotle's terms – a substance, that is, to be a subject who stands in itself in being and is not just a quality or attribute or function of something else. This we saw in the previous chapter. Boethius saw this clearly when he said: "*Persona est rationabilis naturae individua substantia*" (the person is an individual substance of rational nature).[12] Never can functions, or qualities of things be persons. The freedom and consciousness and knowledge and character of an I and self which belong to the essence of the person demand unambiguously a subject who lives and stands in itself in being and does not just inhere in another thing as an accident.

The being of the person, which is the first source of human dignity, requires the rational and intellectual essence as well as the concrete individual existence and life of the subject which we designate as person. Persons are never abstract essences but always existing and incommunicable individuals. This was recognized by Richard of St. Victor when he said that the person is "the incommunicable existence of an intellectual nature" (*persona est intellectualis naturae incommunicabilis existentia*), and that "the person exists in himself alone according to a singular mode of rational existence" (*existens per se solum juxta singularem quendam rationalis existentiae modum*).[13]

The reality of individual existence, and even the absolute uniqueness and non-substitutability of the person as a subject endowed with a rational nature, is a condition of human dignity and of any personal dignity. Thus, the essence of a rational being and the real existence and life of an unsubstitutable individual of such a nature interpenetrate each other in the origin of personal dignity.

We may express this point in a more easily accessible form from a linguistic standpoint which Stephen Schwarz has used in his important recent book on the moral question of abortion.[14] A human being possesses inalienable dignity not only "when he *functions* as a person" but in virtue of "*being* a person."[15] The root of the dignity of persons thus lies in their substantial reality which in turn includes their life, and this excludes that persons possess their dignity only in terms of functioning as persons.

In Aristotelian terms, the substantial being of a human person and its potencies ground this dignity, and not only their actualization. When people are sleeping, they continue to possess this dignity. All embryos who cannot yet use their intellect but possess it as a condition of the possibility of ever using it are endowed with this dignity of the person, too.

These facts – the rootedness of personal dignity in the substantial being of the human person and its independence from its actualizations – are overlooked in the logical consequence of two philosophical positions which do not do justice to the person: I mean an actualism which reduces the person to conscious acts or to a consciously lived center of acts. These positions overlook the great discovery of Aristotle that only the substance can ground properties, and thus also personal dignity, and they overlook the great insight of Boethius that the person is an individual substance. For this reason, it is unfortunate that Scheler thinks, as we have pointed out and examined critically above, that he can save the distinctness of the person from non-personal things only by denying the substantial being of the person as standing in himself or in herself.

Another great error which obscures this insight is any form of materialism which identifies the brain and its functions with the self of the person. Under this assumption, we must take for granted that human beings who cannot function as persons *are not persons* because the organ of their brain is exactly what gives rise to their personhood and dignity. But, as shown in the previous chapter, we can see that the self of the person who thinks and wills must be simple and cannot consist in the ten billions of brain cells, in the billions times billions of their parts and distinct and partly unrelated functions, or in the mere organic life in the brain and in the body which lacks the indivisible unsubstitutable center of the I. Thus, the existence of a spiritual mind, of a soul as source of cognition and of free acts, is necessary to constitute this first and most basic level of human dignity: the dignity of the human substance, a dignity which inalienably belongs to the human being qua human being and qua person and which does not possess degrees. Every human being has it in an equal degree.

B. The Second Source of Human Dignity: Consciousness and Actualization of Personhood

But is this value and dignity truly found in all members of the human species or do we really fall into what Singer calls "speciecism" if we hold that?[16] Singer speaks of his "proposal that we reject the sanctity of human life."[17] He thinks that the value of human beings can only lie in their actual ability to think, to will, etc. He goes as far as to defend the view that retarded and otherwise handicapped children are less endowed with dignity than pigs or chimpanzees.

In rejecting this dignity founded on the very substance of the person, Singer makes an excellent point regarding abortion:

> I will only point out that if we believe it is the potential of the infant that makes it wrong to kill it, we seem to be committed to the view that abortion, however soon after conception it may take place, is as seriously wrong as infanticide.[18]

But Singer denies any intrinsic dignity of human persons in virtue of their life and substantial being, and therefore he justifies both abortion and infanticide. While, for the reasons expounded above, I totally reject Singer's negation of the first and most foundational level of human dignity, I do not deny that actual consciousness and lived conscious life originates a second and new dimension of the dignity of persons.

This second source of the dignity of the human person lies in the conscious actualization of the person, in the awakened personal being. This can be absent in seriously retarded persons or in human beings in the permanent vegetative state. Johann Gottlieb Fichte and H. Tristram Engelhardt, Jr. assume that the state of actualized personhood is reached by normal children only after the second year of life; we could also put it at a much later or earlier date. The consciously awakened being of the person undergoes an infinity of shades and degrees, from the first prenatal experiences in the embryonic state, through the early childhood, and to adulthood. In this consciously awakened being of the human person, we find the root of a new dimension of dignity which expresses itself in the acquisition of human rights that are not grounded – as the right to life – in the very being of a person, in the substantial character of personhood, but in the different degrees of consciousness and maturity. For example, the human rights to freedom of speech and movement, or to education, cannot be attributed to a small child, as little as the human rights to marry, or to educate children. These rights which are grounded only in awakened and consciously lived personhood of an established level of maturity differ from the right not to be subjected to murder, to mutilation, or to undignified treatment, which are rooted in the first source of human dignity, the living human person.[19]

This second source of human dignity and of human rights can be lost through so-called brain death, irreversible coma, or other causes.[20] Thus, this second dimension of the dignity of a human person and the rights grounded in it are not as inalienable as the dignity and rights which are grounded simply in the substance, existence, and essence of the person, in the first source of human dignity. But this second dimension of personal dignity is inalienable as long as a person lives consciously. It does not depend on qualitative values, except in the weak sense explained below; the evil person possesses it just as does the good person.

The second source of dignity of persons can never be substituted for the first and most foundational source of personal dignity, in spite of what Singer suggests.

C. The Third Source and a New Sense of Dignity: Moral Dignity

Thirdly, human dignity is the result only of the good actualizations of the person through love of truth, justice, kindness, etc. These involve an essentially new life and dignity of which Alphonse Gratry rightly says: "Man is dead as soon as he ceases to hope ... and to seek."[21] Similarly, we could describe a human existence full of injustice and evil as a "death." It is a life deprived of the deeper dignity to which the human person is called and which is unattainable for the person without acquiring positive moral qualities.

The mere actualization of personhood and a consciously lived life are not sufficient to ground this moral level of human dignity which also gives rise to many new human rights.

Without the achievement of a minimal level of moral dignity of behavior, the privation of the right to exercise human rights grounded in the conscious existence of the person becomes legitimate, for example, the privation of the freedom of movement. This is the case to which I alluded above: a minimal level of dignity in the third sense is a condition for the fullness of possession of the rights which are rooted in the second level of human dignity. The criminal can be deprived of elementary rights as those to freedom of movement, to marriage, and to educate his or her children. But the criminal must never be deprived of other human rights which are rooted entirely and solely in the second level of personal dignity, for example, the right to a fair trial, to defend oneself in court, to the freedom of conscience and religion. Thus, some of the human rights rooted in the consciousness of living persons are absolutely inalienable as long as those people live, and no matter what crime they might commit. Others rooted in the second level can be lost when their abuse is pushed too far or when the justice of punishment requires it.

Juan-Miguel Palacios has expressed excellently the difference between the second and third level of human dignity:

> Personalistic philosophy thus attributes to the person an ontological dignity which constitutes the foundation of a part of his moral dignity. On the one hand, then, the person is partly endowed with dignity by the mere fact of his existence as person, and this fact makes him merit to be treated in a certain manner, which can already be regarded as a form of moral(ly relevant) dignity. But, on the other hand, any person makes himself worthy or unworthy morally in a more proper sense in turning into such or such a person – into a good or into an evil person, as we say in plain English – in virtue of the moral acts which he performs.[22]

About this level of the moral dignity of the person, Gabriel Marcel says rightly that it is a conquest and not a possession. This would not be true about the first ontological level of personhood and only true in quite a restricted sense about the second level and source of the dignity of a person. Through education, through refinement of thought, but much more, through the acquisition of moral values, this dimension of personal dignity is increased.

The totally new dimension and source of personal dignity meant here emerges clearly in its irreducibility to the first two sources thereof when we contemplate the fact that it depends on the *good* use of freedom. This dignity is not inalienable nor does it automatically belong to us as persons. It is the fruit of morally good acts and thus radically distinct from the first type of dignity. It also has a distinct and unique quality, which, as Kant rightly points out, culminates in holiness. This dignity differs from the purely ontological dignity of persons in that it knows opposites. Dignity constitutes the radical contrast to moral indignity and wretchedness, or to the maliciousness of a Hitler who loses any moral dignity through his actions. Evilness thus can make a person lose temporarily or forever this dignity. Moreover, a completely new type of esteem is owed to a person in virtue of this third source of human dignity, an esteem in a far more literal and deep sense than the one which is the adequate response of respect owed to any being who bears human countenance.

The third level of personal dignity, in this respect like the second one, can undergo innumerable degrees. A minimal degree of it is presupposed for rights, as, for example, that to freedom of movement, which a criminal can therefore lose. New human rights, such as the right to a good moral reputation and to the preservation of your honor in society, have their root in this dignity and cannot be claimed where this dignity in the moral sense of the term is largely or wholly lost.

D. A Fourth Source of Human Dignity: Extrinsic Relations and Individual Gifts of Various Kinds

A fourth source of the value of a personality but also of the dignity of persons themselves in their very being does not depend on what these persons are by nature or by moral acts. It does not depend on their substantial being as persons or on the use of their freedom. Instead, this dimension of the dignity of the person proceeds from gifts that not each person possesses and that each person might not possess. Each person who has these gifts does not necessarily possess them in the same degree. With regard to these gifts and talents, fundamental inequalities exist so that a fraternal recognition of the value of each person stands in stark contrast to the claim to total equality, as thinkers like Gabriel Marcel or Erik Kühnelt-Leddin have pointed out. The cry for *fraternité* of the French Revolution contradicts in some measure the cry for *égalité* of the same revolution, so these thinkers pointed out. As Max Scheler sought to demonstrate, a claim to equality that denies the existing differences of talents and gifts of various kinds would result from a root of *ressentiment*[23] rather than from an insight into a universal equality of human nature. With respect to the fourth source of human dignity, as well as with respect to the second and third, human persons are not equal.

Yet, against intimations to the contrary by Kühnelt-Leddin or Scheler, we must uphold a universal equality of all men, women, and children with regard to their dignity on the level of the first source of human dignity through the substantial character of a human person. This dignity has no other conditions besides human nature and does not come in degrees. We are obliged therefore to oppose any attempts to deny this level of equal human dignity.

We must distinguish every member of the human race being equally a human person, who possesses the same fundamental human rights and is equal to all others, from other respects in which it is just not true that all human beings are equal. To claim an equality of dignity with respect to these inequalities can be the fruit of *ressentiments* and envy rather than of truth. This does not exclude that the fourth source of dignity could in principle also be bestowed upon all human persons through extrinsic gifts – as the religious person believes this to be true of values as, for example, "being the object of divine mercy" or "being redeemed by Christ."

These gifts which endow all or some people with a special dignity can be natural gifts immanent in persons, such as beauty or intelligence, genius or charm, strength of character or exuberant vitality. These gifts constitute a special dignity of the genius, of the artist, and of other persons endowed with specifically ennobling natural gifts. They can also be gifts received through relations with other persons, like the "being tamed" of the fox in *Le petit prince*. St. Exupéry's notion of "*être apprivoisé*" in the *The Little Prince* refers to a uniqueness that a rose or an animal receives in virtue of its being loved by persons. Symbolically, this stands for similar values of uniqueness received by human beings through becoming the object of the love of other persons. Without a doubt, personal uniqueness precedes and motivates human love, but a new dimension of uniqueness results from being loved. To this source of dignity belongs the value the individual receives through being the object of interhuman love or through being the member of a community. The social acceptance of a child through her or his parents or through society also bestows this type of value on the child.

Gabriel Marcel's "existentialist foundation" of human dignity refers to this fourth source of dignity. Marcel sees dignity founded in the gift of a common fatherhood, which also those non-believers in God who defend human dignity may accept unconsciously in a faith that is deeper than their conscious beliefs and opinions. Marcel thinks that only this reference to a common father renders intelligible the sense of kinship which also many atheists feel to other human persons and which is conceived by Marcel as standing in tension to equality. According to Marcel's insights, both *fraternité* (brotherhood and sisterhood) and the ultimate human dignity presuppose the relationship of the bearer of human dignity to a Thou.[24]

Social roles and functions can also give a person new dimensions of dignity and new resulting human rights. For example, the office of the judge bestowed upon a man or woman by society gives rise to a new dignity and to a new human right: the right to the independence of the judge. Likewise, offices of authority, like that of the police officer, or of the person of state, give their bearers new sorts of dignity and rights.

The human dignity which proceeds from gifts that go beyond the immanent rational nature of persons can refer to a religious-theological and simultaneously ontological dimension of these gifts. This notion of dignity of the person lies beyond the reach of philosophical knowledge, but we can see in a philosophy of religion that this deepest religious source of dignity of persons is possible. If it exists, it constitutes quite another type of dignity in comparison with the dignity which immanently proceeds from a person's nature. The dignity of the person on the order of grace and of God's love and presence through grace in a soul, as Christians believe it, belongs to this category. The religious dimension of these gifts which redeem and restore nature, if it exists, as the religious believer accepts, constitutes a completely different dimension of human dignity that results from gifts in comparison with which the new dignity through interpersonal acceptance by society completely fades.

As the second and third source of human dignity, so also this fourth one knows many diverse forms and can be lost because it is not simply immanent to the being and life of a person. I do not deny that the existence and life of a person, too, can be rightly interpreted as gifts, but they do not have the peculiar character of extrinsic gifts intended here. Existence and life of the person are not elements which go beyond the possession of human being and nature. They are not within the power of the human being who is endowed with dignity, as the third source of moral dignity largely is.

5. The Human Being Defined as a Being Capable of Transcending Itself: Human Dignity and Its Immanent and Transcendent Origins

I have insisted elsewhere[25] on the wrongness of a conception of the human being implied in Aristotle's definition of the living animal as *entelechy.* Brilliant as this description is for plants and animals and for many dimensions of human life and soul, it is utterly misleading when used as description of the essence of the human being as person. Inasmuch as human life is personal and mental life, it is in all its aspects governed by a principle of transcendence in various meanings. In knowledge, we find a receptive transcendence, in which the being and essence of things disclose themselves to the mind. We find a reaching of mental life beyond its immanent actuality, an openness of its subject to what is beyond his or her own life, a participation in the essence and existence of things themselves. In absolutely certain knowledge, this transcendence and the discovery of things themselves and of things in themselves, as they exist independently of human consciousness, become indubitable.[26]

In love and in moral acts, we transcend ourselves in quite another sense: through the right use of our freedom, namely, in freely recognizing and acknowledging the being and value of someone else in his or her intrinsic preciousness, dignity, and significance. Works of art or other persons possess their value completely independently of our own interests and of the fulfillment of our desires. We are able to respond to them because admiration, respect, or love are due to these beings and persons. The central discovery of value-response in Dietrich von Hildebrand's ethics and philosophy of love elucidates this profound essential mark of the person.[27]

This value-responding attitude toward beings because of their intrinsic worth culminates in the essence of the religious act within which adoration, a completely transcendent affirmation of the absolute Good, constitutes the central core of all religious acts, as Max Scheler has shown in his highly original philosophy of religion.[28] Think of Scheler's beautiful "definition" of the essence of the human being in terms of transcendence and self-transcendence:

> Thus man's intention beyond himself and all life constitutes his *essence.* This precisely *is* the essential concept of "man": He is a *thing which transcends its own life and all life.* The essential core of his nature – apart from all special organization – is in fact this movement, this spiri-

tual act of transcending himself! "Human" ethics and "biological" ethics both fail to see this.[29]

Five

DIALOGUES WITH SCIENTISTS

I chose the dialogue form to clarify a few statements which occur in the text and which to clarify in the main text itself, even in form of notes, would be cumbersome and difficult. To clarify these issues in the form of dialogues with scientists, dialogues which actually took place in a similar form, will help the reader better understand the present monograph. The following questions were posed to me by prominent scientists after I presented the principal contents of the book for the first time as a paper. I will present the objections of my interlocutors here anonymously and in my slightly adapted version of their questions.[1]

1. On the Significance of Emphasizing the "Many Meanings" of "Life"

Objection: *Some scientists will object: It is superfluous to stress that we speak in many senses of "life" or of being. Not only "life" and being are ambiguous notions, but all other words as well. Any word has many meanings.*

Answer: While virtually every word and philosophical term has many meanings, many words have multiple meanings only for arbitrary linguistic reasons, which can give rise to equivocal terms. For example, the English word "top" can mean a spinning toy for children and a mountain top, or the German word "Schloß" can mean a lock and a castle. But it is hardly meaningful to say, "Of tops we speak in many senses," because no inner reason occurs in the object for a manifold meaning of the word. Other terms have only slight differences in meaning, depending on the species to which you apply the same generic term, as when you apply the word "red" to a light red color or to a dark red color, or the word "dog" to poodles and German shepherds. Here, too, we would be pompous in saying, "Of red or of dogs we speak in many senses, sometimes of dark red, at other times of light red, sometimes of poodles, and other times of German shepherds." Even where the same term expresses radically different meanings, between which only a metaphorical analogy obtains, we do not apply this phrase, as in the case of mathematical triangles and three lovers to which we refer as "triangle." Where good reasons exist to confound two radically different meanings of the same term, however, it is necessary to distinguish the "many senses" of a term. This is even more important where we find some analogous similarity between two terms. The terms "being" or "life" possess at the same time a profound difference in meaning and involve a deeply meaningful unity and similarity between their distinct referents. This "similarity-in-difference," a similarity between objects which belong to quite different kinds of being and whose similarity is not based on some common generic feature, was called "analogy" by ancient and medieval philosophy. With respect to these analogous objects and analogous terms, we must take into consideration the whole spectrum of their meaning and become aware how they are used differently. In our context of a discussion of the origin of life, biologists should realize that the organic life that they investigate is not the only kind of life, and, if they could successfully reduce it to material systems (which I deem impossible), they should not therefore consider also other life, for example, that of the mind, equally reducible to matter. Mental life is much more evidently irreducible to matter than the life of bacteria or of viruses. With regard to viruses, we may well have doubts as to whether they actually live or whether their reproduction is something analogously mechanical or purely physical as the "growth" of crystals. Most biologists today believe that viruses are not alive, although they do possess genetic information and can multiply in other organisms including bacteria. For outside living cells distinct from themselves, they cannot carry on life processes. Viruses show life processes, and specifically metabolism and reproduction, only when they are in the living cell of a plant, an animal, or in bacteria, in which they are called bacteriophages. Philosophically speaking, one can well ask, however, whether the purely parasitic character of viruses is sufficient to deny life to them if they do show all essential signs of life when they inhabit other cells.

Keeping in mind the radically different forms of life and the analogy between them, the biologist will become more cautious in making claims favoring reductionistic models of explaining life.

2. The Autonomy of Philosophy and that of Science with Respect to Life

Objection: *You made intrusions into scientific spheres which I do not completely share. You implied the autonomy of philosophy when you referred to the need for a properly philosophical treatment of the question, "What is life?". Parallel to this claim, I would hold scientific investigations of life to be completely independent of philosophy. Otherwise, if philosophers were in principle to impose limitations on scientific endeavors, we could be faced with a new Galileo case. Philosophers are also autonomous, and they can investigate life independently with their methods. Life lends itself to an exploration from the points of view of many disciplines. Should we then not insist on a complete autonomy and mutual independence of philosophical investigations into life and of scientific biological explanations of life?*

Answer: I agree fully with the idea of the autonomy of the methods of science and of philosophy if this "autonomy" means that the disciplines and methods of both are quite different and have different formal objects. Empirical science uses sense perception, observation, experiments, hypotheses, and complex theories, to explore the factual sides of the world. Philosophers look for highly intelligible and necessary essences and essential features of the world open to evident cognitions and insights, as well as to deductive demonstrations. Mathematicians do the same when they really attend to the principles of numbers, geometric objects, and other data, and when they are not only construing ideas, a procedure which plays a legitimate role in mathematics. The reason for a difference in method between science and philosophy or mathematics lies in differences in the formal objects and purposes of the respective methods. For example, intrinsically necessary essences and essentially necessary states of affairs are grounded in aspects of knowledge, in freedom, in conscious acts, in motion, in matter, and in mind. Philosophy should explore these. But contingent facts and essential structures of complexities also exist which only empirical methods can elucidate. Thus, the clue to why we need different methods lies in an understanding of the different kinds of essences and objects. Non-necessary, contingent essences, the elements of which are held together by some factual, non-necessary although quite meaningful bond, do not allow insights into necessary evident truths. Scientists who explore them must use empirical and experimental methods. But to apply these methods to questions of philosophy and mathematics would be absurd. The mathematician would laugh if she or he were asked to conduct years of experiments to know that 2 x 2 can never equal 5. Equally absurd would it be to solve philosophical questions of ethics and oughtness by means of empirical studies of human or animal behavior. Psychology or sociology can investigate empirical questions of human behavior, but philosophy uses quite different methods designed to give us knowledge about the highly intelligible and necessary aspects of reality.[2]

For philosophers to think that they could interfere in empirical matters would be quite inappropriate. They cannot explore, by means of their methods, the position of the sun or the relationship between the movement of the earth and that of the sun, the empirical marks of life, for example, the different parts of the nutritive or other body systems, the species of insects, or the cellular structure of living organisms and the functions of the parts of cells. They should leave these matters to empirical science to explore. If they do not, a Galileo case may result. Usually, philosophers are less prone to intrude into the sphere of empirical matters than are scientists to speak about philosophical questions. Scientists evidently cannot solve philosophical issues by means of empirical observations; equally evident is that philosophers cannot solve the above-mentioned empirical questions by means of philosophical methods.

Some philosophers, especially those who conducted empirical investigations, like Aristotle, Avicenna, or Albert the Great, exerted a strong influence on science. That influence was inappropriate inasmuch it was based on their general authority in philosophy that was transposed to science, or, because they conflated empirical and philosophical methods. When philosophers try to solve problems of empirical science with their methods, the disastrous result may be a restriction placed upon empirical science that lasts for centuries. Although Aristotle and Albert the Great, in antiquity and in the Middle Ages, conducted empirical science, the Aristotelian idea that all universal natures are necessary has dominated Western thought and impeded for a long time the rise of experimental sciences.

Stanley Jaki, who uses historical, philosophical, and scientific methods and whose education in many disciplines allows him to see their manifold relations, has examined this phenomenon in many perspicacious books. He has shown convincingly many mutual connections between empirical science and philosophical positions. He has demonstrated that only a creationist metaphysics which sees the origin of nature in a free divine act and therefore recognizes contingency in nature, was able in the history of science to provide the proper metaphysical basis for empirical sciences.

This knowledge must not lead us to believe that no absolutely necessary and immutable essences exist which *a priori* sciences as mathematics or philosophy investigate. We should not believe that in the field of objects of these *a priori* sciences empirical methods would be justified, so that it would be possible to establish the morally good by statistics or by behavioral studies of animals. *A priori* is not meant here in the subjectivistic Kantian sense but in the sense of objective essential necessities. I do not deny that philosophy should take its starting point in experience, namely, in a such-being experience in which we come into contact with contingent facts and with essential necessities. I recognize many fruitful mutual relationships between the disciplines and the value of each, but the difference of their methods absolutely forbids philosophers to meddle with the domain of science and to attempt to solve by *a priori* theories those problems that only empirical science can answer.

But what applies to philosophy, applies more so to science. A disaster occurs if ethologists who observe animal behavior deduce ethical conclusions from this, as do Konrad Lorenz, Wolfgang Wickler, and many others. Scientists frequently trespass over the limits of their discipline. This is legitimate if they have a proper philosophical education and only as long as they realize that they are now speaking as philosophers and not as scientists. For example, Einstein's theory of the relativity of time has purely scientific aspects resulting in important formulas regarding mass, acceleration, and energy, such as $E=mc^2$. But he also develops philosophical theories about the essence of time and simultaneity being relative, which in no way follow from his physics. The same is true about Heisenberg who deduces from the physical aspects of his discoveries regarding the uncertainty relation, as well as from Einstein's theory, far-reaching philosophical consequences, which in no way follow from scientific results, regarding indeterminacy, freedom, causality, the first principles of being, and other issues. The same is evident about the theories of evolution and of the Big Bang, which, in most of their forms, are chiefly philosophical theories for which the scientific research provides at best a starting point. This applies still more to the outrageous metaphysical claims about chance, necessity, and God, which Jacques Monod makes in his *Chance and Necessity*. This becomes the source of many errors as soon as scientists become unaware when they are invoking purely philosophical theories which have nothing to do with their science, and when they hold false philosophical theses as if they were empirically demonstrated.

The mutual autonomy of methods and the danger of intruding into the fields of our colleagues, do not imply a complete divorce between scientific and philosophical methods and investigations. Therefore, I would not agree if you proposed the complete independence of philosophy and science from each other as well as the complete distinctness of methods. We have to recognize the described autonomy and the many mutual relations between philosophy and science. For example, biologists presuppose many philosophical categories, like reality, existence, proof, argument, logical laws, matter, space, time, indeterminacy, determinism, and finality, many aspects and the general essence of which they cannot explore by means of their methods but which are objects of philosophical analysis. The same is true about truth, the scope and purpose of each science, the value and limits of scientific knowledge. All these are philosophical problems. The scientist presupposes implicitly some answers to them which only philosophy can give. Jaki showed convincingly that even a metaphysics and theology of contingency and creation was necessary to make empirical sciences possible and to provide their proper philosophical foundation.

The philosopher also profits from science in many ways. Philosophical questions are posed by science to the philosopher. Scientific experiments and results about the brain can widen the scope of philosophy and corroborate or inspire new philosophical discoveries of "*a priori*" structures, which I understand as objective essential necessities and intelligible truths. Many of these become accessible only through a special type of experience. But the role which experience plays for philosophy and for biology is totally different. Experiment has no relevance for philosophy except for corroborating or calling into question from the outside the results of philosophy. Thus, philosophers can be pleased when the results of their philosophical studies are corroborated by empirical sciences,[3] and they are forced to check the adequacy of their methods when their results do not harmonize with the results of empirical science. Yet the experiment is never the philosophical method. The philosophical method is another kind of knowledge: insight (intuition) into highly intelligible and evident essences and states of affairs, and deductive demonstrations.

3. Can We Stand Between or Beyond Reductionism and Anti-Reductionism?

Objection: *Do you make the tacit assumption that the alternative between reductionism and the recognition of irreducibility, between reductionism and non-reductionism or anti-reductionism, is complete? The main philosophical merit of the issues which we discussed during this dialogue (the emergency-of-complexity-problem, dynamical chaos-theory, non-linear thermodynamics), consists in demonstrating that there is a third possibility. Some new systems and ideas about the origin of life are not physicalistic and materialist in the sense of old reductionism. Can we not stand between or beyond reductionism and anti-reductionism? Life cannot be deduced in a predictable mechanistic manner from physical laws. But life can emerge in unpredictable ways from physical systems, whether these are conceived deterministically or indeterministically.*

Answer: Thank you for your interesting objection. I agree with the fact that new forms of theory of matter and of living organisms have emerged, and that these are superior to older ones in that they allow us to account for many more astonishing features of material systems and objects than the older theories had suspected existed. Any theory which opens up to new and verifiable or plausible principles of explanation is less primitively reductionistic than older mechanistic reductionisms which did not include reference to non-mechanical laws like those of teleological (finalistic) principles and purposes, of the "anthropic principle," of dynamic chaos-theories, and of nonlinear thermodynamics. Today most scientists will agree that life cannot be reduced to predictable patterns of mechanics, in terms of which Julien Offray de LaMettrie and René Descartes proposed to explain animal and plant behavior. To admit this and to allow for the unpredictable or for purposes which are not reducible to unpredictable chance, as, for example, the anthropic principle in the cosmos, is less reductionistic than theories which did not admit these forms of phenomena and these principles of the emergence of order. Matter has become far more mysterious in the light of modern physics than it appeared before. Explanations of matter which allow for the unpredictable emergence of phenomena are far less reductionistic than purely mechanical models of explanation which admitted nothing but mechanical causality. But do these new theories cease to be reductionistic? Any form of explanation which does not do full justice to the phenomena and essences of things is reductionistic, when it is offered as a sufficient explanation of these data. A good example would be a chess game. Its explanation in terms of a pure theory of wood of which the pieces consist, and of mechanical causality by means of which the pieces are moved by hands or computers, would not explain anything about the essence of chess. This explanation would not explain the moves because it ignores the principles and rules of chess, including the timeless mathematical, logical, and chess-specific principles. It would ignore, among many other aspects of the royal game, the chess-conventions, the intelligible systems of end-games or of openings, and the computer programs based on these. Even to introduce into the theory of chess the occurrence of non-mechanical, unpredictable patterns of behavior not explicable in terms of classical mechanics would be insufficient as explanation. Such an explanation fails to take into consideration the entirely new sphere of rules, geometrical and logical and chess-specific necessities understood by the players, and the sphere of purposive action and intelligent understanding of chess masters.[4] The most high-level modern physical theory of chess in terms of chaotic and non-chaotic physical systems would be radically reductionistic because it entirely leaves out of consideration the most basic and the more complex principles necessary to explain the moves in a chess game.

To explain life in terms of those same principles which you consider to lead to a theory beyond reductionism would be much more reductionistic than to explain chess games in these terms. For chess does not live. Therefore, in chess, we can admit such categories as conventional rules and logical and mathematical necessities, and then say that the substantial being (the substance) in which all these programs, etc. are stored, for example, the chess computer, is a purely material thing. The material substratum of chess computers or programs like Mephisto or Chess-Base, or the material thing underlying the actual moves of chess pieces are pieces of wood, plastic, or metal. But this explanation would not be enough for a non-reductionist explanation of life or of mental life. Life requires entirely new categories to be understood properly, transcending all those required for explaining a chess game. Life requires new substantial categories, as, for example, entelechies, life-principles, souls, and minds. I do not deny that the properly human personal acts of *understanding* chess games, or of inventing them, require minds and can never be performed by chess computers which understand absolutely nothing of the game though on the basis of purely material causes which are correlated to mental acts in computer programs they simulate a brilliant understanding of chess. I argued in my book on chess philosophy that any *understanding* and *human* playing of chess presupposes minds. Nor do I deny that the invention of chess-computers is a specifically human act. But given the existence of a chess-computer, the explanation of the moves it makes does not require any spiritual substance or mind. Yet we cannot understand its moves or the program it uses and the causes which made it, if we do not understand many conventional and *a priori* rules and principles which go beyond those which dominate physical systems.

We must not only ask: Is modern life-theory in science less reductionistic than classical mechanical models of materialistic life-theories? But: Is it sufficiently non-reductionistic? Do the principles modern physics introduces for the explanation of life, for example, in terms of modern chaos-theory, do justice to life? I would answer: even incomparably less than if these theories were applied to the explanation of chess games. Heisenberg, as expressed in his book *Physics and Philosophy*, could discover analogies between his interpretation of the uncertainty relation, in terms of the alleged indeterminacy of quantum-physical micro-processes, and freedom. This is fascinating, although Heisenberg's philosophical interpretation of his ingenious discoveries in physics involves a confusion between freedom and chance and a conflation of epistemology with metaphysics. Our inability to measure with precision both the speed and location of particles and our resulting ignorance about certain aspects of physical properties and causes of micro-physical events is confounded with the alleged metaphysical absence of any determining cause of material events and their alleged ontological indeterminacy or uncausedness. Matter and material events, I submit, necessarily require an efficient cause through the power of which they are or happen, whether the efficient cause of material events is immanent in nature or transcendent to it, as in the case of free actions upon matter. Inanimate matter cannot be free or act from an inner principle of spontaneous motion. Absolute chance is not possible or a viable substitute of a causal principle of explanation. Therefore, matter is necessarily determined, but in the last analysis, determined by freedom.

In these and similar ways, in spite of the astonishing advances of modern scientific explanations of matter in comparison with older ones, modern theories of life and consciousness in terms of material evolution are just as reductionistic as the older ones. Only the nature of a given object can tell us whether it is an ultimate irreducible datum or explicable in terms of something else. Only the intelligible natures of things themselves dictate whether more sophisticated materialist explanations of life are reductionistic. If life requires an entelechy or *soul,* as Aristotle says, and as I have argued in this book and in other works, then even the most sophisticated materialist models of explaining life, using non-linear equations, chaos-theory, or quantum physics, remain reductionistic and inadequate when they seek to reduce life and consciousness to "nothing but strikingly new phenomena of the physical universe." Basically, these models are then just as reductionistic as the old reductionisms which sought to reduce life and mind to the level of pure machines and to other phenomena known to physics at that time. Life, especially mental life, just cannot be thus reduced. If unpredictable laws or events in the material world are equally unable to explain life or even a chess game as predictable ones, a theory of life or chess in terms of them remains reductionistic. Modern chaos-theoretical explanations of life introduce unexpected laws that explain unexpected events in the physical universe. But if these laws are quantum-mechanically conceived, deterministically or not, and interpreted in terms of chance-events, none of this can change the fundamentally reductionistic character of these theories. De LaMettrie's theory of mind, expounded chiefly in his *L'Homme machine*, 1747, might have been much more primitively reductionistic than these modern theories, but an interpretation of minds in terms of more complex material systems remains equally reductionistic. The matter at hand is this: Can biological life and mental life – can *bios* or *zoee* – be reduced to complex brain-events, brain-processes, cells, modules, and the electrical and chemical occurrences in them? If not, any attempt to explain them in these terms remains reductionistic and different only in degree from older forms of reductionism.

4. The Question of Life as a "Transdisciplinary" Question

Question: *You call the question of life an "interdisciplinary" question, and I am inclined to agree with you. But should we not better introduce the term "transdisciplinary" to indicate the need for a closer cooperation among the disciplines and to avoid a situation in which "interdisciplinary studies" only mean that many disciplines examine the same object from the narrow point of view of their own method? Your use of the term "interdisciplinary" goes against what you have said. Life or death are "transdisciplinary" objects. To explore topics such as life or death requires that one and the same investigation use many methods.*

Answer: I agree with your viewpoint in that we would be quite wrong to conceive of "interdisciplinary" studies thus that each member of a discipline studies an issue or "material" object as, for example, death only from that discipline's point of view and with its methods, without taking into account the results and methods of other disciplines. The term "material object" is not taken from matter but constitutes the opposite of "formal." Interdisciplinary studies should not mean a sum-total of studies which remain each enclosed in only one discipline. Instead, the goal of interdisciplinary studies is to arrive at a more comprehensive understanding of the issues at stake, by leaving the narrowness of your own discipline. In this respect, we can legitimately speak of transdisciplinary studies rather than of interdisciplinary ones, although the term "transdisciplinary" and "interdisciplinary" stand in need of explanation.

"Transdisciplinary studies" would be most undesirable if "transdisciplinary" meant that we no longer respect the different methods of different disciplines, or that scientists do amateur philosophy and wrong philosophy which they pass for "scientific" or "transdisciplinary," or that philosophers should engage themselves in amateur scientific theories. We should approach an issue by the methods which are appropriate to it and which pertain to a discipline which we master and whose methods we use conscientiously and rigorously, without attempting an amateurish crossing of the borders. Interdisciplinary or transdisciplinary studies should not mean, for example, that scientists get involved in forms of unfounded opinion as does Jacques Monod, who in his *Chance and Necessity* philosophizes in the most hair-raisingly amateurish way, talking about the highest matters of metaphysics. The sophisticated and adequate scientific knowledge on which Monod's success in micro-biology and other sciences depended did not prepare him in the least for philosophical theories. "Transdisciplinary" cannot mean a "*nihil obstat*" to incredibly naive pseudo-philosophies of scientists or to similarly naive scientific theories of philosophers. In a properly interdisciplinary or transdisciplinary study, we should check with a representative of another discipline whether we interpret its results correctly, and we should never falsely claim authority in fields and methods outside the scope of our competence. If we are unprepared to pursue philosophical investigations, we should leave those to the philosopher and not engage in audacious philosophical theories without the necessary rigor of properly philosophical methods.

The greater danger is for scientists to think they know philosophy than for philosophers to think they know science. While philosophy does not turn a philosopher into a scientist, many people think that anyone is prepared to philosophize. This is true in that every woman and man has some philosophical assumptions and can in principle know philosophical truths. But the proper exposition and understanding of philosophical truth is not an easy task and it requires deep reflection and proper training, as well as philosophical talent and a fundamental attitude of openness toward being. The illusion whereby all people who know something else easily come to think that they are also good philosophers, is basically the problem of *doxa* described by Socrates in the *Apology*. Whereas Socrates, the philosopher, knows quite well that he does not understand the several crafts, poetry, and the intricacies of political life, the craftsmen and craftswomen, the poets, and the politicians think they know all philosophy. Socrates knows his limits, whereas the representatives of other fields think that, because they know some things which the philosopher does not understand, they know all others and the most important objects of philosophy as well, even if Socrates can easily show that they know nothing about them. This does not exclude that some individual scientists were also great philosophers and that many scientists who have not been great philosophers nevertheless gained many philosophical insights, as I tried to show elsewhere of Sir John Eccles with respect to the "self-conscious mind."[5]

5. Mental Life Cannot Be Identified with the Brain

Objection: *You presented a critique of reducing thought and will to the individual brain, to which indeed they cannot be reduced. But deducing from this that mental life cannot be reduced at all to brains is to take too big of a step. The irreducibility of thought to individual brains and brain-events does not yet prove that mental phenomena are irreducible to a community of evolving brains which develop in a cultural environment which programs these brains. We can note the tremendous influence of learning on brains, and isolated brains would never develop in these ways, even in purely physiological terms. Our brains would never have developed many of their functions if they had been left in an isolated state. We need a new phenomenological method to explore emergent aspects of brains, as members of a society of brains. Therefore, how can your objections refer to an emergent community of brains? Why could we not say instead that the individual brain in its uninfluenced state is insufficient to explain thought? But the brain which has been subjected to a process of brain-programming can explain thought, social life, language, and all other human activities. The mere physical organ of the brain, the consequence of the genetic code and of a hardware-program can none of them explain the mind. An explanation is however provided by the multiple effects of the "software-program" which comes to our brain from the world, from the objects of perception, experience, and memory, and even more from the interactions of our brain with other brains in schooling, learning of any kind from others.*

Answer: I fully agree with you on the idea that the "programming" of the brain as well as the complex spatio-temporal patterns in the modules of the brain occur by the immanent individual structures of the brain yet include manifold changes of brain-activity and of something like "brain-programs," changes which are consequences of experience and of manifold external influences. Memory in all its forms gives a splendid example of this, but so does any form of learning or understanding.

Analogous to the above remarks about the more subtle reductionisms of life to phenomena explored by quantum-physics and chaos-theory, reductionism still occurs in reducing mental life to the sum-total of complex brain-events. Whether you have many brains or one, brains which function according to teleologically conceived patterns of modular programs or according to primitive chance and necessity, explanations of mental life in terms of distinct principles of explanation are only different degrees, although perhaps essentially different degrees, of reductionism. None of this influences the central philosophical question: Whether any conceivable material substance which can store programs, with its billions of brain cells, can be the substantial subject or substratum evidently required for thought? If my arguments against this are valid, your theory remains essentially reductionistic. We cannot possibly assume that the *subject* of thought and will, which can be shown to be an indivisible, simple, and spiritual substance, the personal self, could be identified with a brain subjected to manifold external influences from the world and from other brains, or to a plurality of brains. If it is essentially and necessarily impossible, as I tried to show, that the personal self be identical with one brain or with a part of a brain which, in its physical complexity of cells and of parts thereof, is utterly incapable of producing even the tiniest thought or conscious act, then it is equally impossible that the mind be reduced to one brain modified by other brains.

Programs or spatio-temporal patterns of brain-activity influenced by them, are less capable of being the ontological subjects of intellectual or free acts than a brain. They are not substantial entities like persons. The fundamental brain-physiological reductionism does not cease to be reductionistic if we add to our brain other brains and their interaction with our brain-events. In the final analysis, none of the phenomena discussed in this book in the context of the proofs for a spiritual soul are more explainable in terms of many brains than in terms of one brain, or in terms of a brain programmed by external influences as opposed to an isolated brain. I have tried to show this in several books and articles on the body-soul problem. Consciousness cannot be an emergent or a supervenient property of a brain or of a "society of brains," just as little as conscious life can be an epiphenomenon of a single brain.

6. "Can" and "Cannot" in Philosophical Knowledge

Question: *You used terms such as "can" or "cannot" in your critique of reductionism. But can we determine these limits, can we establish in some* a priori *fashion the limits of what empirical science is going to be able to show? I put "can" and "cannot" in quotation marks because in many examples complex structures require completely new categories to be explained. It would be impossible to write equations for these higher structural properties. Thus, philosophers must be extremely cautious in using terms as "can" or "cannot" or "can never" in a discussion.*

Answer: I fully agree with your opinion about the dangers of saying "can" or "cannot" too quickly. In the object of natural science the most astonishing forms of "reductions" are possible, even where our experience seems to refute the possibility of reductions, as the example of a feasible "reduction" of diamond to carbon proves. Philosophers must be cautious not to raise illegitimate obstacles to the freedom of experimental research. They should abstain from assertions of impossibility wherever only empirical methods can determine what is possible or impossible.

But where we meet intelligible and necessary data, as, for example, the question as to whether the number 11 is prime, or whether minds can emerge from brains, for us to say that not enough experiments have been made to verify this assumption would be quite untenable. No experiments are needed or able to prove these supremely intelligible and necessary truths.

This is not to exclude that some empirical methods and guess-work could apply to spheres that in principle are open to *a priori* knowledge, for example, to aspects of number theory. Empirical methods and guess-work apply only where immediate insight and deduction is impossible regarding *a priori* questions, as in aspects of the theory of prime numbers or of chess-openings, which cover vast fields and where so many possibilities exist that limited human minds need to "try out" what is the correct answer and learn by trial and error. In these cases the experiment has a role relative to our incapacity of understanding matters by *a priori* insights, "mathematical inductions," or deductive arguments.[6]

That we do not need empirical observations and experiments for our knowledge, applies to philosophy, and to mathematics and logic. Not because philosophy makes blind and unverifiable as well as unfalsifiable assumptions, but because the intrinsic objective evidence of objects makes empirical experimental methods and their objects unnecessary. Because we can understand essential necessities, we can say: never can minds be reduced to brains, never can justice be reduced to *ressentiments* of the weak against the strong, never can moral values be reduced to conventions, never can promises be reduced to declarations of wills or to their social acceptance.[7] Due to the intelligibility of the object of our demonstrations of minds as spiritual substances, we can justifiably say that a reduction is never admissible.[8] Here the untenability of a similar reduction is strictly evident. But wherever the contingent, non-necessary structure of an object does not allow for a reduction, we should abstain from it.

For example, we would be wrong to reduce the whole poetic activity of Johann Wolfgang von Goethe to "nothing but his will to fame."

Obstacles erected by philosophers blocked the progress of science for many centuries. The spheres which are legitimately explored empirically, apart from certain results which are established beyond the shadow of a doubt,[9] are always open in principle to refutations and to new possibilities the existence of which no philosophy can demonstrate or hypothetically exclude. This must not lead to our overlooking the rationality and reliability of empirical scientific knowledge. Karl Popper holds a falsificationistic concept of science which calls into radical doubt the method of induction and has many other problematic implications. Also Thomas Kuhn and Larry Laudan have proposed theories of science in which the rationality of inductive methods is denied.[10]

Yet empirical knowledge, experimental methods, and hypotheses open to falsification, are not all that exists in the sphere of knowledge. Even if we admit induction that proceeds from repeated observation as a legitimate and reliable method of scientific knowledge, the empirical knowledge based on this type of experience is not the only kind of science. Properly philosophical methods also exist which grasp highly intelligible and necessary truths. These truths can never be overthrown by empirical research. If philosophical methods of insight and demonstration make evident that a free act can never be produced by a brain but that the brain can only be its condition or be in other ways compatible with freedom related to the brain, then the necessity of this fact holds for the real and for any possible world. Then to prove empirically the materiality of the subject of thought is as impossible as to prove that mathematical or philosophical or any empirical results would ever show that 2 x 2=12, or that envy is morally good, or that a being can at the same time not be, and innumerably many other necessary falsities. When dealing with necessary truths, we can rightly say that things which are in contradiction to philosophical knowledge of essences can never happen. Here we are able to determine parameters of what can and cannot be.

NOTES

Acknowledgements

1. The results of this research will be published shortly. See Patricia Donohue-White, Kateryna Fedoryka, Paulina Taboada (eds.), *Towards a Personalistic Conception of Health*, forthcoming in the *Philosophy and Medicine* Book Series (Dordrecht: Kluwer); and James M. DuBois (ed.), *Moral Issues in Psychology* (Lanham/New York/London: University Press of America, 1996).

2. The Proceedings of this Meeting, to be published by the Pontifical Academy for the Sciences, contain their names as well as some of their contributions to the discussion of my paper.

3. This paper was presented by Valery Atlas at the International Academy of Philosophy in the Principality of Liechtenstein. See Niels Bohr, *Collected Works*, ed. J. R. Nielsen (Amsterdam: North-Holland-Elsevier, 1972-1985), vols. 1, 4, 5.

4. See Duns Scotus, *Grammatica speculativa*, p. 52; cf. also Martin Heidegger, *Die Kategorien- und Bedeutungslehre des Duns Scotus*, in: Martin Heidegger, *Gesamtausgabe*, I. Abteilung, Veröffentlichte Schriften 1914-1970, vol. 1, *Frühe Schriften* (Frankfurt a. M.: Vittorio Klostermann, 1978), pp. 189-412.

Introduction

1. Erwin Schrödinger, *What Is Life?* (Cambridge, England: Cambridge University Press, 1944).

2. See Schrödinger, *Was ist Leben?* (Munich and Zurich: Piper, 3rd ed., 1987), p. 137; see also Ernst Peter Fischer, "Was ist Leben? – mehr als vierzig Jahre später," in: Schrödinger, *Was ist Leben?*, pp. 10 ff. See also Bernd-Olaf Küppers, *Der Ursprung biologischer Information. Zur Naturphilosophie der Lebensentstehung*, Preface by Carl Friedrich von Weizsäcker (Munich/Zurich: Piper, 1986), p. 266, n. 50; and Hans Günter Gassen, Andrea Martin, Gabriele Sachse, *Der Stoff, aus dem die Gene sind: Bilder und Erklärungen zur Gentechnik* (Munich: J. Schweitzer Verlag, 1986), pp. 13 ff. See also Josef Seifert, "Genetischer Code und Teleologie, Information, Kausalität und Finalität: Kurzer Abriß naturwissenschaftlicher genetischer Erkenntnisse als Hintergrund neuer philosophischer Probleme," *Arzt und Christ* 34 (1988), pp. 185-200.

3. See Hedwig Conrad-Martius, "Präformismus in der Natur," in: Conrad-Martius, *Schriften zur Philosophie*, ed. Eberhard Avé-Lallement, vol. 2 (Munich: Kösel, 1964), pp. 164 ff.

4. See Ludwig von Bertalanffy, *General System Theory* (New York, 4th ed., 1972).

5. See, for example, *ibid.*, pp. 15 ff. See on this also Paulina Taboada, "Bedeutung der 'Allgemeinen Systemtheorie' in der heutigen Debatte über den Gesundheitsbegriff," to be published in Patricia Donohue-White, Kateryna Fedoryka, and Paulina Taboada (eds.), "Towards a Personalistic Concept of Health," forthcoming in the *Philosophy and Medicine* Book Series (Dordrecht: Kluwer).

6. See, for example, Hedwig Conrad-Martius, *Die Seele der Pflanze*, in: Conrad-Martius, *Schriften zur Philosophie*, vol. 1. See also Helmuth Plessner, *Die Stufen des Organischen und der Mensch: Einleitung in die philosophische Anthropologie* (Berlin/New York: Walter de Gruyter, 3rd unchanged ed., 1975; 1st ed. 1928), esp. pp. 123 ff.; and Stephan Pietrowicz, *Helmuth Plessner* (Freiburg/Munich: Verlag Karl Alber, 1992), pp. 303 ff.

7. See, for example, Plessner, *Die Stufen des Organischen und der Mensch*, pp. 111-218. See also Pietrowicz, *Helmuth Plessner*, esp. pp. 354-426; see also Emil-Heinz Hocevar, *Die Seinsstruktur der Pflanzen* (unpublished dissertation: Salzburg 1972) (published by Anton Pustet, Salzburg, 1975), and Hans-Eduard Hengstenberg, *Evolution und Schöpfung* (Salzburg: Anton Pustet, 1963).

8. Hans Jonas, *The Phenomenon of Life: Toward a Philosophical Biology* (New York: Harper & Row, 1966), p. 11.

9. See esp. Hans Jonas, "The Nobility of Sight," *ibid.*, pp. 135-156.

10. The present book represents an enlarged and modified version of a lecture presented at the Plenary Session of The Pontifical Academy of Sciences on "The Emergence of Complexity in Mathematics, Physics, Chemistry, and Biology" (26-31 October 1992), Rome.

11. See John Crosby, "Evolutionism and the Ontology of the Human Person," *Review of Politics*, 38 (April 1976), pp. 208-243. See also Hengstenberg, *Evolution und Schöpfung*. See likewise Josef Seifert, *Leib und Seele. Ein Beitrag zur philosophischen Anthropologie* (Salzburg: A. Pustet, 1973), pp. 71 ff., 157 ff.

12. Cf. Erich Blechschmidt, *Wie beginnt das menschliche Leben?* (Stein am Rhein: Christiana Verlag, 4th ed., 1983).

13. See Stanley L. Jaki, *Cosmos and Creator* (Chicago: Regnery Gateway, 1980), pp. 69-86; cf. also by the same author, *The Origin of Science and the Science of Origin* (South Bend, Ind.: University of Notre Dame Press, 1979).

14. See on this Josef Seifert, *Das Leib-Seele Problem und die gegenwärtige philosophische Diskussion: Eine kritisch-systematische Analyse* (Darmstadt: Wissenschaftliche Buchgesellschaft, 2nd ed., 1989), ch. 6. This book will be published soon in English.

15. Michael Polanyi, "Life Transcending Physics and Chemistry," *Chemical and Engineering News*, 45 (1967), p. 64 f.

16. On the method of such a phenomenological realist philosophy, compare Josef Seifert, *Back to Things in Themselves: A Phenomenological Foundation for Classical Realism* (London: Routledge, 1987), chs. 1-4.

Chapter One

1. Aristotle, *Metaphysics*, Book 4, 1003 a 33.

2. See A. Müller, "Bios (Leben, Lebensform)," *Historisches Wörterbuch der Philosophie*, ed. Joachim Ritter, vol. 1, A-C (Basel/Stuttgart: Schwabe & Co., 1971), pp. 948-949.

3. Josef Seifert, "Das Unsterblichkeitsproblem aus der Sicht der philosophischen Ethik und Anthropologie," *Franziskanische Studien*, 3 (1978), and "Gibt es ein

Leben nach dem Tod?", *Forum Katholische Theologie*, 5:4 (1989). See also Helmut Plessner, "Homo Absconditus," *Philosophische Anthropologie heute*, eds. R. Rocek, Oskar Schatz (Munich: Anton Pustet, 1972), p. 39.

4. See Hans Jonas, "Immortality and the Modern Temper," in: *The Phenomenon of Life: Toward a Philosophical Biology* (New York: Harper & Row, 1966), pp. 262 ff.

5. Jonas, *The Phenomenon of Life*, p. 22.

6. See Antonio Millán-Puelles, *The Theory of the Pure Object*, trans. and ed. by Jorge García-Gómez, in: *Philosophy and Realist Phenomenology. Studies of the International Academy of Philosophy in the Principality Liechtenstein*, vol. 2, eds. Rocco Buttiglione and Josef Seifert, The International Academy of Philosophy in the Principality Liechtenstein (Heidelberg: Universitätsverlag C. Winter, 1996).

7. See Josef Seifert, *Back to Things in Themselves: A Phenomenological Foundation for Classical Realism* (London: Routledge, 1987), and *Erkenntnis objektiver Wahrheit. Die Transzendenz des Menschen in der Erkenntnis* (Salzburg: A. Pustet, 2nd ed., 1976).

8. See Plato, *Phaedrus*, 245 e 2-6.

9. See Plato, *ibid.*, 245 c 5 – 246 a 1.

10. Aristotle, *De Anima*, Book 1, 403 b 25 ff.; and 404 a 8-9.

11. *Ibid.*, 406 a 1-5.

12. See Thomas Aquinas, *Summa Theologica*, Book 1, q. 18, a. 1, resp.

13. Max Scheler, *Die Stellung des Menschen im Kosmos*, (1928), in: Scheler, *Gesammelte Werke*, vol. 9, ed. Manfred Frings (Bern: A. Francke Verlag, 1976), p. 13. See also Scheler's "Biologievorlesung," *Schriften aus dem Nachlaß*, vol. 5, *Varia* (Bonn: Bouvier-Verlag, 1993), p. 314 ff.

14. Scheler, "Biologievorlesung," p. 314 ff., p. 324.

15. *Ibid.*, p. 327.

16. *Ibid.*, p. 328, pp. 342 ff., pp. 354 ff. See also Scheler, "Altern und Tod," *Schriften aus dem Nachlaß*, vol. 3 (Bonn: Bouvier-Verlag Herbert Grundmann, 1987), p. 260 ff.

17. Immanuel Kant, *Träume eines Geistersehers*, Akademieausgabe, vol. 4, p. 544.

18. Augustine, *De Civitate Dei*, Book 5, 9-10.

19. Augustine, *ibid.*, Book 5, 9.

20. See Plato, *Phaedrus*, 245, c 5 ff.

21. See Jonas, *The Phenomenon of Life*, pp. 3 ff.

22. See esp. *ibid.*, pp. 4, 38 ff.

23. *Ibid.*, pp. 12-16, 19-23, 25 f., 55 f.

24. Hans Jonas, *Macht oder Ohnmacht der Subjektivität? Das Leib-Seele-Problem im Vorfeld des Prinzips Verantwortung* (Frankfurt a. M.: Insel Verlag, 1981).

25. See also Gabriel Marcel, *Sein und Haben*, trans. Ernst Gehler (Paderborn: Ferdinand Schöningh, 2nd ed., 1968). Cf. Josef Seifert, *Leib und Seele: Ein Beitrag zur philosophischen Anthropologie* (Salzburg: A. Pustet, 1973), pp. 170-182, and

Josef Seifert, *Das Leib-Seele-Problem und die gegenwärtige philosophische Diskussion: Eine kritisch-systematische Analyse* (Darmstadt: Wissenschaftliche Buchgesellschaft, 2nd ed., 1989), pp. 158-162.

26. Jonas, *The Phenomenon of Life*, pp. 95-96.

27. *Ibid.*, p. 22.

28. See Josef Seifert, *Essere e persona: Verso una fondazione fenomenologica di una metafisica classica e personalistica* (Milan: Vita e Pensiero, 1989), chs. 8-15, and *ibid.*, ch. 10. See, besides Duns Scotus and Suarez's *Metaphysical Investigation V* "Individual Unity and Its Principle", trans. Jorge J. E. Gracia (Milwaukee: Marquette University Press, 1982), also Edith Stein, *Endliches und Ewiges Sein* (Freiburg: Herder, 3rd ed., 1986).

29. See Thomas Aquinas, *Summa Theologica*, Book 1, q. 18, a. 3, resp.

30. Aristotle, *Metaphysics*, Book 12, 1072 b 27 ff.

31. See Josef Seifert, *Erkenntnis objektiver Wahrheit: Die Transzendenz des Menschen in der Erkenntnis* (Salzburg: A. Pustet, 2nd ed., 1976), chs. 1-3.

32. George Edward Moore, *Principia Ethica* (1903) (London, 1971, 14th ed.), ch. 1.

33. See Josef Seifert, "Essence and Existence: A New Foundation of Classical Metaphysics on the Basis of 'Phenomenological Realism,' and a Critical Investigation of 'Existentialist Thomism'," *Aletheia* 1:1 (1977), pp. 17-157; 1:2 (1977), pp. 371-459, ch. 1. See also Josef Seifert, *Sein und Wesen* (Heidelberg, Universitätsverlag C. Winter, 1996), ch. 1.

34. In Aristotle, *De Anima*, 415 a 13-14; or *ibid.*, 415 a 14-20.

35. See Aristotle, *Posterior Analytics*, Book 2, 99 b 20 ff., 100 b 10 ff.

36. See on this Adolf Reinach, "Concerning Phenomenology," trans. Dallas Willard, *The Personalist*, 50 (Spring 1969), pp. 194-221, reprinted in *Perspectives in Philosophy*, ed. Robert N. Beck (New York: Holt, Reinhart, & Winston, 1961 and 1969); Reinach, "Über Phänomenologie," in: Adolf Reinach, *Sämtliche Werke.* Textkritische Ausgabe in zwei Bänden, vol. 1: *Die Werke*, Teil 1: Kritische Neuausgabe (1905-1914), Teil 2: Nachgelassene Texte (1906-1917), eds. Karl Schuhmann and Barry Smith (Munich and Vienna: Philosophia Verlag, 1989), pp. 531-550. See also Max Scheler, *Formalism in Ethics and Non-Formal Ethics of Values*, trans. Manfred S. Frings and Roger L. Funk (Evanston, Ill.: Northwestern University Press, 1973), esp. the part "Formalism and Apriorism"; Dietrich von Hildebrand, *What Is Philosophy?* (Milwaukee: Bruce, 1960; 2nd ed. Chicago: Franciscan Herald Press, 1973; 3rd ed., with a new introductory essay by Josef Seifert, London and New York: Routledge, 1991), esp. pp. xii ff., and ch. 4; Fritz Wenisch, *Die Philosophie und ihre Methode* (Salzburg: A. Pustet, 1976); Seifert, *Back to Things in Themselves.*

37. See George Edward Moore, *Principia Ethica*, ch. 1; Dietrich von Hildebrand, *Ethics* (Chicago: Franciscan Herald Press, 2nd ed., 1978), chs. 1-10.

38. Johann Wolfgang von Goethe, *Farbenlehre*, in: Goethe, *Sämmtliche Werke* in 40 Bänden (Stuttgart and Tübingen: J. G. Cotta'scher Verlag, 1840), 2. Abtheilung, no. 177, vol. 37, p. 68. Here, and in the following quotes from Goethe, I use my own translation from the German original.

39. *Goethes Gespräche mit Eckermann* (Leipzig: Insel-Verlag, 1921), p. 448.

40. Goethe, *Farbenlehre*, no. 177, vol. 37, p. 68.

41. See also Goethe, *Gespräche mit Eckermann*, p. 639. Cf. also *ibid.*, pp. 432, 514, 567, 591.

42. *Farbenlehre*, Introduction, vol. 37, p. 9.

43. *Ibid.*, 5. Abtheilung, nos. 716, 720, vol. 37, pp. 232-233.

44. *Ibid.*, no. 175, vol. 37, p. 67.

45. *Ibid.*

46. For example *ibid.*, vol. 37, no. 247, p. 90. See also Hans Leisegang, *Goethes Denken* (Leipzig: Felix Meiner, 1932), pp. 157-159; 168 f.

47. See Goethe, *Farbenlehre*, no. 177, vol. 37, p. 68.

48. *Ibid.*, vol. 37, no. 752, p. 246.

49. *Ibid.*, 752, p. 246.

50. *Ibid.*, 754, p. 247.

51. See Goethe, *Nachträge zur Farbenlehre*, *ibid.*, vol. 40, pp. 423-425.

52. Cf. Helmut Plessner, *Die Stufen des Organischen und der Mensch: Einleitung in die philosophische Anthropologie* (Berlin/New York: Walter de Gruyter, 3rd unchanged ed., 1975; 1st ed. 1928), p. 108, n.

53. Plessner, *Die Stufen*, p. 107.

54. See against such a reductionism Goethe, "Über den Granit", quoted by Leisegang, in his *Goethes Denken*, p. 90.

55. Goethe, *Farbenlehre*, vol. 37, no. 754, p. 247.

56. See Anselm of Canterbury, *Monologion*, 15. Thomas Aquinas, *De Veritate*, Q. 1. Duns Scotus, *Oxon* (or *Ordinatio*) 1, d. 1-3, ff., *Oxon.* 1, d. 8, q. 1, n. 7; 4, d. 8, q. 1; 1, d. 7, q. un.; *Quodl.* q. 5, n. 9; *ibid.*, n. 13; 25, 216a. Allan Wolter, *The Transcendentals and Their Function in the Metaphysics of Duns Scotus* (St. Bonaventure University, N. Y.: Franciscan Institute Publications, 1946). Seifert, *Essere e persona*, ch. 5.

57. See also Josef Seifert, "Die verschiedenen Bedeutungen von 'Sein': Dietrich von Hildebrand als Metaphysiker und Martin Heideggers Vorwurf der Seinsvergessenheit," in: *Wahrheit, Wert und Sein: Festgabe für Dietrich von Hildebrand zum 80. Geburtstag*, ed. Balduin Schwarz (Regensburg: Habbel, 1970), pp. 301-332. See Seifert, "Zur Herkunft des Glaubens. Gründe und Hintergründe. Reflexionen über das Problem einer Theodizee angesichts der Leiden und Übel in der Welt," *Glaube im Unglauben der Zeit* (Augsburg: Dialogsekretariat, 1983).

58. Dietrich von Hildebrand, *Ethics*, chs. 1-3. Cf. also John F. Crosby, "The Idea of Value and the Reform of the Traditional Metaphysics of Bonum," *Aletheia*, 1 (1977), pp. 231-339.

59. Cf., for example, R. W. Southern, *Saint Anselm: A Portrait in a Landscape* (Cambridge, England: Cambridge University Press, 1991).

60. See Wolter, *The Transcendentals and Their Function in the Metaphysics of Duns Scotus.* See Josef Seifert, *Essere e persona*, ch. 5.

61. See Josef Seifert, "Essere persona come perfezione pura," *De Homine* (Rome: Herder/Università Lateranense, 1994).

62. See Seifert, *Essere e persona*, ch. 5.

63. Anselm of Canterbury, *Monologion*, ch. 15, 29-31 (my translation).

64. Cf. also Bonaventure, *Opera*, vol. 3, p. 617 d. 1.

65. See for an ample bibliography and proof of this Giovanni Reale, *Verso una nuova interpretazione di Platone* (Milan: Jaca Book, 16th ed., 1996), chs. 15 20.

66. See Aristotle, *Metaphysics*, Book 12, 1072b 27 ff.

67. See Seifert, *Essere e persona*, ch. 10.

68. See also Marcel, *Sein und Haben*, pp. 213 ff.

69. See Josef Seifert, *Essere e persona*, ch. 10-15.

70. See Josef Seifert, *Gott als Gottesbeweis. Eine phänomenologische Neubegründung des ontologischen Arguments* (Heidelberg: Universitätsverlag C. Winter, 1996).

71. See Josef Seifert, "Is 'Brain Death' actually Death?", *The Monist*, 76 (1993), pp. 175-202.

72. See Conrad-Martius, *Die Seele der Pflanze*, in: Hedwig Conrad-Martius, *Schriften zur Philosophie*, ed. Eberhard Avé-Lallement, vol. 1 (Munich: Kösel, 1963), pp. 276-362. See Seifert, *Leib und Seele.*

73. Seifert, *Essere e persona*, ch. 7.

74. *Ibid.*, ch. 10.

75. Aristotle, *De Anima* 412 a 14 f.

76. See also Georg Wilhelm Friedrich Hegel, *Vorlesungen über die Geschichte der Philosophie*, in: *Werke*, ed. Glockner (Stuttgart: Friedrich Fromann/Günter Holzboog, 1959), vol. 18, p. 343. See also Robert Spaemann, "Zum Begriff des Lebens," p. 86. See likewise Spaemann and Reinhard Löw, *Die Frage Wozu? Geschichte und Wiederentdeckung des teleologischen Denkens* (Munich: Bertelsmann, 1981). See also Löw, *Philosophie des Organischen* (Munich: C. Bertelsmann, 1980).

77. Georg Wilhelm Friedrich Hegel, *Wissenschaft der Logik*, vol. 2, ed. Glockner (Stuttgart: Friedrich Fromann/Günter Holzboog, 4th ed., 1964).

78. See Ludger Hölscher, *The Reality of the Mind: St. Augustine's Arguments for the Human Soul as Spiritual Substance* (London: Routledge and Kegan Paul, 1986); and Seifert, *Back to Things in Themselves*, ch. 4 ff.

79. Martin Heidegger, *Sein und Zeit* (my translation), quoted by Spaemann in: "Zum Begriff des Lebens," p. 84.

80. See Balduin Schwarz, *Wahrheit, Irrtum und Verirrungen. Die sechs großen Krisen und sieben Ausfahrten der abendländischen Philosophie*, in: *Philosophie und Realistische Phänomenologie. Studien der Internationalen Akademie für Philosophie im Fürstentum Liechtenstein*, eds. Rocco Buttiglione and Josef Seifert, vol. 5 (Heidelberg: Universitätsverlag C. Winter, 1996).

81. See Dietrich von Hildebrand, *What Is Philosophy?*, chs. 2-4.

82. See Josef Seifert, "Objektivismus in der Wissenschaft und Grundlagen philosophischer Rationalität. Kritische Überlegungen zu Karl Poppers Wissenschafts-, Erkenntnis- und Wahrheitstheorie," *Die Gedankenwelt Sir Karl Poppers: Kritischer Rationalismus im Dialog*, eds. Norbert Leser, Josef Seifert, K. Plitzner (Heidelberg: Uni-

versitätsverlag C. Winter, 1991), pp. 31-74, and "Diskussion," pp. 75-82. See also Josef Seifert, "Wissen und Wahrheit in Naturwissenschaften, Philosophie und Glauben," *Naturwissenschaft und Weltbild*, eds. H.-C. Reichel, E. Prat de la Riba (Vienna: Hölder-Pichler-Tempsky, 1992).

83. See Reinach, "Über Phänomenologie"; von Hildebrand, *What Is Philosophy?*, ch. 4; and Seifert, *Back to Things in Themselves.*

84. See Seifert, "Objektivismus in der Wissenschaft und Grundlagen philosophischer Rationalität."

85. See von Hildebrand, *What Is Philosophy?*, esp. ch. 4; see also Balduin Schwarz, "Dietrich von Hildebrands Lehre von der Soseinserfahrung in ihren philosophiegeschichtlichen Zusammenhängen," *Wahrheit, Wert und Sein*, pp. 33-51. See also Seifert, *Back to Things in Themselves*, chs. 1, 2, 4-5, and Seifert, *Erkenntnis objektiver Wahrheit*, Part 2, ch. 1.

Chapter Two

1. See Max Scheler, *Der Formalismus in der Ethik und die materiale Wertethik* (Bern and Munich: Francke, 5th ed., 1966), pp. 124, 172, 281.

2. See also Elisabeth Lukas, *Psychotherapie in Würde. Sinnorientierte Lebenshilfe nach Viktor E. Frankl* (Berlin/Munich: Quintessenz, 1994).

3. George Edward Moore, *Principia Ethica* (1903); 14th ed. (London, 1971), chs. 1, 6; p. 6.

4. Cf. Josef Seifert, "Essence and Existence: A New Foundation of Classical Metaphysics on the Basis of 'Phenomenological Realism,' and a Critical Investigation of 'Existentialist Thomism'," *Aletheia* 1:1 (1977), pp. 17-157; 1:2 (1977), pp. 371-459, ch. 1. See also Seifert, *Sein und Wesen* (Heidelberg: Universitätsverlag C. Winter, 1996), ch. 1.

5. Seifert, "Essence and Existence," pp. 56 ff.

6. See Josef Seifert, "Genetischer Code und Teleologie, Information, Kausalität und Finalität: Kurzer Abriß naturwissenschaftlicher genetischer Erkenntnisse als Hintergrund neuer philosophischer Probleme," *Arzt und Christ*, 34 (1988), pp. 185-200.

7. For example, N. Jessop, in *Zoology: Theory and Problems.*

8. Carroll Lane Fenton, "Living Things," *Compton's Interactive Encyclopedia*, 1995.

9. See Aristotle, *De Anima*, Book 3, 433 b 23 ff.

10. In Seifert, "Genetischer Code und Teleologie," pp. 187 ff.

11. See Bruno Vollmert, "Die Frage nach der Entstehung der Lebewesen in naturwissenschaftlicher Sicht. Darwins Lehre im Lichte der makromolekularen Chemie," *Schriftenreihe der Gustav-Siewerth-Akademie*, vol. 5 (Weilheim-Bierbronnen, 1995), esp. p. 9.

12. Robert Spaemann, "Zum Begriff des Lebens," *Sichtweisen der Psychiatrie*, eds. G. Kockott, Hermann Joseph Muller (Munich: Zuckerschwertverlag, 1994), p. 86.

13. See Seifert, "Essence and Existence," particularly ch. 1.

14. See Hans Driesch, *Philosophie des Organischen* (Gifford Lectures) (Leipzig: Verlag von Quelle & Meyer, 4th ed., 1928), pp. 109 ff.

15. *Ibid.*, pp. 124 ff.

16. *Ibid.*, pp. 129 ff.

17. *Ibid.*, pp. 175 ff.

18. See also Hans André, *Urbild und Ursache in der Biologie* (Munich/Berlin, 1931). See Klaus Michael Meyer-Abich, "Der Holismus im 20. Jahrhundert," *Klassiker der Naturphilosophie: Von den Vorsokratikern bis zur Kopenhagener Schule*, ed. Gernot Böhme (Munich: Verlag C. H. Beck, 1989), esp. pp. 314 ff., 318 ff., 326 ff.

19. Alejandro Serani, *et al.*, *Nociones fundamentales y aplicadas de etica clinica* (Santiago, Chile: Catholic University of Chile, 1991).

20. See Kenneth B. Storey and Janet M. Storey, "Frozen and Alive," *Scientific America* (1990), pp. 62-67.

21. *Ibid.*, p. 63.

22. *Ibid.*, p. 64.

23. *Ibid*, p. 67.

24. *Ibid.*

25. *Ibid.*, pp. 62-63.

26. Cf. Adolf Reinach, "Concerning Phenomenology," trans. from the German ("Über Phänomenologie") by Dallas Willard, *The Personalist*, 50 (Spring 1969), pp. 194-221. Reprinted in *Perspectives in Philosophy*, ed. Robert N. Beck (New York: Holt, Reinhart, & Winston, 1961 and 1969); Dietrich von Hildebrand, *What Is Philosophy?* (Milwaukee: Bruce, 1960; 2nd ed. Chicago: Franciscan Herald Press, 1973; 3rd ed., with a new introductory essay by Josef Seifert, London and New York: Routledge, 1991), ch. 4.

27. See Helmuth Plessner, *Die Stufen des Organischen und der Mensch: Einleitung in die philosophische Anthropologie* (Berlin/New York: Walter de Gruyter, 3rd unchanged ed., 1975), 1st ed. 1928, p. 107.

28. See, for example, Descartes, part 5 of the *Discours de la méthode*, in: *Oeuvres de Descartes*, eds. Charles Adam and Paul Tannery, vol. 6, 1-78. See also Descartes, *Treatise on Man* and numerous passages in his correspondence. See likewise, Descartes, *Passions of the Soul*, vol. 1, 50; *Letter to the Marquis of Newcastle* of November 1646. These and many other texts are collected in Leonora Cohen Rosenfield, *From Beast-Machine to Man-Machine. Animal Soul in French Letters from Descartes to LaMettrie* (New York: Oxford University Press, 1941). See also Hans Jonas, *The Phenomenon of Life: Toward a Philosophical Biology* (New York: Harper & Row, 1966), pp. 55 ff.

29. Josef Simon, "Leben," *Handbuch philosophischer Grundbegriffe*, vol. 3, eds. Hermann Krings, Hans Michael Baumgartner, and C. Wild (Munich: Kösel, 1973), p. 847.

30. Descartes, *Letter to Mersenne*, 13 July 1640.

31. Descartes, *Letter to Mersenne*, 11 June 1640.

32. Alice von Hildebrand, "On the Pseudo-Obvious," *Wahrheit, Wert und Sein: Festgabe für Dietrich von Hildebrand zum 80. Geburtstag*, ed. Balduin Schwarz (Regensburg: Josef Habbel, 1970), pp. 25-32.

33. See Aristotle, *De Anima*, Book 2, 412b 11 ff.

34. *Ibid.*, 414a 19-20.

35. See also Josef Seifert, "Organismus," *Evangelisches Lexikon für Theologie und Gemeinde*, eds. H. Burkhardt and U. Swarat, vol. 3 (Wuppertal and Zurich: R. Brackhausverlag, 1994), pp. 1484-1485.

36. See Josef Seifert, *Erkenntnis objektiver Wahrheit: Die Transzendenz des Menschen in der Erkenntnis* (Salzburg: A. Pustet, 2nd ed., 1976), Part 2.

37. Wojciech Zełaniec, "Fathers, Kings, and Promises: Husserl and Reinach on the *A Priori*," *Husserl Studies*, 9 (1992), pp. 147-149, 160 ff., and 172-173.

38. Plato, *Phaedrus*, 245c 5 ff.

39. Aristotle, *De Anima*, 404a 9; 406a 1-5. See likewise St. Thomas Aquinas, *Summa Theologica*, Book 1, q. 18.

40. Immanuel Kant, *Träume eines Geistersehers*, Akademieausgabe, vol. 4, p. 544.

41. See Hedwig Conrad-Martius, *Die Seele der Pflanze*, in: Conrad-Martius, *Schriften zur Philosophie*, ed. Eberhard Avé-Lallement, vol. 1 (Munich: Kösel, 1963), pp. 276-362, pp. 313 ff.

42. Aristotle, *Eudemian Ethics*, 1223 a.

43. See Augustine, *De libero Arbitrio*, Book 2, and *De Civitate Dei*, Book 5.

44. See Bonaventure, *Opera omnia*, vol. 2, p. 744 arg. 7.

45. See Reinhard Löw, *Leben aus dem Labor: Gentechnologie und Verantwortung – Biologie und Moral* (Munich: C. Bertelsmann, 1985); Löw, *Philosophie des Organischen* (Munich: C. Bertelsmann, 1980); Löw, "Herder und die Evolution," in: Reinhard Löw (ed.), *Oikeiosis. Festschrift für Robert Spaemann* (Weinheim: VCH Verlagsgesellschaft, 1987), pp. 131-147; see also Robert Spaemann and Reinhard Löw, *Die Frage Wozu? Geschichte und Wiederentdeckung des teleologischen Denkens* (Munich: Bertelsmann, 1981). Also Johannes von Uexcüll, *Umwelt und Innenwelt der Tiere* (Berlin: Verlag 5. Julius Springer, 1921), Hans Driesch, *Philosophie des Organischen* (Gifford Lectures) (Leipzig: Verlag von Quelle & Meyer, 4th ed., 1928), Claude Bernard, *Leçons sur les phénomènes de la vie communs aux animaux et aux végétaux* (Paris: J.-B. Baillière, 1879-1985; Paris: J. Vrin, 1966, reprod. photomécanique de l'éd. de 1885), and Etienne Gilson, *D'Aristote à Darwin et retour* (Paris: J. Vrin, 1971). See also Eugenio Rignano, *Qu'est-ce que la vie? Nouveaux essais de synthèse biologique* (Paris: Librairie Félix Alcan, 1926), pp. 1 ff.

46. Johannes von Uexcüll, *Umwelt und Innenwelt der Tiere*; F. J. J. Buytendijk, *Mensch und Tier: Ein Beitrag zur vergleichenden Psychologie* (Hamburg: Rowohlt, 1958).

47. See T. Purola, "A Systems Approach to Health and Health Policy," *Medical Care*, 10:5 (1972).

48. See Hedwig Conrad-Martius, "Präformismus in der Natur," in: Conrad-Martius, *Schriften zur Philosophie*, pp. 153-173; and Paulina Taboada, "Bedeutung

der 'allgemeinen Systemtheorie' in der heutigen Debatte über den Gesundheitsbegriff' (Schaan, Principality of Liechtenstein: The International Academy of Philosophy, 1995, forthcoming), pp. 19 ff.

49. Cf. Conrad-Martius, "Präformismus," p. 160. See also Conrad-Martius, *ibid.*, p. 159.

50. Kant, *Kritik der Urteilskraft*, B 287-289.

51. Conrad-Martius, *Die Seele der Pflanze*, p. 284.

52. Aristotle, *De Anima*, Book 2, 415 b 12-14.

53. Max Scheler, *Die Stellung des Menschen im Kosmos* (1928), in: Scheler, *Gesammelte Werke*, vol. 9, ed. Manfred Frings (Bern: A. Francke Verlag, 1976), p. 12.

54. Aristotle, *De Anima.* See also Franz Brentano, *Psychology from an Empirical Standpoint* (1973) (*Psychologie vom empirischen Standpunkt*, vol. 1-2, ed. Oskar Kraus, unveränderter Nachdruck der Ausgabe von 1924, 1st ed. 1874, Hamburg: Felix Meiner, 1973), p. 179.

55. See Seifert, *Leib und Seele*, pp. 71 ff.

56. See Conrad-Martius, *Die Seele der Pflanze*, esp. pp. 337, and 327, note 51.

57. See Storey, "Frozen and Alive," p. 62.

58. *Ibid.*, p. 62.

59. *Ibid.* See David Weissmann, *Dispositional Properties* (Carbondale and Edwardsville, Ill.: Southern Illinois University Press, 1965), p. 67.

60. *Ibid.*, pp. 129 ff., 159-193.

61. My translation of Plato, *Phaedo*, 105b f.

62. See Plato, *Phaedo* 105 f., and *Phaedrus* 245c 5 ff.

63. Aristotle, *De Anima*, Book 2, 412 a 1-5; 14-15; 17-21.

64. See J. L. Mackie, *Ethics: Inventing Right and Wrong* (New York: Penguin Books, 1977), pp. 39 ff., 147.

65. *Ibid.*, p. 39.

66. *Ibid.*

67. John Finnis, *Fundamentals of Ethics* (Oxford: Clarendon Press, 1983), p. 59.

68. See Josef Seifert, *Back to Things in Themselves: A Phenomenological Foundation for Classical Realism* (London: Routledge, 1987); and Seifert, *Erkenntnis objektiver Wahrheit.*

69. Cf. Bonaventure, *Opera omnia*, vol. 1, p. 625, arg. 4.

70. *Ibid.*, vol. 3, p. 445 3*.

71. Aristotle, *De Anima* ch. 4, 4, 415b 13.

72. Thomas Aquinas, *Summa Theologica*, Book 1, q. 18 a. 2, 3. Cf. *ibid.*, *ad primum* and *ad tertium.*

73. Bonaventure, *Opera*, Book 2, p. 49 f.

74. *Ibid.*, vol. 3, p. 451 f. 4.

75. See Seifert, "Essence and Existence," ch. 1 and chs. 4-7.

76. See Thomas Aquinas, *Summa Theologica*, Book 1, q. 18, 2c; q. 57, 1, 2m.

77. Cf. Bonaventure, *Opera*, vol. 2, p. 562 b, I, p. 767 5*.

78. Seifert, "Essence and Existence," chs. 8 and 9.

79. See Bonaventure, *Opera*, vol. 2, p. 562 b.

80. *Ibid.*, vol. 2, p. 641 arg. 2.

81. *Ibid.*, vol. 12, p. 864 f. 2.

82. See Alejandro Serani, *L'Etre vivant selon la perspective réaliste: Propos pour les fondements d'une biophilosophie* (Toulouse: Université de Toulouse le Mirail U.E.R. d'Etudes philosophiques et politiques, 1986).

83. Plato, *Phaedo* 106b 4-5.

84. *Ibid.*, 105 b 5 – 107 a 1; 106 b 4-5. See Josef Seifert, *Das Leib-Seele Problem und die gegenwärtige philosophische Diskussion. Eine kritisch-systematische Analyse* (Darmstadt: Wissenschaftliche Buchgesellschaft, 2nd ed., 1989).

85. Cf. George Edward Moore, *Principia Ethica*, ch. 1.

86. Cf. Dietrich von Hildebrand, *Ethics* (Chicago: Franciscan Herald Press, 2nd ed., 1978), chs. 1-3, 17-18. See also Josef Seifert, "Die verschiedenen Bedeutungen von 'Sein' – Dietrich von Hildebrand als Metaphysiker und Martin Heideggers Vorwurf der 'Seinsvergessenheit'," *Wahrheit, Wert und Sein*, pp. 301-332. See likewise, John Crosby, "The Idea of Value and the Reform of the Traditional Metaphysics of Bonum," *Aletheia*, 1 (1977), pp. 231-339.

87. See Bonaventure, *Opera*, vol. 1, p. 625, arg. 4. See also Edith Stein, *Endliches und ewiges Sein* (Freiburg: Herder, 3rd ed., 1986), pp. 390-392. See also Scheler, *Der Formalismus*, p. 280-281.

88. See *ibid.*, pp. 280 ff.

89. See Jay Roth, "The Piling of Coincidence on Coincidence," *Cosmos, Bios, Theos: Scientists Reflect on Science, God, and the Origins of the Universe, Life, and Homo sapiens*, eds. Henry Margenau and Roy Abraham Varghese (LaSalle, Ill.: Open Court, 1992), p. 199.

90. Henry Margenau, "The Laws of Nature are Created by God," *Cosmos, Bios, Theos*, eds. Margenau and Varghese (LaSalle, Ill.: Open Court, 1992), p. 63.

91. Johannes von Uexcüll, *Umwelt und Innenwelt der Tiere*, pp. 19 ff.

92. Cf. Erwin Schrödinger, *What Is Life?* (Cambridge, England: Cambridge University Press, 1944), chs. 6-7.

93. See Ludwig von Bertalanffy, *General System Theory* (New York, 1972).

94. See Schrödinger, *Was ist Leben?*, ch. 6, pp. 120 ff., esp. pp. 128 ff.; also p. 134.

95. Roger Penrose, *The Emperor's New Mind: Concerning Computers, Minds, and the Law of Physics* (Oxford: Oxford University Press, 6th ed., 1989), p. 302.

96. Max Planck, *Vorlesungen über Thermodynamik* 1930 (Berlin: de Gruyter, 11th enlarged ed. 1964).

97. Ilya Prigogine, *From Being to Becoming: Time and Complexity in the Physical Sciences* (New York: W. H. Freeman, 1980).

98. See Schrödinger, *What Is Life?*, p. 139.

99. *Ibid.*, ch. 6, no. 57, pp. 127; no. 65, pp. 138 f.

100. See *ibid.*, 65, p. 139.

101. Margenau and Varghese (eds.), *Cosmos*, *Bios*, *Theos*, p. 29.

102. See Gregory J. Chaitin, "Zahlen und Zufall – Algorithmische Informationstheorie: Neueste Resultate über die Grundlagen der Mathematik," *Naturwissenschaft und Weltbild*, eds. H.-C. Reichel, E. Prat de la Riba (Vienna: Hölder-Pichler-Tempsky, 1992), pp. 30-44.

103. See also James P. Crutchfield, "Chaos 1: Chaos and Complexity," *Handbook of Metaphysics and Ontology*, eds. Hans Burkhardt and Barry Smith, 1 (Munich/Philadelphia/Vienna: Philosophia, 1991), p. 142.

104. Ilya Prigogine, "The Universe Started from an Instability in the Quantum Vacuum," *Cosmos*, *Bios*, *Theos*, p. 189. Cf. also Friedrich Cramer, *Chaos und Unordnung* (Stuttgart: DVA, 1988).

105. Robert Jastrow, "What Forces Filled the Universe with Energy Fifteen Billion Years Ago?", *Cosmos*, *Bios*, *Theos*, esp. p. 47.

106. See Eugene Linden, "Can We Really Understand Matter?", *Science* (16 April 1990), p. 43.

107. Adam Morton, "Chaos 2: Fractals and Chaos," *Handbook of Metaphysics and Ontology*, p. 145.

108. Cf. Seifert, *Leib und Seele*, pp. xxv ff., 71-115.

109. Margenau, Varghese (eds.), *Cosmos.*

110. See Morton, "Chaos 2," p. 145. Cf. also *ibid.*, pp. 144-146.

111. Crutchfield, "Chaos 1," p. 141.

112. *Ibid.*, p. 142.

113. Schrödinger, *Was ist Leben?*, ch. 7, nos. 66-71, in the German edition pp. 140-147.

114. *Ibid*, no. 68, p. 144.

115. *Ibid.*, no.71, p. 147.

116. See Reinach, "Concerning Phenomenology." See also von Hildebrand, *What Is Philosophy?*, pp. xii ff., and ch. 4; Seifert, *Back to Things in Themselves*, esp. ch. 1.

117. See, for example, Andrej D. Linde, "Chaotic Inflation," *Physics Letters* 129B: 177-181 (1983). See also S. H. Keller, M. A. Stone, and A. Fine, "Models, Chaos, and Goodness of Fit," *Philosophical Topics*, 18:2 (1990), pp. 85-105. See likewise, Willem B. Drees, *Beyond the Big Bang: Quantum Cosmologies and God* (LaSalle, Ill.: Open Court, 1990), p. 48.

118. Ilya Prigogine and Edgard Gunzig, "Cosmology 2: The Reasons for the Cosmos," *Handbook of Metaphysics and Ontology*, vol. 1, p. 186. Cf. also *ibid.*, pp. 186-189.

119. See John Crosby, "Evolutionism and the Ontology of the Human Person," *Review of Politics*, 38 (April 1976), pp. 208-243.

120. Cf. Josef Seifert, "Friedrich Nietzsches Verzweiflung an der Wahrheit und sein Kampf gegen die Wahrheit," *Rehabilitierung der Philosophie*, ed. Dietrich von Hildebrand (Regensburg: J. Habbel, 1974), pp. 197 ff.

121. See, for example, Drees, *Beyond the Big Bang*, pp. 22 ff. See also *ibid.*, pp. 18 ff.

122. Giovanni Reale, *Platone. Verso una nuova interpretazione di Platone* (Milan: Jaca Book, 16th ed., 1996); Giovanni Reale, *Platon*, trans. Ludger Hölscher, with an introduction by Hans Krämer, ed. and with a postface by J. Seifert (Paderborn: Schöningh, 1993), chs. 15-21.

123. See Cornelio Fabro, *L'uomo e il Rischio di Dio* (Rome: Editrice Studium, 1967); Josef Seifert, *Essere e persona: Verso una fondazione fenomenologica di una metafisica classica e personalistica* (Milan: Vita e Pensiero, 1989), chs. 10-15; and Seifert, *Leib und Seele*, chs. 1-2.

124. See Seifert, *Leib und Seele*, pp. 140-159.

125. Cf. also Drees, *Beyond the Big Bang*, pp. 24 ff.

126. Seifert, *Essere e persona*, chs. 10-15.

127. See von Hildebrand, *What Is Philosophy?*, esp. pp. xii ff., and ch. 4; Seifert, *Back to Things in Themselves*, chs. 1-2.

128. Scheler, *Formalism*, p. 68.

129. See Josef Seifert, "Is 'Brain Death' actually Death?", *The Monist*, 76 (1993), pp. 175-202; Seifert, "Is 'Brain Death' actually Death? A Critique of Redefining Man's Death in Terms of 'Brain Death'," *Working Group on the Determination of Brain Death and Its Relationship to Human Death*, eds. Robert J. White, Heinz Angstwurm, Ignacio Carasco de Paola (Vatican City: Pontifical Academy of the Sciences, 1992), pp. 95-143; Seifert, "Hirntod: Ein Beitrag zur Kritik der philosophischen Korrumpierung der medizinischen Technik," *Ethik und Technik* (Zurich: M&T ed., 1988); and Seifert, "Ist 'Hirntod' wirklich der Tod?", *WMW Diskussionsforum Medizinische Ethik*, 4 (October 1990), D 2. Cf. also Seifert, "Abortion and Euthanasia as Legal and as Moral Issues: Some Reflections on the Relationship between Morality, Church and State," *Bioethics Update, Proceedings of the 1987 Annual Conference on Bioethics*, ed. N. Tonti-Filippini (Melbourne: St. Vincent's Bioethics Centre, 1988), pp. 162-212.

130. See Seifert, *Back to Things in Themselves*, chs. 4-5.

131. See von Hildebrand, *What Is Philosophy?*; Seifert, *Leib und Seele*, "Prolegomena."

132. See Conrad-Martius, *Seele der Pflanze*.

Chapter Three

1. Hans Jonas, "Against the Stream: Comments on the Definition and Redefinition of Death," in *Philosophical Essays: From Ancient Creed to Technological Man* (Chicago and London: The University of Chicago Press, 1974); Jonas, *Technik, Medizin und Ethik: Zur Praxis des Prinzips Verantwortung* (Frankfurt a. M.: Insel Verlag, 1985); see also Jonas, "Gehirntod und menschliche Organbank: Zur pragmatischen Umdefinierung des Todes," in: Jonas, *Technik, Medizin und Ethik*, pp. 219-241. See also Josef Seifert, "Is 'Brain Death' actually Death? A Critique of Redefining Man's Death in Terms of 'Brain Death'," *Working Group on the Determination of Brain Death and Its Relationship to Human Death*, eds. Robert J. White, Heinz Angstwurm,

Ignacio Carasco de Paola (Vatican City: Pontifical Academy of the Sciences, 1992), pp. 95-143; "Is 'Brain Death' actually Death?", *The Monist*, 76 (1993), pp. 175-202; "Hirntod: Ein Beitrag zur Kritik der philosophischen Korrumpierung der medizinischen Technik," *Ethik und Technik* (Zurich: M&T ed., 1988); "Ist 'Hirntod' wirklich der Tod?", *Ethik und Technik*; "Erklären heute Medizin und Gesetze Lebende zu Toten?", *Organspende: Kritische Ansichten zur Transplantationsmedizin*, eds. R. Greinert and G. Wuttke (Göttingen: Lamuv Verlag, 1991), pp. 185-208; "Menschenwürde und unbedingte Achtung menschlichen Lebens: Einige Fragen der Bioethik und die Grundlagen der Moral," *Essener Gespräche zum Thema Staat und Kirche*, 22 (Aschendorff, 1988).

2. Bonaventure, *Commentary on the Sentences* (*Opera*, vol. 3, p. 38 a).

3. *Ibid*., vol. 1, p. 170 f. 3.

4. See Augustine, *De Trinitate*, Book 10, x, 14. Cf. also Ludger Hölscher, *The Reality of the Mind: St. Augustine's Arguments for the Human Soul as Spiritual Substance* (London: Routledge and Kegan Paul, 1986).

5. Cf. Karol Wojtyła, *The Acting Person* (Boston: Reidel, 1979).

6. See Josef Seifert, *Leib und Seele: Ein Beitrag zur philosophischen Anthropologie* (Salzburg: A. Pustet, 1973); *Das Leib-Seele Problem und die gegenwärtige philosophische Diskussion Person: eine kritisch-systematische Analyse* (Darmstadt: Wissenschaftliche Buchgesellschaft, 2nd ed. 1989), pp. 111 ff., 180 ff.; cf. also Hölscher, *The Reality of the Mind.*

7. See Aristotle, *Metaphysics; Categories.* See also Josef Seifert, *Essere e persona: Verso una fondazione fenomenologica di una metafisica classica e personalistica* (Milan: Vita e Pensiero, 1989), ch. 8.

8. See Thomas Aquinas, *De Ente et Essentia;* see also Josef Seifert, "Essence and Existence: A New Foundation of Classical Metaphysics on the Basis of 'Phenomenological Realism,' and a Critical Investigation of 'Existentialist Thomism'," *Aletheia*, 1:1 (1977), pp. 17-157; 1:2 (1977), pp. 371-459, chs. 1, 2, 4, 5.

9. Roderick M. Chisholm, *Person and Object* (London: Allen & Unwin, 1976); *The First Person* (Minneapolis: University of Minnesota Press, 1982); "Brentano's Conception of Substance and Accident," *Die Philosophie Franz Brentanos* (*Grazer philosophische Studien*) (Amsterdam: Rodopi, 1978), pp. 197-210.

10. See Roderick Chisholm, "Is There a Mind-Body Problem?", *Philosophic Exchange*, 2 (1978), pp. 25-32; and Seifert, *Das Leib-Seele Problem*, pp. 65, 80, 123, 129.

11. See Max Scheler, *Die Stellung des Menschen im Kosmos* (1928), in: Scheler, *Gesammelte Werke*, vol. 9, ed. Manfred Frings (Bern: A. Francke Verlag, 1976), pp. 7-72, p. 39.

12. Gottfried Wilhelm Leibniz, *Monadology*, no. 17.

13. See Chisholm, *Person and Object.*

14. See Aristotle, *De Anima*, Book 1, 407 a 7 ff.

15. Hans Jonas, *Macht oder Ohnmacht der Subjektivität?*

16. James P. Crutchfield, "Chaos 1," *Handbook of Metaphysics and Ontology*, eds. Hans Burkhardt and Barry Smith, 1 (Munich/Philadelphia/Vienna: Philosophia, 1991), p. 143.

17. Max Scheler, *Formalism in Ethics and Non-Formal Ethics of Values*, trans. Manfred S. Frings and Roger L. Funk (Evanston, Ill.: Northwestern University Press, 1973), p. 289.

18. See the following works by Dietrich von Hildebrand: *Ethics* (Chicago: Franciscan Herald Press, 2nd ed., 1978), chs. 17, 26-28; *Das Wesen der Liebe*, in: Hildebrand, *Gesammelte Werke*, vol. 3 (Regensburg/Stuttgart: Habbel/Kohlhammer, 1971), chs. 1-2.

19. See Seifert, "Essence and Existence", pp. 379-385.

20. See on this H. T. Engelhardt, Jr., *The Foundation of Bioethics* (New York and Oxford: Oxford University Press, 1986, 2nd ed. 1996).

21. See Seifert, *Das Leib-Seele Problem*; Seifert, "Is 'Brain Death' actually Death?".

22. See Seifert, *Das Leib-Seele Problem.*

Chapter Four

1. Peter Singer, *Muß dieses Kind am Leben bleiben?* (Erlangen: Harald Fischer Verlag, 1993).

2. See Dietrich von Hildebrand, *Ethics* (Chicago: Franciscan Herald Press, 2nd ed., 1978), chs. 1-3, 4-7, 9, 17-18. Von Hildebrand, *Moralia*, in: Hildebrand, *Gesammelte Werke*, vol. 9 (Regensburg: Verlag Josef Habbel, 1980). See also John F. Crosby, "The Idea of Value and the Reform of the Traditional Metaphysics of Bonum," *Aletheia*, 1 (1977), pp. 231 ff.

3. Immanuel Kant, *Foundations of the Metaphysics of Morals*, A 68, p. 48.

4. Alexander of Hales, *Glossa*, 1, 23, 9.

5. Kant, *Grundlegung zur Metaphysik der Sitten* (1785), 434.

6. Kant, *ibid.*; *Metaphysik der Sitten* (1797).

7. Cf. Josef Seifert, "Absolute Moral Obligations toward Finite Goods as Foundation of Intrinsically Right and Wrong Actions: A Critique of Consequentialist Teleological Ethics: Destruction of Ethics through Moral Theology?", *Anthropos*, 1 (1985), pp. 57-94.

8. Anselm of Canterbury, *Proslogium*, chs. 2-3.

9. See on this Josef Seifert, *Gott als Gottesbeweis. Eine phänomenologische Neubegründung des ontologischen Arguments*, in: *Philosophie und Realistische Phänomenologie. Studien der Internationalen Akademie für Philosophie im Fürstentum Liechtenstein*, eds. Rocco Buttiglione and Josef Seifert (Heidelberg: Universitätsverlag C. Winter, 1996), chs. 9-10.

10. Cf. Rudolf Otto, *Das Heilige: Über das Irrationale in der Idee des Göttlichen und sein Verhältnis zum Rationalen* (Munich: Verlag C. H. Beck, Sonderauflage, 1962), pp. 14 ff., 66 ff. Cf. also Otto, "Wert, Würde und Recht," *Zeitschrift für*

Theologie und Kirche, 12 (1931), pp. 1-67; reprinted in: Otto, *Aufsätze zur Ethik*, ed. J. S. Boozer (Munich: Verlag C. H. Beck, 1981), pp. 53-106, as well as his "Wertgesetz und Autonomie," in: Otto, *Aufsätze zur Ethik*, ed. J. S. Boozer (Munich: Verlag C. H. Beck, 1981), pp. 107-126. See also Max Scheler, "Probleme der Religion," in: Scheler, *Vom Ewigen im Menschen* (Bern and Munich: Francke Verlag, 5th ed., 1968), pp. 101-354.

11. See Janusz Korczak, *Das Recht des Kindes auf Achtung* (Göttingen: Vandenhoeck & Ruprecht, 3rd ed., 1979), esp. pp. 7 ff., p. 372.

12. Boethius, *Contra Eutychen et Nestorium*, cap. 3.

13. Richard of St. Victor, *Trin.* 4, 22; 4, 25.

14. See Stephen Schwarz, *The Moral Question of Abortion* (Chicago: Loyola University Press, 1990).

15. *Ibid.*, pp. 100-113.

16. Peter Singer, "Unsanctifying Human Life," in: Singer, *Ethical Issues Relating to Life and Death* (Melbourne, 1979), pp. 41 ff.

17. *Ibid.*, pp. 59, 43, 50.

18. *Ibid.*, p. 50.

19. Cf. J.-M. Palacios, "El problema de la fundación de los derechos humanos," in: *Revista de Filosofía*, 2:6 (1983), p. 262.

20. Cf. Hans Jonas, "Gehirntod und menschliche Organbank: Zur pragmatischen Umdefinierung des Todes" (abbr. "Gehirntod"), in: Jonas, *Technik, Medizin und Ethik: Zur Praxis des Prinzips Verantwortung* (Frankfurt a. M.: Insel Verlag, 1985), pp. 219-241. Cf. also Hans Jonas, *Philosophical Essays: From Ancient Creed to Technological Man*, and Jonas, "Against the Stream: Comments on the Definition and Redefinition of Death," in: Jonas, *Philosophical Essays*, pp. 132 ff. See also Josef Seifert, "Is 'Brain Death' actually Death? A Critique of Redefining Man's Death in Terms of 'Brain Death'," *Working Group on the Determination of Brain Death and Its Relationship to Human Death*, eds. Robert J. White, Heinz Angstwurm, Ignacio Carasco de Paola (Vatican City: Pontifical Academy of the Sciences, 1992), pp. 95-143. See Seifert, "Is 'Brain Death' actually Death?", *The Monist*, 76 (1993), pp. 175-202.

21. Alphonse Gratry, *Was ist die Seele? Von dem Geheimnisse der Seele und von der menschlichen Sprache* (Munich/Salzburg/New York: Stifterbibliothek, 1953), 7, p. 17.

22. J. M. Palacios, "El problema de la fundación de los derechos humanos," p. 261.

23. Cf. Max Scheler, *Das Ressentiment im Aufbau der Moralen*, in: Scheler, *Vom Umsturz der Werte* (Bern and Munich: Francke-Verlag, 1955). Cf. also Siegfried Johannes Hamburger, "Kritische Reflexionen über Max Schelers *Ressentiment im Aufbau der Moralen*", *Aletheia*, 6 (1993/1994), pp. 28-67.

24. Cf. Gabriel Marcel, *The Existential Background of Human Dignity*, in: Max Scheler, *Vom Umsturz der Werte* (Bern and Munich: Francke-Verlag, 1955). Cf. Marcel, *Die Menschenwürde und ihr existentieller Grund* (Frankfurt a. M.: Josef Knecht, 1965), pp. 139-162, 163 ff. Cf. also Erik Kühnelt-Leddin, *Liberty or Equality: The Challenge of Our Time* (London: Hollis and Carter, 1952).

25. See Josef Seifert, *Essere e persona: Verso una fondazione fenomenologica di una metafisica classica e personalistica* (Milan: Vita e Pensiero, 1989), ch. 9.

26. See Josef Seifert, *Back to Things in Themselves: A Phenomenological Foundation for Classical Realism* (London: Routledge, 1987).

27. See Dietrich von Hildebrand, *Ethics*, chs. 1-3, 17-18, and *Das Wesen der Liebe*, in: Hildebrand, *Gesammelte Werke*, vol. 3 (Regensburg/Stuttgart: Habbel/Kohlhammer, 1971), chs. 1-5, 9.

28. Scheler, "Probleme der Religion," pp. 101 ff.

29. See Max Scheler, *Formalism in Ethics and Non-Formal Ethics of Values*, trans. Manfred S. Frings and Roger L. Funk (Evanston, Ill.: Northwestern University Press, 1973), p. 289. See likewise von Hildebrand, *Ethics*, chs. 1-3, 17-18. See also Seifert, *Essere e persona*, ch. 9.

Chapter Five

1. The original version of my paper, "The Irreducibility of Life to Chaotic and Non-Chaotic Physical Systems," and the discussion – with the names of the scientists – will be published by the Pontifical Academy of the Sciences in the Proceedings of a Meeting dedicated to Life and Chaos Theory.

2. See Dietrich von Hildebrand, *What Is Philosophy?* (Milwaukee: Bruce, 1960; 2nd ed. Chicago: Franciscan Herald Press, 1973; 3rd ed., with a new introductory essay by Josef Seifert, London and New York: Routledge, 1991), 7, pp. xii ff., and ch. 4; see also Balduin Schwarz, "Dietrich von Hildebrands Lehre von der Soseinserfahrung in ihren philosophiegeschichtlichen Zusammenhängen," *Wahrheit, Wert und Sein: Festgabe für Dietrich von Hildebrand zum 80. Geburtstag*, ed. Balduin Schwarz (Regensburg: Habbel, 1970), pp. 33-51; and Josef Seifert, *Back to Things in Themselves: A Phenomenological Foundation for Classical Realism* (London: Routledge, 1987).

3. Josef Seifert, *Das Leib-Seele Problem und die gegenwärtige philosophische Diskussion: eine kritisch-systematische Analyse* (Darmstadt: Wissenschaftliche Buchgesellschaft, 2nd ed. 1989).

4. See Josef Seifert, *Schachphilosophie* (Darmstadt: Wissenschaftliche Buchgesellschaft, 1989), ch. 2 ff.

5. In Seifert, *Das Leib-Seele Problem* (soon to be published in English).

6. See Gregory J. Chaitin, "Zahlen und Zufall – Algorithmische Informationstheorie: Neueste Resultate über die Grundlagen der Mathematik," *Naturwissenschaft und Weltbild*, eds. H.-C. Reichel, E. Prat de la Riba (Vienna: Hölder-Pichler-Tempsky, 1992), pp. 30-44. See also Seifert, *Schachphilosophie*, ch. 2.

7. See A. Reinach, "The Apriori Foundations of the Civil Law," trans. J. F. Crosby, *Aletheia*, 3 (1983), pp. xxxiii-xxxv; 1-142.

8. See Ludger Hölscher, *The Reality of the Mind: St. Augustine's Arguments for the Human Soul as Spiritual Substance* (London: Routledge and Kegan Paul, 1986).

9. See Josef Seifert, "Wissen und Wahrheit in Naturwissenschaften, Philosophie und Glauben," *Naturwissenschaft und Weltbild.*

10. Cf. Josef Seifert, "Objektivismus in der Wissenschaft und Grundlagen philosophischer Rationalität: Kritische Überlegungen zu Karl Poppers Wissenschafts-, Erkenntnis- und Wahrheitstheorie," pp. 31-74, pp. 75-82; cf. also Agnieska Lekka-Kowalik, *Rationality: A Preliminary Philosophical Account* (Schaan, Liechtenstein: Unpublished Doctoral Dissertation, 1993).

BIBLIOGRAPHY

The Bibliography only contains works cited in the present book. The ancient and medieval philosophical authors are cited according to the standard editions and systems of quotation, and, where no reference to a specific edition or translation is made, their works are presumed to be known universally.

André, Hans, *Urbild und Ursache in der Biologie* (Munich/Berlin, 1931).

Arendt, Hannah, *The Life of the Mind*, vol. 1: *Thinking*; vol. 2: *Willing* (New York: Harcourt Brace Jovanovich, 1971, 1977, 1978).

———, *Vom Leben des Geistes*, vol. 1, *Das Denken* (Munich/Zurich: R. Piper & Co. Verlag, 1979).

Aristotle, *Works*, 23 vols., Greek-English, Loeb Classical Library (Cambridge, Mass., and London: Harvard University Press/William Heinemann Ltd.).

———, *Metaphysics*, Loeb ed., vols. 17 and 18, trans. Hugh Tredennick (Cambridge, Mass./London: Harvard University Press/William Heinemann Ltd., 1968, 1976).

———, *Eudemian Ethics*, trans. H. Rackham, Loeb ed., vol. 20 (Cambridge, Mass.: Harvard University Press, 1961), pp. 190-477.

———, *De Anima*, On the Soul, trans. J. A. Smith, *The Basic Works of Aristotle*, ed. Richard McKeon (New York: Random House, 1971), pp. 533-603.

Atlas, Valery, "On the Principle of Complementarity," unpublished paper (Schaan, Principality of Liechtenstein: The International Academy of Philosophy, 1994).

Bernard, Claude, *Leçons sur les phénomènes de la vie communs aux animaux et aux végétaux* (Paris: J.-B. Baillière, 1879-1885; Paris: J. Vrin, 1966, reprod. photomécanique de l'éd. de 1885).

Bertalanffy, Ludwig von, *General System Theory* (New York, 4th ed., 1972).

Blechschmidt, Erich, *Wie beginnt das menschliche Leben?* (Stein am Rhein: Christiana Verlag, 4th ed., 1983).

Bogdanov, Grichka and Igor: see under Guitton.

Bohr, Niels, *Collected Works*, 5 vols., ed. J. R. Nielsen (Amsterdam: North-Holland-Elsevier, 1972-1985).

Bollnow, O. F., *Die Lebensphilosophie F. H. Jacobis* (Stuttgart/Berlin/Köln/Mainz: Kohlhammer, 1933/1966).

Bonaventure, *Opera omnia*, eds. PP. Collegium a S. Bonaventura, ad Claras Aquas (Quarracchi) ex Typographia Collegii S. Bonaventura, 10 vols. (1882-1902).

Brentano, Franz, *Psychologie vom empirischen Standpunkt*, vol. 1-2, ed. O. Kraus, unchanged reprint of the 1924 ed. (1st ed. 1874), (Hamburg: Felix Meiner, 1973). Also in English translation as: *Psychology from an Empirical Standpoint* (1973).

Buytendijk, F. J. J., *Mensch und Tier: Ein Beitrag zur vergleichenden Psychologie* (Hamburg: Rowohlt, 1958).

Chaitin, Gregory J., "Zahlen und Zufall – Algorithmische Informationstheorie: Neueste Resultate über die Grundlagen der Mathematik," *Naturwissenschaft und Weltbild*, eds. H.-C. Reichel, E. Prat de la Riba (Vienna: Hölder-Pichler-Tempsky, 1992), pp. 30-44.

Chisholm, Roderick M., "Brentano's Conception of Substance and Accident," *Die Philosophie Franz Brentanos (Grazer philosophische Studien)* (Amsterdam: Rodopi, 1978), pp. 197-210.

———, "Is There a Mind-Body Problem?", *Philosophic Exchange*, 2 (1978), pp. 25-32.

———, *The First Person* (Minneapolis: University of Minnesota Press, 1981).

———, *Person and Object* (London: Allen & Unwin, 1976).

Conrad-Martius, Hedwig, *Die Seele der Pflanze*, in: Conrad-Martius, *Schriften zur Philosophie*, ed. Eberhard Avé-Lallement, vol. 1 (Munich: Kösel, 1963), pp. 276-362.

———, "Präformismus in der Natur," in: Conrad-Martius, *Schriften zur Philosophie*, ed. Eberhard Avé-Lallement, vol. 2 (Munich: Kösel, 1964), pp. 153-173.

Cramer, Friedrich, *Chaos und Unordnung* (Stuttgart: DVA, 1988).

Crosby, John F., "The Idea of Value and the Reform of the Traditional Metaphysics of Bonum," *Aletheia*, 1 (1977), pp. 231-339.

———, "Evolutionism and the Ontology of the Human Person," *Review of Politics*, 38 (April 1976), pp. 208-243.

Crutchfield, James P., "Chaos 1: Chaos and Complexity," *Handbook of Metaphysics and Ontology*, eds. Hans Burkhardt and Barry Smith, 1 (Munich/Philadelphia/Vienna: Philosophia, 1991), pp. 139-144.

Darwin, Charles, *The Origin of Species by Way of Natural Selection or the Preservation of Favoured Races in the Struggle for Life* (1st ed.: London, 1858), Mentor ed., with an Introduction by Julian Huxley (New York: New American Library, 1958).

Descartes, René, *Discours de la Méthode*, in: *Oeuvres de Descartes*, eds. Charles Adam & Paul Tannery (Paris: J. Vrin, 1982), vol. 6, pp. 1-78.

———, *Meditationes de Prima Philosophia*, *Oeuvres de Descartes*, eds. Charles Adam & Paul Tannery (Paris: J. Vrin, 1983), vol. 7, pp. 1-561.

———, *Treatise on Man*, quoted in Leonora C. Rosenfield, *From Beast-Machine to Man-Machine.*

———, *Passions of the Soul*, quoted in Leonora C. Rosenfield, *From Beast-Machine to Man-Machine.*

———, *Letter to the Marquis of Newcastle*, quoted in Leonora C. Rosenfield, *From Beast-Machine to Man-Machine.*

Donohue-White, Patricia, Kateryna Fedoryka, and Paulina Taboada (eds.), "Towards a Personalistic Concept of Health," forthcoming in the *Philosophy and Medicine* Book Series (Dordrecht: Kluwer).

Drees, Willem B., *Beyond the Big Bang: Quantum Cosmologies and God* (LaSalle, Ill.: Open Court, 1990).

Driesch, Hans, *Philosophie des Organischen* (Gifford-Lectures) (Leipzig: Verlag von Quelle & Meyer, 4th ed., 1928).

DuBois, James M. (ed.), *Moral Issues in Psychology* (Lanham/New York/London: University Press of America, 1996).

Engelhardt, H. Tristram, Jr., *The Foundation of Bioethics* (New York and Oxford: Oxford University Press, 1986; 2nd ed. 1996).

Fabro, Cornelio, *L'uomo e il Rischio di Dio* (Rome: Editrice Studium, 1967).

Fedoryka, Kateryna: see under Donohue-White, Patricia.

Fenton, Carroll Lane, "Living Things," *Compton's Interactive Encyclopedia*, 1995.

Fine, A.: see under Keller, S. H.

Finnis, John, *Fundamentals of Ethics* (Oxford: Clarendon Press, 1983).

Fischer, Ernst Peter, "Was ist Leben? – mehr als vierzig Jahre später," in: E. Schrödinger, *Was ist Leben?* (Munich/Zurich: Piper, 3rd ed. 1987), pp. 9-15.

Frankl, Viktor E., "Der Mensch auf der Suche nach Sinn: Anthropologische Grundlagen der Psychotherapie," in: Viktor E. Frankl, *Logotherapie und Existenzanalyse. Texte aus sechs Jahrzehnten* (Berlin/Munich: Quintessenz Verlag, 2nd ed., 1994), "In memoriam 1938," pp. 298-299.

Gassen, Hans Günter, Andrea Martin, and Gabriele Sachse, *Der Stoff, aus dem die Gene sind: Bilder und Erklärungen zur Gentechnik* (Munich: J. Schweitzer Verlag, 1986).

Gehlen, Arnold, *Der Mensch. Seine Natur und Stellung in der Welt* (Frankfurt a. M./Bonn: Athenäum Verlag, 1962).

Gilson, Etienne, *D'Aristote à Darwin et retour* (Paris: J. Vrin, 1971).

Goethe, Johann Wolfgang von, *Zur Farbenlehre. Didaktischer Theil. Der Farbenlehre polemischer Theil. Geschichte der Farbenlehre. Nachträge zur Farbenlehre,* in: Johann Wolfgang von Goethe, *Sämmtliche Werke* in 40 Bänden (Stuttgart and Tübingen: J. G. Cotta'scher Verlag, 1840), vols. 37-40.

———, *Goethes Gespräche mit Eckermann* (Leipzig: Insel-Verlag, 1921).

———, "Über den Granit," quoted in Hans Leisegang, *Goethes Denken*, p. 90.

Gratry, Alphonse, *De la connaissance de l'âme* (Paris: 3rd ed., 1861).

———, *Was ist die Seele? Von dem Geheimnisse der Seele und von der menschlichen Sprache* (Munich/Salzburg/New York: Stifterbibliothek, 1953).

Grene, Marjorie, "Positionality in the Philosophy of Helmuth Plessner," *The Review of Metaphysics* 20 (1966), pp. 250-277.

Guitton, Jean, Grichka Bogdanov, Igor Bogdanov, *Dieu et la science* (Paris: B. Grasset, 1991).

Gunzig, Edgard: see under Prigogine, Ilya.

Hamburger, Siegfried Johannes, "Kritische Reflexionen über Max Schelers *Ressentiment im Aufbau der Moralen*," *Aletheia*, 6 (1993/1994), pp. 28-67.

Hegel, Georg Friedrich Wilhelm, *Vorlesungen über die Geschichte der Philosophie*, in: *Werke*, ed. Glockner (Stuttgart: Friedrich Fromann/Günter Holzboog, 1959), vol. 18.

———, *Wissenschaft der Logik*, vol. 2, ed. Glockner (Stuttgart: Friedrich Fromann/ Günter Holzboog, 4th ed., 1964).

Heidegger, Martin, *Die Kategorien- und Bedeutungslehre des Duns Scotus*, in: Martin Heidegger, *Gesamtausgabe*, I. Abteilung, Veröffentlichte Schriften 1914-1970, vol. 1, *Frühe Schriften* (Frankfurt a. M.: Vittorio Klostermann, 1978).

———, *Sein und Zeit*, quoted in Robert Spaemann, "Zum Begriff des Lebens," p. 84.

Heisenberg, Werner, *Physics and Philosophy: The Revolution in Modern Science* (New York: Harper & Row, 1962).

Hengstenberg, Hans-Eduard, *Evolution und Schöpfung* (Salzburg: Anton Pustet, 1963).

Hildebrand, Alice von, "On the Pseudo-Obvious," *Wahrheit, Wert und Sein*, ed. Balduin Schwarz, pp. 25-32.

Hildebrand, Dietrich von, *Ethics* (Chicago: Franciscan Herald Press, 2nd ed., 1978).

———, *Moralia*, in: Hildebrand, *Gesammelte Werke*, vol. 9 (Regensburg: Verlag Josef Habbel, 1980).

———, *What Is Philosophy?* (Milwaukee: Bruce, 1960; 2nd ed. Chicago: Franciscan Herald Press, 1973; 3rd ed., with a new introductory essay by Josef Seifert, London and New York: Routledge, 1991).

———, *Das Wesen der Liebe*, in: Hildebrand, *Gesammelte Werke*, vol. 3 (Regensburg/Stuttgart: Habbel/Kohlhammer, 1971).

Hocevar, Heinz-Emil, *Die Seinsstruktur der Pflanzen* (doctoral diss., published in Salzburg, 1975).

Hölscher, Ludger, *The Reality of the Mind: St. Augustine's Arguments for the Human Soul as Spiritual Substance* (London: Routledge and Kegan Paul, 1986), 2nd ed. forthcoming.

Huxley, Julian, *Evolution, the Modern Synthesis* (London: Allen & Unwin, 1943).

Jaki, Stanley L., *Cosmos and Creator* (Chicago: Regnery Gateway, 1980).

———, *The Origin of Science and the Science of Origin* (South Bend, Ind.: University of Notre Dame Press, 1979).

Jastrow, Robert, "What Forces Filled the Universe with Energy Fifteen Billion Years Ago?", *Cosmos, Bios, Theos*, eds. Margenau and Varghese, pp. 45-49.

Jessop, N., *Zoology: Theory and Problems.*

Jonas, Hans, "Against the Stream: Comments on the Definition and Redefinition of Death," in: Jonas, *Philosophical Essays*, pp. 132-140.

———, "Gehirntod und menschliche Organbank: Zur pragmatischen Umdefinierung des Todes" (abbr. "Gehirntod"), in: Jonas, *Technik, Medizin und Ethik*, pp. 219-241.

———, "Immortality and the Modern Temper," in: Jonas, *The Phenomenon of Life.*

———, *The Phenomenon of Life: Toward a Philosophical Biology* (New York: Harper & Row, 1966).

———, *Macht oder Ohnmacht der Subjektivität? Das Leib-Seele-Problem im Vorfeld des Prinzips Verantwortung* (Frankfurt a. M.: Insel Verlag, 1981).

———, *Philosophical Essays: From Ancient Creed to Technological Man* (Chicago and London: The University of Chicago Press, 1974).

———, "The Nobility of Sight," in: Jonas, *The Phenomenon of Life.*

———, *Technik, Medizin und Ethik: Zur Praxis des Prinzips Verantwortung* (Frankfurt a. M.: Insel Verlag, 1985).

Kant, Immanuel, *Kant's Gesammelte Schriften*, ed. 5. der Preußischen Akademie der Wissenschaften (Berlin and Leipzig: Walter de Gruyter & Co., 1938).

———, *Grundlegung zur Metaphysik der Sitten*, Akademieausgabe, vol. 4.

———, *Metaphysik der Sitten*, Akademieausgabe, vol. 5.

———, *Foundations of the Metaphysics of Morals* (With Critical Essays), ed. Robert P. Wolff, trans. by Lewis W. Beck (Indianapolis: Bobbs-Merrill, 1976).

———, *Foundations of the Metaphysics of Morals*, trans. and introd. by Lewis White Beck (Indianapolis: Bobbs-Merrill, 1959).

———, *Opus postumum*, Akademieausgabe, vols. 21 and 22, Kant's handschriftlicher Nachlaß, vols. 8 and 9, Opus postumum.

———, *Träume eines Geistersehers*, Akademieausgabe, vol. 4.

Keller, S. H., M. A. Stone, and A. Fine, "Models, Chaos, and Goodness of Fit," *Philosophical Topics*, 18:2 (1990), pp. 85-105.

Korczak, Janusz, *Das Recht des Kindes auf Achtung* (Göttingen: Vandenhoeck & Ruprecht, 3rd ed., 1979).

Kühnelt-Leddin, Erik, *Liberty or Equality: The Challenge of Our Time* (London: Hollis and Carter, 1952).

Küppers, Bernd-Olaf, *Der Ursprung biologischer Information. Zur Naturphilosophie der Lebensentstehung*. Introduced by Carl Friedrich von Weizsäcker (Munich/Zurich: Piper, 1986).

Leisegang, Hans, *Goethes Denken* (Leipzig: Felix Meiner, 1932).

Lekka-Kowalik, Agnieska, *Rationality: A Preliminary Philosophical Account* (Schaan, Liechtenstein: Unpublished Doctoral Dissertation, 1993).

Linde, Andrej D., "Chaotic Inflation," *Physics Letters*, 129B: 177-181 (1983).

Linden, Eugene, "Can We Really Understand Matter?", *Science* (16 April 1990), p. 43.

Löw, Reinhard, "Herder und die Evolution," in: *Oikeiosis. Festschrift für Robert Spaemann*, ed. Reinhard Löw (Weinheim: VCH Verlagsgesellschaft, 1987).

———, *Leben aus dem Labor: Gentechnologie und Verantwortung – Biologie und Moral* (Munich: C. Bertelsmann, 1985).

———, *Philosophie des Organischen* (Munich: C. Bertelsmann, 1980).

———, (ed.), *Oikeiosis. Festschrift für Robert Spaemann* (Weinheim: VCH Verlagsgesellschaft, 1987).

———; see also under Robert Spaemann.

Lukas, Elisabeth, *Psychotherapie in Würde. Sinnorientierte Lebenshilfe nach Viktor E. Frankl* (Berlin/Munich: Quintessenz, 1994).

Mackie, J. L., *Ethics: Inventing Right and Wrong* (New York: Penguin Books, 1977).

Marcel, Gabriel, *The Existential Background of Human Dignity*, in: Max Scheler, *Vom Umsturz der Werte* (Bern and Munich: Francke-Verlag, 1955).

———, *Die Menschenwürde und ihr existentieller Grund* (Frankfurt a. M.: Josef Knecht, 1965).

———, *Sein und Haben*, trans. by Ernst Gehler (Paderborn: Ferdinand Schöningh, 2nd ed., 1968).

Margenau, Henry and Roy Abraham Varghese (eds.), *Cosmos, Bios, Theos: Scientists Reflect on Science, God, and the Origins of the Universe, Life, and Homo sapiens* (LaSalle, Ill.: Open Court, 1992).

Margenau, Henry, "The Laws of Nature Are Created by God," *Cosmos, Bios, Theos*, ed. Margenau and Varghese.

Martin, Andrea: see under Gassen, Hans Günter.

Meyer-Abich, Klaus Michael, "Der Holismus im 20. Jahrhundert," *Klassiker der Naturphilosophie: Von den Vorsokratikern bis zur Kopenhagener Schule*, ed. Gernot Böhme (Munich: Verlag C. H. Beck, 1989), pp. 313-329.

Millán-Puelles, Antonio, *Teoría del objeto puro.* Colecciones Cuestiones Fundamentales (Madrid: Ediciones RIALP, 1990).

———, *The Theory of the Pure Object*, trans. and ed. Jorge García-Gómez, in: *Philosophy and Realist Phenomenology. Studies of the International Academy of Philosophy in the Principality Liechtenstein*, eds. Rocco Buttiglione and Josef Seifert, vol. 2 (Heidelberg: Universitätsverlag C. Winter, 1996).

Monod, Jacques, *Chance and Necessity* (New York: Random House Inc., 1972).

Moore, G. E., *Principia Ethica* (1903); 14th ed. (London, 1971).

Morton, Adam, "Chaos 2: Fractals and Chaos," *Handbook of Metaphysics and Ontology*, eds. Hans Burkhardt and Barry Smith (Munich/Philadelphia/Vienna: Philosophia, 1991), vol. 1, pp. 144-146.

Müller, A., "Bios (Leben, Lebensform)," *Historisches Wörterbuch der Philosophie*, ed. Joachim Ritter, vol. 1, A-C (Basel/Stuttgart: Schwabe & Co., 1971), pp. 948-949.

Otto, Rudolf, *Das Heilige: Über das Irrationale in der Idee des Göttlichen und sein Verhältnis zum Rationalen* (Munich: Verlag C. H. Beck, Sonderauflage, 1962).

———, "Wert, Würde und Recht," *Zeitschrift für Theologie und Kirche*, 12 (1931), pp. 1-67; reprinted in: Otto, *Aufsätze zur Ethik*, ed. J. S. Boozer (Munich: Verlag C. H. Beck, 1981), pp. 53-106.

———, "Wertgesetz und Autonomie," in: Otto, *Aufsätze zur Ethik*, ed. J. S. Boozer (Munich: Verlag C. H. Beck, 1981), pp. 107-126.

Palacios, J. M., "El problema de la fundación metafísica de los derechos humanos," in: *Revista de Filosofía*, 2:6 (1983), pp. 257-273.

Penrose, Roger, *The Emperor's New Mind: Concerning Computers, Minds, and the Law of Physics* (Oxford: Oxford University Press, 6th ed., 1989).

Pietrowicz, Stephan, *Helmuth Plessner* (Freiburg/Munich: Verlag Karl Alber, 1992).

Planck, Max, *Vorlesungen über Thermodynamik* 1930 (Berlin: de Gruyter, 11th enlarged ed. 1964).

Plato, *Platonis Opera*, vol. 1, ed. J. Burnet (Oxford: Clarendon Press, 1961); vol. 2 (Oxford, 1960).

———, *The Collected Dialogues of Plato including the Letters*, ed. Huntington Cairns and Edith Hamilton (Princeton: Princeton University Press, 1961, 10th printing 1980).

———, *Phaedrus*, trans. W. C. Helmbold and W. G. Rabinowitz (Indianapolis/New York: Bobbs-Merrill Co., 1956).

———, *Phaedo*, trans. F. J. Church (Indianapolis/New York: Bobbs-Merrill Co., 1951).

Plessner, Helmut, *Die Stufen des Organischen und der Mensch: Einleitung in die philosophische Anthropologie* (Berlin/New York: Walter de Gruyter, 3rd unchanged ed., 1975), 1st ed. 1928.

———, "Homo Absconditus," *Philosophische Anthropologie heute*, eds. R. Rocek and O. Schatz (Munich: Anton Pustet, 1972).

Polanyi, Michael, "Life's Irreducible Structure," *Science*, 160 (1968), p. 1308.

———, "Life Transcending Physics and Chemistry," *Chemical and Engineering News*, 45 (1967), p. 56 ff.

Prigogine, Ilya and Edgard Gunzig, "Cosmology 2: The Reasons for the Cosmos," *Handbook of Metaphysics and Ontology*, eds. Hans Burkhardt and Barry Smith (Munich/Philadelphia/Vienna: Philosophia, 1991), vol. 1, pp. 186-189.

Prigogine, Ilya, "The Universe Started from an Instability in the Quantum Vacuum," *Cosmos, Bios, Theos*, eds. Margenau and Varghese, pp. 188-192.

Ilya Prigogine, *From Being to Becoming: Time and Complexity in the Physical Sciences* (New York: W. H. Freeman, 1980).

Purola, T., "A Systems Approach to Health and Health Policy," *Medical Care*, 10:5 (1972).

Reale, Giovanni, *Verso una nuova interpretazione di Platone* (Milan: Jaca Book, 16th ed., 1996); Giovanni Reale, *Platon*, trans. Ludger Hölscher, introduced by Hans Krämer, ed. and with a postface by Josef Seifert (Paderborn: Schöningh, 1993).

Reinach, Adolf, *Sämtliche Werke: Textkritische Ausgabe in zwei Bänden*, vol. 1: *Die Werke*, Teil 1: Kritische Neuausgabe (1905-1914), Teil 2: Nachgelassene Texte (1906-1917); eds. Karl Schuhmann and Barry Smith (Munich and Vienna: Philosophia Verlag, 1989).

———, "The Apriori Foundations of the Civil Law," trans. J. F. Crosby, *Aletheia*, 3 (1983), pp. xxxiii-xxxv; 1-142.

———, "Concerning Phenomenology," trans. from the German ("Über Phänomenologie") by Dallas Willard, *The Personalist*, 50 (Spring 1969), pp. 194-221.

Reprinted in *Perspectives in Philosophy*, ed. Robert N. Beck (New York: Holt, Reinhart, & Winston, 1961 and 1969).

———, "Über Phänomenologie," in: Adolf Reinach, *Sämtliche Werke*, vol. 1, pp. 531-550.

Rignano, Eugenio, *Qu'est-ce que la vie? Nouveaux essais de synthèse biologique* (Paris: Librairie Félix Alcan, 1926).

Roux, Wilhelm, "Das Wesen des Lebens," *Die Kultur der Gegenwart. Ihre Entwicklung und ihre Ziele*, III. Teil, ed. Paul Hinneberg (Leipzig/Berlin, 1915), pp. 173-187.

Rosenfield, Leonora C., *From Beast-Machine to Man-Machine: Animal Soul in French Letters from Descartes to LaMettrie* (New York: Oxford University Press, 1941).

Roth, Jay, "The Piling of Coincidence on Coincidence," *Cosmos, Bios, Theos*, eds. Margenau and Varghese.

Sachse, Gabriele: see under Gassen, Hans Günter.

Scheler, Max, "Altern und Tod," in: Scheler, *Schriften aus dem Nachlaß*, vol. 3 (Bonn: Bouvier-Verlag Herbert Grundmann, 1987), pp. 251-327.

———, *Philosophische Anthropologie*, in: Scheler, *Schriften aus dem Nachlaß*, vol. 3 (Bonn: Bouvier-Verlag Herbert Grundmann, 1987), pp. 314-353.

———, "Biologievorlesung," in: Scheler, *Schriften aus dem Nachlaß*, vol. 5, *Varia* (Bonn: Bouvier-Verlag, 1993), pp. 257-361.

———, "Biologie und Physik. Materielle Mengen und lebendige Körper," in: Scheler, *Schriften aus dem Nachlaß*, vol. 5, *Varia* (Bonn: Bouvier-Verlag, 1993), pp. 285-313.

———, *Der Formalismus in der Ethik und die materiale Wertethik* (Bern and Munich: Francke, 5th ed., 1966).

———, *Formalism in Ethics and Non-Formal Ethics of Values*, trans. Manfred S. Frings and Roger L. Funk (Evanston, Ill.: Northwestern University Press, 1973).

———, "Instinktbewegungen," in: Scheler, *Schriften aus dem Nachlaß*, vol. 5, *Varia* (Bonn: Bouvier-Verlag, 1993), pp. 354-361.

———, "Phänomenologie des Lebens und organischen Geschehens," in: Scheler, *Schriften aus dem Nachlaß*, vol. 5, *Varia* (Bonn: Bouvier Verlag, 1993), pp. 314-353.

———, *Die Stellung des Menschen im Kosmos* (1928), in: Scheler, *Gesammelte Werke*, vol. 9, ed. Manfred Frings (Bern: A. Francke Verlag, 1976), pp. 7-72.

———, *Man's Place in Nature*, trans. and introd. by Hans Meyerhoff (New York: The Noonday Press, 10th printing 1979).

———, "Probleme der Religion," in: Scheler, *Vom Ewigen im Menschen* (Bern and Munich: Francke Verlag, 5th ed., 1968), pp. 101-354.

———, *Das Ressentiment im Aufbau der Moralen*, in: Scheler, *Vom Umsturz der Werte* (Bern and Munich: Francke-Verlag, 1955).

Schrödinger, Erwin, *What Is Life?* (Cambridge, England: Cambridge University Press, 1944).

———, *Was ist Leben?* (Munich and Zurich: Piper, 3rd ed., 1987).

———, *Mind and Matter* (Cambridge, England: Cambridge University Press, 1958).

———, *Geist und Materie* (Vienna/Hamburg: Paul Zsolnay Verlag, 1986).

Schwarz, Balduin, "Dietrich von Hildebrands Lehre von der Soseinserfahrung in ihren philosophiegeschichtlichen Zusammenhängen," *Wahrheit, Wert und Sein*, ed. Schwarz, pp. 33-51.

———, *Das Problem des Irrtums in der Philosophie* (Münster: Aschaffenburg, 1934).

———, (ed.) *Wahrheit, Wert und Sein: Festgabe für Dietrich von Hildebrand zum 80. Geburtstag* (Regensburg: Habbel, 1970).

———, *Wahrheit, Irrtum und Verirrungen. Die sechs großen Krisen und sieben Ausfahrten der abendländischen Philosophie*, in: *Philosophie und Realistische Phänomenologie. Studien der Internationalen Akademie für Philosophie im Fürstentum Liechtenstein*, eds. Rocco Buttiglione and Josef Seifert, vol. 5 (Heidelberg: Universitätsverlag C. Winter, 1996).

Schwarz, Stephen, *The Moral Question of Abortion* (Chicago: Loyola University Press, 1990).

Scotus, Duns, *Grammatica speculativa* (today attributed to Thomas of Erfurt), Luca Wading (1639), L. Vives 1891-1895, reprint of the 1639 edition (Hildesheim: Olms, 1968).

Seifert, Josef, "Abortion and Euthanasia as Legal and as Moral Issues: Some Reflections on the Relationship between Morality, Church, and State," *Bioethics Update, Proceedings of the 1987 Annual Conference on Bioethics*, ed. N. Tonti-Filippini (Melbourne: St. Vincent's Bioethics Centre, 1988), pp. 162-212.

———, "Absolute Moral Obligations towards Finite Goods as Foundation of Intrinsically Right and Wrong Actions: A Critique of Consequentialist Teleological Ethics: Destruction of Ethics through Moral Theology?", *Anthropos*, 1 (1985), pp. 57- 94.

———, *Back to Things in Themselves: A Phenomenological Foundation for Classical Realism* (London: Routledge, 1987), 2nd edition forthcoming.

———, "Is 'Brain Death' actually Death? A Critique of Redefining Man's Death in Terms of 'Brain Death'," *Working Group on the Determination of Brain Death and Its Relationship to Human Death*, eds. Robert J. White, H.

Angstwurm, Ignacio Carasco de Paola (Vatican City: Pontifical Academy of the Sciences, 1992), pp. 95-143.

———, "Is 'Brain Death' actually Death?", *The Monist*, 76 (1993), pp. 175-202.

———, *Erkenntnis objektiver Wahrheit: Die Transzendenz des Menschen in der Erkenntnis* (Salzburg: A. Pustet, 2nd ed., 1976).

———, "Essence and Existence: A New Foundation of Classical Metaphysics on the Basis of 'Phenomenological Realism,' and a Critical Investigation of 'Existentialist Thomism'," *Aletheia*, 1:1 (1977), pp. 17-157; 1:2 (1977), pp. 371-459.

———, *Essere e persona: Verso una fondazione fenomenologica di una metafisica classica e personalistica* (Milan: Vita e Pensiero, 1989).

———, "Genetischer Code und Teleologie, Information, Kausalität und Finalität: Kurzer Abriß naturwissenschaftlicher genetischer Erkenntnisse als Hintergrund neuer philosophischer Probleme," *Arzt und Christ*, 34 (1988), pp. 185-200.

———, *Gott als Gottesbeweis. Eine phänomenologische Neubegründung des ontologischen Arguments*, in: *Philosophie und Realistische Phänomenologie. Studien der Internationalen Akademie für Philosophie im Fürstentum Liechtenstein*, eds. Rocco Buttiglione and Josef Seifert, vol. 4 (Heidelberg: Universitätsverlag C. Winter, 1996).

———, "Zur Herkunft des Glaubens. Gründe und Hintergründe: Reflexionen über das Problem einer Theodizee angesichts der Leiden und Übel in der Welt," *Glaube im Unglauben der Zeit* (Augsburg: Dialogsekretariat, 1983).

———, "Erklären heute Medizin und Gesetze Lebende zu Toten?", *Organspende: Kritische Ansichten zur Transplantationsmedizin*, eds. R. Greinert and G. Wuttke (Göttingen: Lamuv Verlag, 1991), pp. 185-208.

———, "Ist 'Hirntod' wirklich der Tod?", *Ethik und Technik* (Zurich: M&T ed., 1988).

———, "Hirntod: Ein Beitrag zur Kritik der philosophischen Korrumpierung der medizinischen Technik," *Ethik und Technik* (Zurich: M&T ed., 1988).

———, "Gibt es ein Leben nach dem Tod?", *Forum Katholische Theologie*, 5:4 (1989).

———, *Das Leib-Seele Problem und die gegenwärtige philosophische Diskussion: eine kritisch-systematische Analyse* (Darmstadt: Wissenschaftliche Buchgesellschaft, 2nd ed. 1989).

———, *Leib und Seele: Ein Beitrag zur philosophischen Anthropologie* (Salzburg: A. Pustet, 1973).

———, "Menschenwürde und unbedingte Achtung menschlichen Lebens: Einige Fragen der Bioethik und die Grundlagen der Moral," *Essener Gespräche zum Thema Staat und Kirche*, 22 (Aschendorff, 1988).

———, "Objektivismus in der Wissenschaft und Grundlagen philosophischer Rationalität. Kritische Überlegungen zu Karl Poppers Wissenschafts-, Erkenntnis- und Wahrheitstheorie," *Die Gedankenwelt Sir Karl Poppers: Kritischer Rationalismus im Dialog*, eds. Norbert Leser, Josef Seifert, K. Plitzner (Heidelberg: Universitätsverlag C. Winter, 1991), pp. 31-74, and "Diskussion," pp. 75-82.

———, "Organismus", *Evangelisches Lexikon für Theologie und Gemeinde*, eds. H. Burkhardt and U. Swarat, vol. 3 (Wuppertal and Zurich: R. Brackhausverlag, 1994), pp. 1484-1485.

———, "Essere persona come perfezione pura," *De Homine* (Rome: Herder/ Università Lateranense, 1994).

———, "Friedrich Nietzsches Verzweiflung an der Wahrheit und sein Kampf gegen die Wahrheit," *Rehabilitierung der Philosophie*, ed. Dietrich von Hildebrand (Regensburg: J. Habbel, 1974), pp. 197 ff.

———, *Schachphilosophie* (Darmstadt: Wissenschaftliche Buchgesellschaft, 1989).

———, "Die verschiedenen Bedeutungen von 'Sein': Dietrich von Hildebrand als Metaphysiker und Martin Heideggers Vorwurf der Seinsvergessenheit," *Wahrheit, Wert und Sein*, ed. Balduin Schwarz, pp. 301-332.

———, "Transcendentals and Pure Perfections," *Handbook of Metaphysics and Ontology*, vol. 2, eds. Hans Burkhardt and Barry Smith (Munich: Philosophia Verlag, 1991), pp. 909-911.

———, "Das Unsterblichkeitsproblem aus der Sicht der philosophischen Ethik und Anthropologie," *Franziskanische Studien*, 3 (1978).

———, "Wissen und Wahrheit in Naturwissenschaften, Philosophie und Glauben," *Naturwissenschaft und Weltbild*, eds. H.-C. Reichel, E. Prat de la Riba (Vienna: Hölder-Pichler-Tempsky, 1992).

———, *Widerspruchsfreiheit: Versuch einer philosophischen Lösung des Antinomienproblems als eines Grundproblems der "Kritik der reinen Vernunft" und der Philosophie überhaupt* (Heidelberg: Universitätsverlag Winter, 1996).

Sepper, Dennis L., *Goethe contra Newton: Polemics and the Project for a New Science of Color* (Cambridge, England: Cambridge University Press, 1988).

Serani, Alejandro, *L'Etre Vivant selon la perspective réaliste: Propos pour les fondements d'une biophilosophie* (Toulouse: Université de Toulouse le Mirail U.E.R. d'Etudes philosophiques et politiques, 1986).

———, *et al.*, *Nociones fundamentales y aplicadas de etica clinica* (Santiago, Chile: Catholic University of Chile, 1991).

———, "The Origin of Species as a Biological and Philosophical Problem," unpublished lecture (Schaan, Principality of Liechtenstein: The International Academy of Philosophy, 1993).

Simon, Josef, "Leben," *Handbuch philosophischer Grundbegriffe*, vol. 3, eds. Hermann Krings, Hans Michael Baumgartner, and C. Wild (Munich: Kösel, 1973), pp. 844-859.

Singer, Peter, *Muß dieses Kind am Leben bleiben?* (Erlangen: Harald Fischer Verlag, 1993).

———, "Unsanctifying Human Life," in: Peter Singer, *Ethical Issues Relating to Life and Death* (Melbourne, 1979), pp. 41-61.

Southern, R. W., *Saint Anselm: A Portrait in a Landscape* (Cambridge, England: Cambridge University Press, 1991).

Spaemann, Robert, "Zum Begriff des Lebens," *Sichtweisen der Psychiatrie*, eds. G. Kockott, H. J. Müller (Munich: Zuckerschwertverlag, 1994), pp. 84-89.

Spaemann, Robert and Reinhard Löw, *Die Frage Wozu? Geschichte und Wiederentdeckung des teleologischen Denkens* (Munich: Bertelsmann, 1981).

Stein, Edith, *Endliches und Ewiges Sein* (Freiburg: Herder, 3rd ed., 1986).

Stone, M. A.: see under Keller, S. H.

Storey, Kenneth B. and Janet M., "Frozen and Alive," *Scientific America* (1990), pp. 62-67.

Suárez, Francis, *Metaphysical Investigation V* "Individual Unity and Its Principle," (1592), trans. Jorge J. E. Gracia (Milwaukee: Marquette University Press, 1982).

Szostak, Walter, *Teleologie des Lebendigen: Zu Karl Poppers und H. Jonas' Philosophie des Geistes.* Dissertation zur Erlangung des akademischen Grades eines Doktors der Philosophie der Philosophischen Fakultät der Universität des Saarlandes (Saarbrücken 1994).

Taboada, Paulina, "Bedeutung der 'Allgemeinen Systemtheorie' in der heutigen Debatte über den Gesundheitsbegriff" (Schaan, Principality of Liechtenstein: The International Academy of Philosophy, to be published).

———, see under Patricia Donohue-White.

Thomas Aquinas, *Summa Theologica*, Complete American ed. in 2 vols., trans. Fathers of the English Dominican Province (New York: Benziger Brothers, without year).

———, "Summa Theologica," *S. Thomae Opera Omnia. Ut sunt in Indice Thomistico* (Stuttgart/Bad Cannstadt: Frommann/Holzboog, 1980), vol. 2.

Toulmin, Stephen and June Goodfield, *The Architecture of Matter* (London: Kutchinson & Co., 1966).

———, *Materie und Leben* (Munich: W. Goldmann Verlag, 1970).

Uexcüll, Johannes von, *Umwelt und Innenwelt der Tiere* (Berlin: Verlag 5. Julius Springer, 1921).

Varghese, Roy: see under Henry Margenau.

Vollmert, Bruno, "Die Entstehung von Lebewesen in naturwissenschaftlicher Sicht – Darwins Lehre im Lichte der Makromolekularen Chemie," *Schriftenreihe der Gustav-Siewerth-Akademie*, vol. 5 (Weilheim-Bierbronnen, 1995).

Weissmann, David, *Dispositional Properties* (Carbondale and Edwardsville, Ill.: Southern Illinois University Press, 1965).

Wenisch, Fritz, *Die Philosophie und ihre Methode* (Salzburg: A. Pustet, 1976).

Whitehead, Alfred North, *The Concept of Nature* (Cambridge, England: University Press, 1971).

Wojtyła, Karol, *The Acting Person* (Boston: Reidel, 1979); cf. also the corrected text, authorized by the author (unpublished), Library of the International Academy of Philosophy in the Principality of Liechtenstein, Schaan.

Wolter, Allan, *The Transcendentals and Their Function in the Metaphysics of Duns Scotus* (St. Bonaventure University, N. Y.: Franciscan Institute Publications, 1946).

Załaniec, Wojciech, "Fathers, Kings, and Promises: Husserl and Reinach on the *A Priori*," *Husserl Studies*, 9 (1992), 147-177.

ABOUT THE AUTHOR

Born 1945, married to Mary K. Seifert (Heyne), six children (aged 6-20). Full Professor of Philosophy and Founding Rector of *Internationale Akademie für Philosophie im Fürstentum Liechtenstein* (International Academy of Philosophy in the Principality Liechtenstein), 1986 - . Full Professor of Philosophy and Founding Rector of International Academy of Philosophy (in Irving, Texas, 1980-1985). Associate Professor, and before that, Assistant Professor, at the University of Dallas, Texas (1973-1981); Assistant Professor of Philosophy at the University of Salzburg (1969-1973).

Books: 1. *Erkenntnis objektiver Wahrheit. Die Transzendenz des Menschen in der Erkenntnis* (Knowledge of Objective Truth: The Transcendence of Man in Knowledge), first edition (Salzburg: Universitätsverlag A. Pustet, 1972), 340 pp., second improved and enlarged edition (Salzburg: Universitätsverlag A. Pustet, 1976), 398 pp. 2. *Leib und Seele. Ein Beitrag zur philosophischen Anthropologie* (Body and Soul: A Contribution towards a Philosophical Anthropology) (Salzburg: Universitätsverlag A. Pustet, 1973), 380 pp. 3. *Was ist und was motiviert eine sittliche Handlung?* (What Is and What Motivates a Moral Action?) (Salzburg: Universitätsverlag A. Pustet, 1976), 88 pp., also in Polish 1984 and in Spanish 1995. 4. *Das Leib-Seele-Problem in der gegenwärtigen philosophischen Diskussion. Eine kritische Analyse* (The Body/Mind Problem in Contemporary Philosophical Discussion. A Critical Analysis) (Darmstadt: Wissenschaftliche Buchgesellschaft, 1979), 162 pp. Second and enlarged edition. 5. *Das Leib-Seele Problem und die gegenwärtige philosophische Diskussion. Eine kritisch-systematische Analyse* (The Body/Mind Problem and the Contemporary Philosophical Discussion: A Critical and Systematic Investigation) (Darmstadt: Wissenschaftliche Buchgesellschaft, 2nd edition, 1989), 327 pp. 6. *Back to Things in Themselves: A Phenomenological Foundation for Classical Realism*, in: "Studies in Phenomenological and Classical Realism" (Boston and London: Routledge and Kegan Paul, 1987), 364 pp. 7. *Essere e persona. Verso una fondazione fenomenologica di una metafisica classica e personalistica* (Being and Person: Toward a Phenomenological Foundation of a Classical and Personalistic Metaphysics) (Milan: Vita e Pensiero, 1989), 621 pp. 8. *Schachphilosophie* (Chess-Philosophy) (Darmstadt: Wissenschaftliche Buchgesellschaft, 1989), 146 pp. 9. *Sein und Wesen* (Being and Essence) (Heidelberg: Universitätsverlag C. Winter, 1996), 578 pp. 10. *Gott als Gottesbeweis. Eine phänomenologische Neubegründung des ontologischen Arguments* (God as Proof of God's Existence: A Phenomenological Rethinking of the Ontological Argument) (Heidelberg: Universitätsverlag C. Winter, 1996), 715 pp. Editor of seven other books.

Author of 238 articles in philosophy: on epistemology, philosophy of science, philosophy of life and health, philosophy of psychology, metaphysics, ethics and bioethics, philosophy of religion, aesthetics, logic, history of philosophy and individual philosophers.

Editor of three Series of Monographs in Philosophy with Routledge and Universitätsverlag C. Winter, Heidelberg, and Editor of the International Journal of Philosophy *Aletheia.* Member of the European Academy of Sciences, of the New York Academy of Sciences, of other Academies and many Philosophical Societies. 1994-1996: Director of a Research Project, supported by the Swiss Nationalfonds (National Endowment for the Humanities), on the philosophical concept of health and the health definition of the World Health Organization.

INDEX

VIBS

The **Value Inquiry Book Series** is co-sponsored by:

American Maritain Association
American Society for Value Inquiry
Association for Personalist Studies
Association for Process Philosophy of Education
Center for East European Dialogue and Development, Rochester Institute of Technology
Centre for Cultural Research, Aarhus University
College of Education and Allied Professions, Bowling Green State University
Concerned Philosophers for Peace
Conference of Philosophical Societies
International Academy of Philosophy of the Principality of Liechtenstein
International Society for Universalism
International Society for Value Inquiry
Natural Law Society
Philosophical Society of Finland
Philosophy Seminar, University of Mainz
R.S. Hartman Institute for Formal and Applied Axiology
Society for Iberian and Latin-American Thought
Society for the Philosophic Study of Genocide and the Holocaust
Yves R. Simon Institute.

Titles Published

1. Noel Balzer, *The Human Being as a Logical Thinker.*

2. Archie J. Bahm, *Axiology: The Science of Values.*

3. H. P. P. (Hennie) Lötter, *Justice for an Unjust Society.*

4. H. G. Callaway, *Context for Meaning and Analysis: A Critical Study in the Philosophy of Language.*

5. Benjamin S. Llamzon, *A Humane Case for Moral Intuition.*

6. James R. Watson, *Between Auschwitz and Tradition: Postmodern Reflections on the Task of Thinking.* A volume in **Holocaust and Genocide Studies.**

7. Robert S. Hartman, *Freedom to Live: The Robert Hartman Story,* edited by Arthur R. Ellis. A volume in **Hartman Institute Axiology Studies.**

8. Archie J. Bahm, *Ethics: The Science of Oughtness.*

9. George David Miller, *An Idiosyncratic Ethics; Or, the Lauramachean Ethics.*

10. Joseph P. DeMarco, *A Coherence Theory in Ethics.*

11. Frank G. Forrest, *Valuemetrics: The Science of Personal and Professional Ethics.* A volume in **Hartman Institute Axiology Studies.**

12. William Gerber, *The Meaning of Life: Insights of the World's Great Thinkers.*

13. Richard T. Hull, Editor, *A Quarter Century of Value Inquiry: Presidential Addresses of the American Society for Value Inquiry.* A volume in **Histories and Addresses of Philosophical Societies.**

14. William Gerber, *Nuggets of Wisdom from Great Jewish Thinkers: From Biblical Times to the Present.*

15. Sidney Axinn, *The Logic of Hope: Extensions of Kant's View of Religion.*

16. Messay Kebede, *Meaning and Development.*

17. Amihud Gilead, *The Platonic Odyssey: A Philosophical-Literary Inquiry into the* Phaedo.

18. Necip Fikri Alican, *Mill's Principle of Utility: A Defense of John Stuart Mill's Notorious Proof.* A volume in **Universal Justice.**

19. Michael H. Mitias, Editor, *Philosophy and Architecture.*

20. Roger T. Simonds, *Rational Individualism: The Perennial Philosophy of Legal Interpretation.* A volume in **Natural Law Studies.**

21. William Pencak, *The Conflict of Law and Justice in the Icelandic Sagas.*

22. Samuel M. Natale and Brian M. Rothschild, Editors, *Values, Work, Education: The Meanings of Work.*

23. N. Georgopoulos and Michael Heim, Editors, *Being Human in the Ultimate: Studies in the Thought of John M. Anderson.*

24. Robert Wesson and Patricia A. Williams, Editors, *Evolution and Human Values.*

25. Wim J. van der Steen, *Facts, Values, and Methodology: A New Approach to Ethics.*

26. Avi Sagi and Daniel Statman, *Religion and Morality.*

27. Albert William Levi, *The High Road of Humanity: The Seven Ethical Ages of Western Man,* edited by Donald Phillip Verene and Molly Black Verene.

28. Samuel M. Natale and Brian M. Rothschild, Editors, *Work Values: Education, Organization, and Religious Concerns.*

29. Laurence F. Bove and Laura Duhan Kaplan, Editors, *From the Eye of the Storm: Regional Conflicts and the Philosophy of Peace.* A volume in **Philosophy of Peace.**

30. Robin Attfield, *Value, Obligation, and Meta-Ethics.*

31. William Gerber, *The Deepest Questions You Can Ask About God: As Answered by the World's Great Thinkers.*

32. Daniel Statman, *Moral Dilemmas.*

33. Rem B. Edwards, Editor, *Formal Axiology and Its Critics.* A volume in **Hartman Institute Axiology Studies.**

34. George David Miller and Conrad P. Pritscher, *On Education and Values: In Praise of Pariahs and Nomads.* A volume in **Philosophy of Education.**

35. Paul S. Penner, *Altruistic Behavior: An Inquiry into Motivation.*

36. Corbin Fowler, *Morality for Moderns.*

37. Giambattista Vico, *The Art of Rhetoric* (*Institutiones Oratoriae,* 1711-1741), from the definitive Latin text and notes, Italian commentary and introduction by Giuliano Crifò, translated and edited by Giorgio A. Pinton and Arthur W. Shippee. A volume in **Values in Italian Philosophy.**

38. W. H. Werkmeister, *Martin Heidegger on the Way,* edited by Richard T. Hull. A volume in **Werkmeister Studies.**

39. Phillip Stambovsky, *Myth and the Limits of Reason.*

40. Samantha Brennan, Tracy Isaacs, and Michael Milde, Editors, *A Question of Values: New Canadian Perspectives in Ethics and Political Philosophy.*

41. Peter A. Redpath, *Cartesian Nightmare: An Introduction to Transcendental Sophistry.* A volume in **Studies in the History of Western Philosophy.**

42. Clark Butler, *History as the Story of Freedom: Philosophy in Intercultural Context,* with Responses by sixteen scholars.

43. Dennis Rohatyn, *Philosophy History Sophistry.*

44. Leon Shaskolsky Sheleff, *Social Cohesion and Legal Coercion: A Critique of Weber, Durkheim, and Marx.*

45. Alan Soble, Editor, *Sex, Love, and Friendship: Studies of the Society for the Philosophy of Sex and Love, 1977-1992.* A volume in **Histories and Addresses of Philosophical Societies.**

46. Peter A. Redpath, *Wisdom's Odyssey: From Philosophy to Transcendental Sophistry.* A volume in **Studies in the History of Western Philosophy.**

47. Albert A. Anderson, *Universal Justice: A Dialectical Approach.* A volume in **Universal Justice.**

48. Pio Colonnello, *The Philosophy of José Gaos.* Translated from Italian by Peter Cocozzella. Edited by Myra Moss. Introduction by Giovanni Gullace. A volume in **Values in Italian Philosophy.**

49. Laura Duhan Kaplan and Laurence F. Bove, Editors, *Philosophical Perspectives on Power and Domination: Theories and Practices.* A volume in **Philosophy of Peace.**

50. Gregory F. Mellema, *Collective Responsibility.*

51. Josef Seifert, *What Is Life? The Originality, Irreducibility, and Value of Life.* A volume in **Central-European Value Studies.**